MW01630453

JENNY HOLZER

FONDATION BEYELER
Museum of Contemporary Art

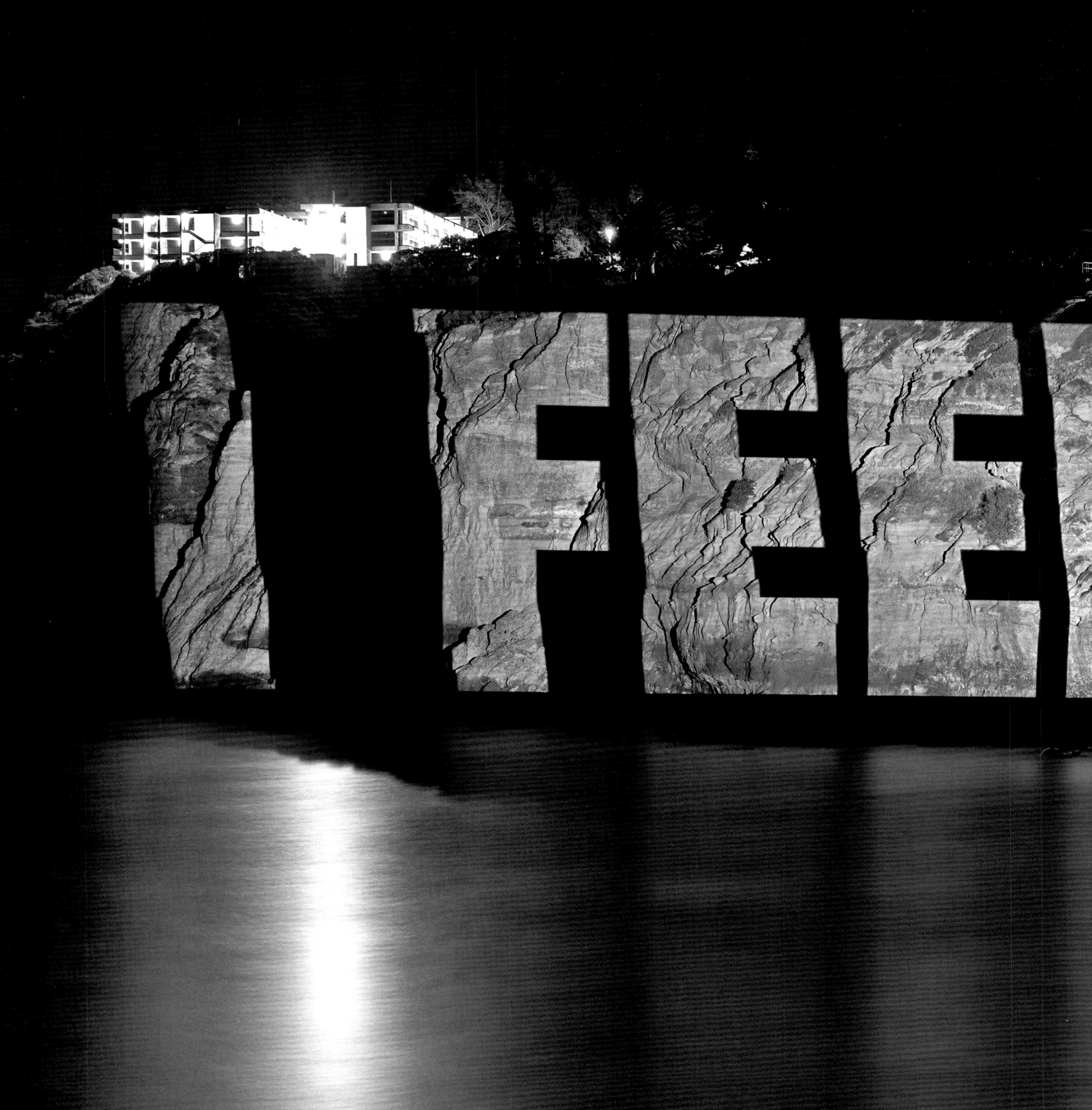
I FEE

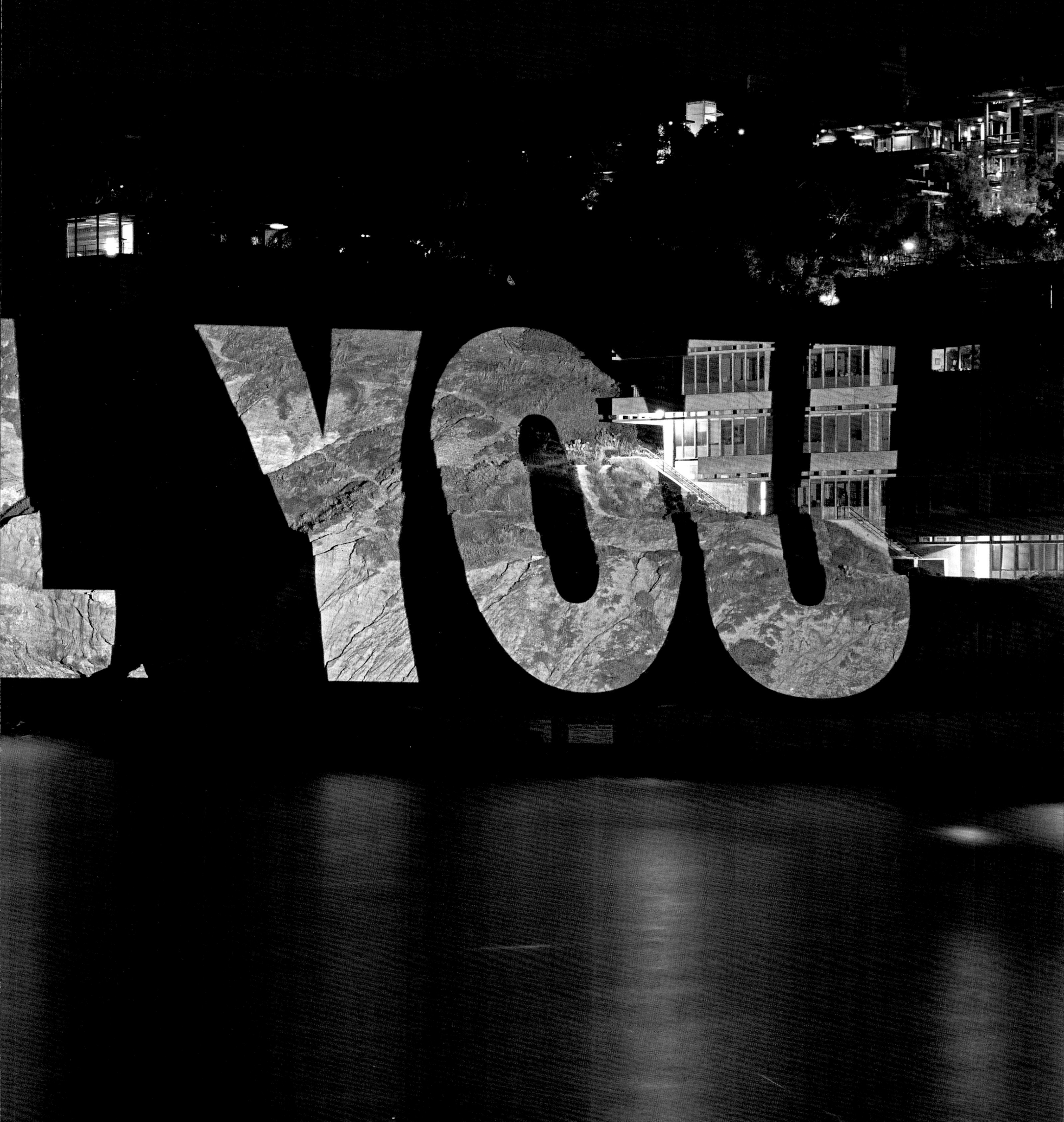
YOU

CONTENTS

JENNY HOLZER'S commitment to making work that is conceptually and aesthetically resonant is revealed in her unflinching address of power and violence as well as vulnerability and tenderness, and in her work's physical embodiment of these concerns. Centering on the artist's work since the 1990s, this exhibition reveals the way in which Holzer continues to innovate formally while building upon and extending a vision of art that encompasses the individual, the body, and politics. This marks the first major exhibition of Holzer's work in an American museum in nearly two decades and extends the strong presence that her work has consistently enjoyed in Europe.

The Museum of Contemporary Art, Chicago and Fondation Beyeler are delighted to partner on this survey of one of the most compelling and pioneering artists of today. In an unprecedented collaboration between our two institutions, the staff of both museums have worked closely together, and also with the artist herself, to realize the project. On the MCA's side, Elizabeth Smith, James W. Alsdorf Chief Curator and Deputy Director for Programs, conceived the idea to invite Jenny Holzer to present a major exhibition and has spearheaded the project from its outset, working with many colleagues inside and outside of our institutions to do so. At Fondation Beyeler, Philippe Büttner, Curator, and Delia Ciuha, Publications Department, played crucial roles in many aspects of the partnership and, above all, in the production of the catalogue. To them and to their colleagues at both museums, including former MCA Pritzker Director Robert Fitzpatrick, who encouraged the initiation of this project, we extend thanks and congratulations.

We are profoundly grateful to the donors who generously supported the exhibition's realization. The Andy Warhol Foundation for the Visual Arts and the National Endowment for the Arts provided crucial early assistance. In the United States, Donald and Brigitte Bren, Anne and Burt Kaplan, Andrea and Jim Gordon, Penny Pritzker and Bryan Traubert, Gretchen and Jay Jordan, the Kovler Family Foundation, Cari and Michael Sacks, Howard and Donna Stone, Kathy and Steven Taslitz, Helen and Sam Zell, Lannan Foundation, the Graham Foundation for Advanced Studies in the Fine Arts, Barbara Ruben, Irving Stenn, Jr., Lynn and Allen Turner, and The Orbit Fund graciously contributed additional funds. We warmly thank Sara Szold, Cheim & Read, Monika Sprüth Philomene Magers, and Yvon Lambert for their generosity regarding the exhibition catalogue. The MCA is also delighted to have commissioned a major work from Jenny Holzer, *For Chicago* (2007), which features prominently in the exhibition and which has entered our collection through the generosity of the Edlis/Neeson Art Acquisition Fund.

Our deep appreciation is extended to the lenders of important works in the show, including The Broad Art Foundation, The David Roberts Art Foundation, Cari and Michael Sacks, Cheim & Read, Yvon Lambert, and Monika Sprüth Philomene Magers.

We are honored that the exhibition will travel to the Whitney Museum of American Art, New York, and wish to thank our colleagues Adam Weinberg and Donna De Salvo for their participation.

To the artist Jenny Holzer, we extend our warmest and most heartfelt thanks for the privilege of allowing the MCA, Chicago and Fondation Beyeler to present this most recent survey of her work at such a significant time in her own career as an artist, and at a critical moment in the culture at large.

Madeleine Grynsztejn
Pritzker Director
Museum of Contemporary Art, Chicago

Sam Keller
Director
Fondation Beyeler, Riehen/Basel

JENNY HOLZER'S work is among the most significant contributions to the art of our time. Her fluency with language, the intellectual rigor that underlies her work, and the way she makes sensate the messages in her chosen texts have been a source of inspiration for many other artists, as have her uses of innovative technologies and embrace of the public sphere for the presentation of art. Blending form and content seamlessly, Holzer's work is characterized by a formal beauty and use of stunning effects ranging from scale and motion to color and light that expands and reinforces the way it communicates meaning through language.

It is a great honor and privilege to have worked with Holzer, a figure whom I have long admired, on this exhibition and book, and I wish to thank the many individuals who have played important roles in realizing this project. At Fondation Beyeler, I extend profound thanks to Sam Keller, Director, for his warm embrace of the project and the partnership with the MCA. To Philippe Büttner and Delia Ciuha, I express deep appreciation for their gracious collegiality and for their important work with regard to production of the catalogue, in particular. Ulf Küster, Curator, also deserves thanks for his participation in the early discussions surrounding our institutional collaboration.

At the MCA, I would like to thank Madeleine Grynsztejn, Pritzker Director, for her encouragement of the project's direction and her predecessor, Robert Fitzpatrick, who enthusiastically endorsed the idea to present a major show of Holzer's work. My colleagues in the Exhibitions area Jennifer Draffen, Meridith Grey, Dennis O'Shea, and Scott Short provided careful stewardship and oversight of the exhibition logistics and its complex physical and technical requirements. Karla Loring in Media Relations and Angelique Power in Marketing undertook key efforts to publicize the exhibition and extend its reach to audiences. Lisa Key, Julie Havel, Rob Sherer, and Jonathan Lehman in Development worked tirelessly to raise the necessary funds. Erika Hanner, Marissa Reyes, and Jackie Terrassa in Education created a series of public programs and educational components that illuminated the exhibition's content and the artist's significance for our public. Gwen Infusino, Kate Kraczon, Celine Kopp, and Tricia Van Eck in Curatorial provided crucial assistance and support for my own efforts. Deputy Director Janet Alberti and her predecessor, Greg Cameron, offered helpful guidance from the outset.

In addition to those already named, the following Fondation Beyeler staff members contributed to the success of the project: Fausto De Lorenzo, Managing Director; Raphaël Bouvier, Publications Department; Nicole Rüegsegger and Tanja Narr, Registrars; Markus Gross, Conservator; Catherine Schott, Public Relations; Claudia Carrara, Corporate Communications; and Ben Ludwig, Exhibition Services.

At the Holzer studio, David Breslin was an invaluable partner to our staff at the MCA and Fondation Beyeler. His essential contributions to all phases of this project's development as well as his professionalism, attention to detail, and congeniality are deeply appreciated. Additionally, we wish to warmly thank Kerin Sulock and Alanna Gedgaudas for providing vital assistance, Brenda Phelps and Jon Grizzle for their diligent and excellent work creating this catalogue, Carolyn Padwa for her careful overseeing of the artwork, and Marc Breslin for his eye and attention.

The catalogue could not have been realized to such a high standard without the participation of designer Mark Nelson and his partner, David Zaza, of Anthony McCall Associates; we thank them for their sensitivity and flexibility in all aspects of this process. We are most grateful to Benjamin H. D. Buchloh and Joan Simon for their insightful writings about Holzer's work in this catalogue. Annette Kulenkampff of Hatje Cantz deserves special mention for her role in catalogue production.

We are delighted that the exhibition will travel to additional museums in the United States and Europe. At the Whitney Museum of American Art in New York, we extend profound thanks to Joan Simon and David Kiehl, in particular, for championing the exhibition and for their roles in the project there.

I wish to join Madeleine Grynsztejn and Sam Keller in warmly acknowledging the support of the lenders, who graciously parted with important works for the duration of the tour, and the donors to the project. Without their crucial assistance, we could not have realized this exhibition. I would also like to extend personal thanks to Joel Wachs, and to Jenny Holzer's gallerists Howard Read, John Cheim, and Adam Sheffer of Cheim & Read; Yvon Lambert, Séverine Waelchli, Olivier Belot, and Nicolas Nahab of Yvon Lambert; and Monika Sprüth, Philomene Magers, and Eva-Maria Haenlein of Monika Sprüth Philomene Magers, all of whom provided valuable assistance and advice. Tania Bruguera, Sarah Herda, Joanne Heyler, Tony Karman, Nathan Mason, Randy Michaels, W.J.T. Mitchell, Anne Pasternak, Janet Carl Smith, and Joe Thompson helped in realizing various aspects of the project; to all of the above, we are most grateful.

Finally, my collaborators and I wish to express our deepest appreciation to Jenny Holzer, whose insight and guidance have been vital in developing this project. We are honored to present her work to our public.

Elizabeth A.T. Smith
James W. Alsdorf Chief Curator and Deputy Director for Programs
Museum of Contemporary Art, Chicago

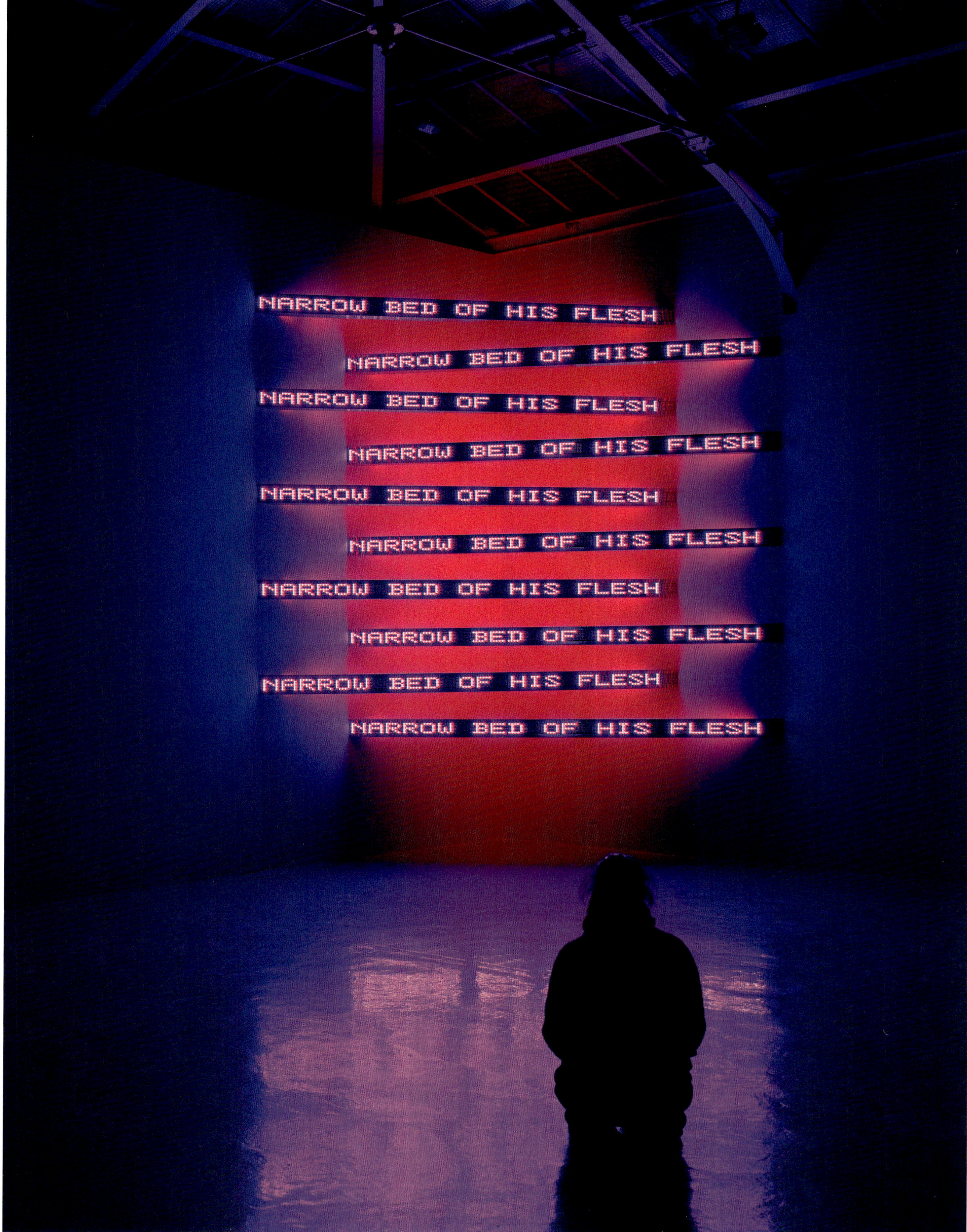
NARROW BED OF HIS FLESH
NARROW BED OF HIS FLESH
NARROW BED OF HIS FLESH
NARROW BED OF HIS FLESH
NARROW BED OF HIS FLESH
NARROW BED OF HIS FLESH
NARROW BED OF HIS FLESH
NARROW BED OF HIS FLESH
NARROW BED OF HIS FLESH
NARROW BED OF HIS FLESH

OTHER VOICES, OTHER FORMS

JOAN SIMON

I gravitate to works like Goya's Black Paintings, and I stay in awe of Matisse's The Joy of Life.
I've spent more time in Goya territory, but I've always wanted at least to understand that Matisse . . .
— Jenny Holzer

THE MARRIAGE OF FORM AND CONTENT has often been divorced in the critical address of Jenny Holzer's work, with content extensively parsed and form presented as an adjunct if necessary element. In good part because Holzer's practice has been recognized as that of a Conceptualist, her words have been privileged. Yet it is how Holzer situates her texts in space that makes for an experience different from — though critically based in — reading. As the artist herself has said: "People talk about the content, and that's right, but very few mention how the stuff looks, and that's important."[1]

Holzer's body of work for the past 30 years has centered on the articulation of speech, and as the subjects, phrasing, tone, duration, and authorship of her expressions have changed, so, too, have their embodiments. At times she uses a correlate to the tone of her voicings, as in the plain, inexpensive, offset-printed posters that initially, in 1977, carried her own vernacular-sounding, epigrammatic *Truisms* into the streets, or via the thin, five-foot-high white LED (light-emitting diode) strips mounted behind glass that carry more than 30 hours of an anthology of centuries of New York stories (beginning with a 1670 text) in the glass-fronted lobby of 7 World Trade Center, a 2006 commission in a new office building near the lost Twin Towers that expresses what Holzer has called the "sometime wistful" ambience of the site in writing that is "slow and white and floating."

But at other times, Holzer's work gains by employing a dissonance between medium and message. Her recent series of sculptures, begun in 2004, are handsome and, as she says, "shapely." For *Rib Cage* (2004), whose arcs span the corner of a room, Holzer invokes the wall-bound serial repetitions of Donald Judd's stacks along with the aura of Dan Flavin's fluorescent-light illuminations to create a hypnotic intervention that is at once ephemeral and muscularly architectonic. The subtext for this work, and one of Holzer's starting points, is the metal frame of a torture cage that Holzer abstracted from drawings and a photograph, while the literal text that sails around both the interior and exterior of its bands is the poem "Beach Walk," by Henri Cole.[2] Still more dramatic in its spatial play and in the disjunction between sculptural presence and illuminating text is *Red Yellow Looming* (2004), where 13 horizontal LED signs ascend from floor to ceiling, creating a plane that tips forward into the room and dwarfs the viewer under its looming topmost edge. Deploying red and amber electronic diodes in concert with their perceived greenish after-images, Holzer shapes a space both ominously threatening and seductively inviting, one that broadcasts a selection of declassified U.S. government documents and bathes the room in a red that is part ethereal Rothko, part holy fires of purgatory.

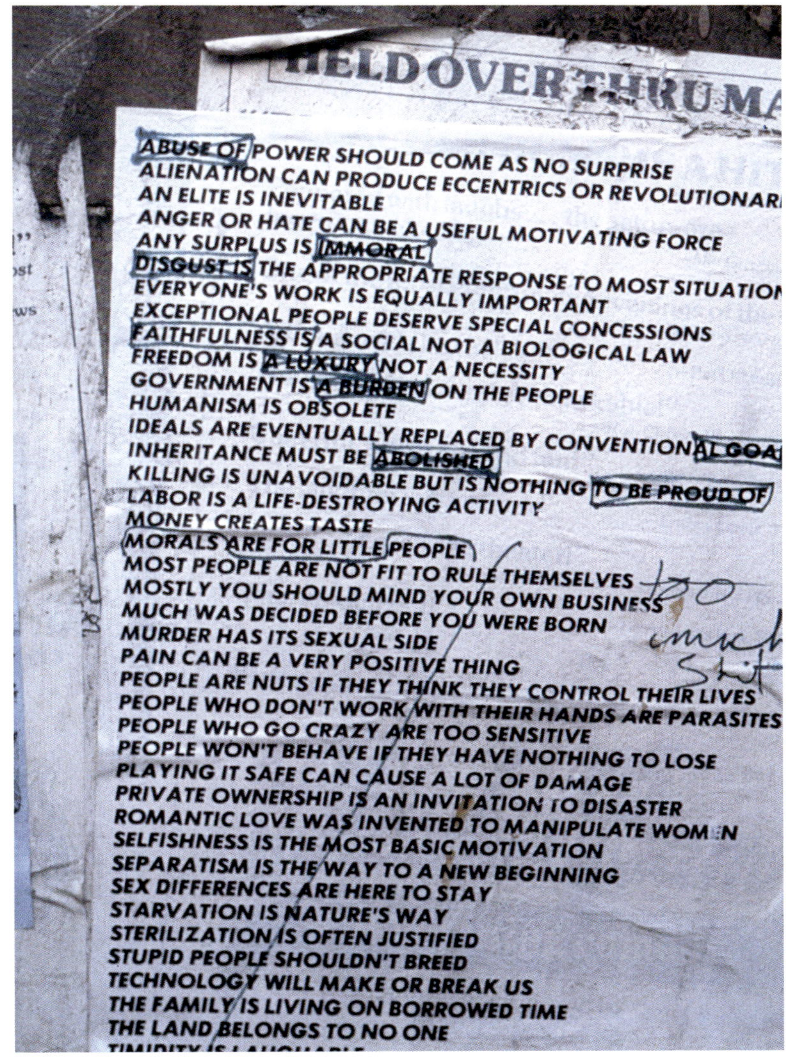

opposite: ***Purple Cross*, 2004**; above: **from *Truisms*, 1977**

For recent paintings that employ traditional oil on linen, which she began to make in 2005, Holzer takes up a different but equally evocative palette for the ground, which, because it is often at odds with the disturbing matters that are figured upon it, amplifies brute details of interrogation, military strategies, and first-person prisoner and soldier accounts. These paintings bear the particulars of documented if intentionally secret abuses of governmental power that Holzer had in mind very early on and which she flagged in more generalized phrasing as a daily motto on a host of items, including caps, T-shirts, posters, cash-register receipts, dinner plates, stone benches, golf balls, a race car, and on a banner trailing a small plane: ABUSE OF POWER COMES AS NO SURPRISE.

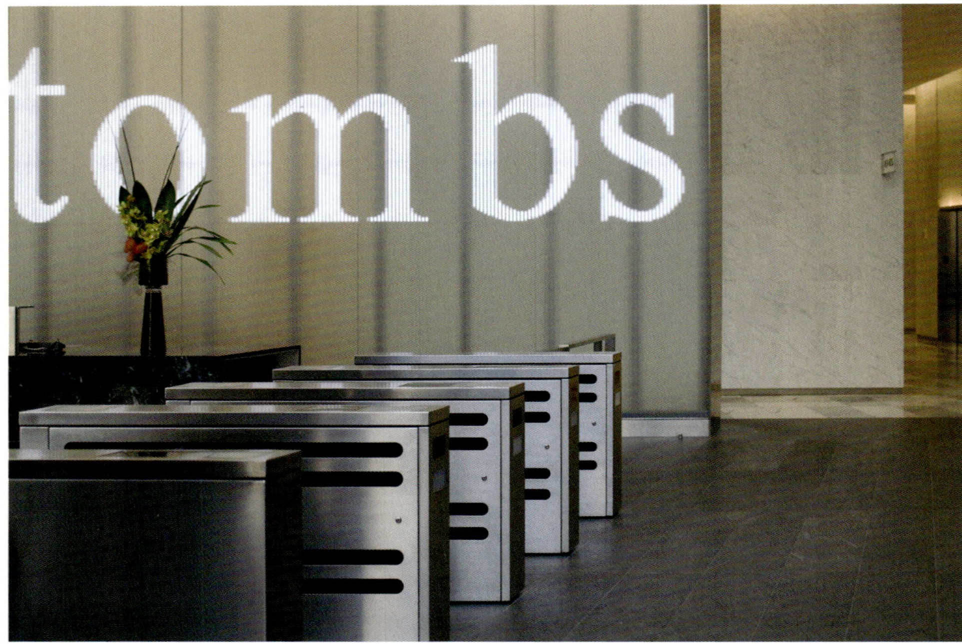

***For 7 World Trade*, 2006**

That Holzer more than ever speaks truth to power comes as no surprise, but the sensuous beauty of many of her works in recent years, in particular her shift to painting and her creation of electronic sculptures with their overriding painterly auras, are turns that could not have been easily predicted. Her use of vaporous light in the new sculptures may be traced to the large-scale film projections that she began to present outdoors in 1996, while the choice of painting may be related to her graduate work of 1976–77, when overall painted canvas fields were inflected with a single line of text or when a whole room glowed with washes of color.

Now, though, the medium of painting is used to translate, illuminate, and revalue pages of declassified government documents and to frame the escalated political and emotional import of her subjects. The paintings also reinforce in new ways the rigorous conceptual strategies she has long employed, for though they appear to depart from her use of standard "found" forms of public address — such as the changing news flashes of her electronic signs, first used in 1982 (and related to the iconic news "zipper" of Times Square) or memorialized inscriptions chiseled into stone for the ages (benches beginning in 1986, sarcophagi in 1987)[3] — Holzer's paintings remain keyed to the vernacular in her systematic reuse of the format of a standard 8½-by-11-inch sheet of paper for any of the five different sizes to which Holzer scales them.

Yet despite the continuity of her use of text within these new paintings and sculptures, two changes that came a few years prior to their introduction in 2004–5 inform these works and ought to be mentioned at the outset. One change, largely unnoticed, came in 2001, when Holzer decided to stop writing her own texts after completing perhaps the most emotional and autobiographical of her writings — the lengthy *Oh* that was displayed in 2001 on ceiling-mounted LED signs in the otherwise empty glass-framed modernist gallery of Berlin's Neue Nationalgalerie, designed by Mies van der Rohe. Used in their stead have been Holzer's collections of her readings of others, initially quotations from Viennese diaries and letters of the mid-19th century for the Biedermeier room that she was invited to re-install

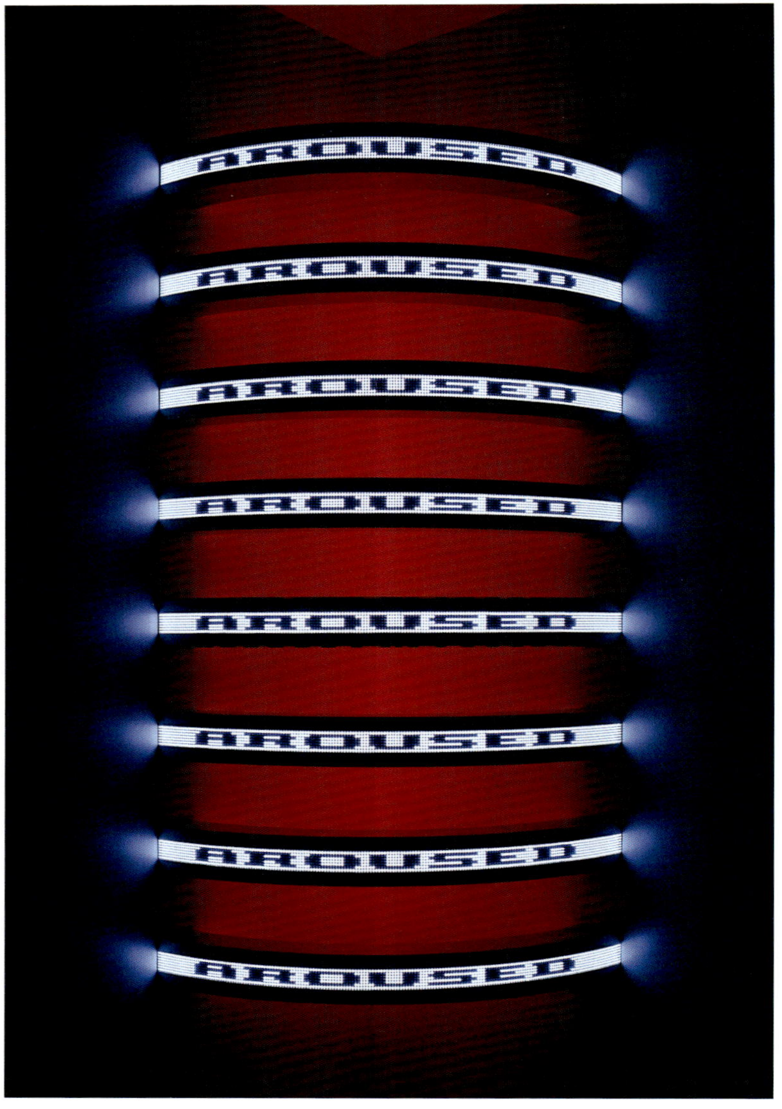

***Rib Cage*, 2004**

at Vienna's Museum für Angewandte Kunst (MAK), followed by her projection of a Yehuda Amichai poem, the first poem Holzer used, on the Jüdisches Museum Berlin on February 8, 2001. Holzer has gone on to use a wide range of material, from entire novels to her many series of declassified, redacted government communications, in addition to poetry from a significant number of international poets.[4]

The second change can also be seen in the 2001 Neue Nationalgalerie installation where Holzer created for her audience a rapturous immersion in text and light as she reckoned the architectural space itself:

> As close as I've come to *The Joy of Life* was to have the NNG turn pretty amber and melt. When I lit the ceiling signs there, they made a fire and had the museum glow from outside. The text would stream, and the ceiling appeared to bow down or become vaulted. The bowing was faintly ominous, and the vaulting uplifting.

One could liken this new dynamic in Holzer's work to Roland Barthes's characterization of a "desiring reading," where "all the body's emotions are present, mingled, coiled up: fascination, emptiness, pain, voluptuousness," and where the question turns to "*what the reader understands*" from the establishment of "*what the author meant*."[5] Her new play of text and field —

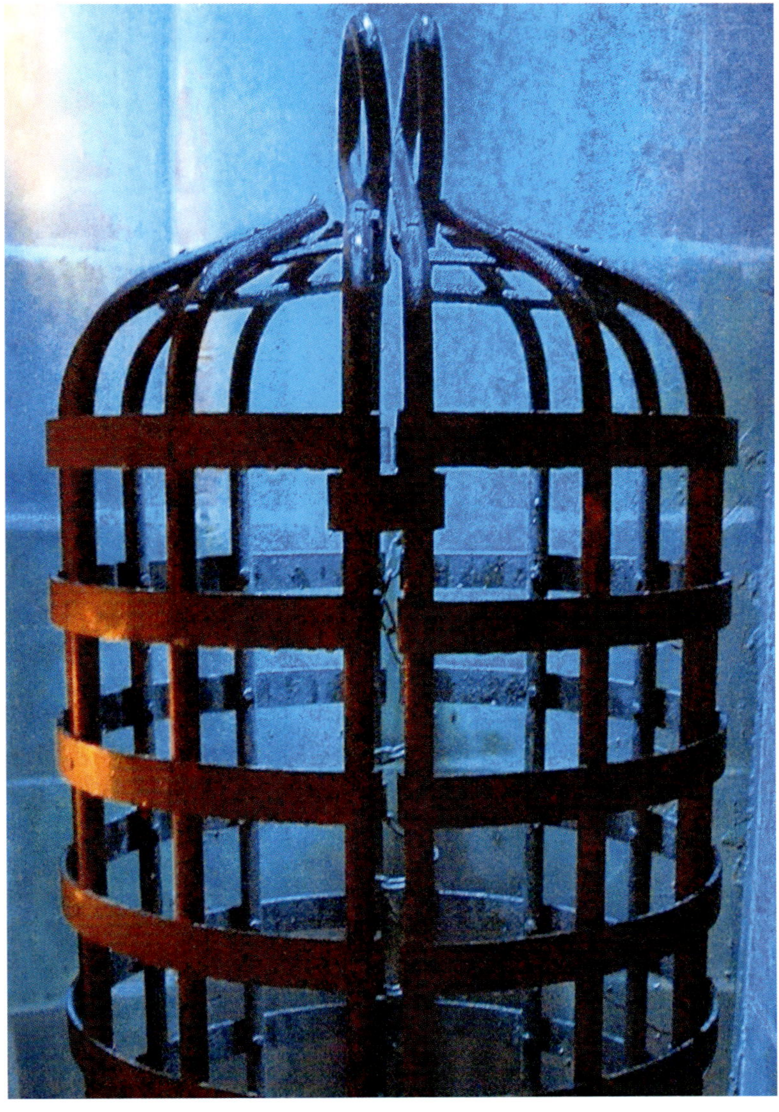

Hanging cage

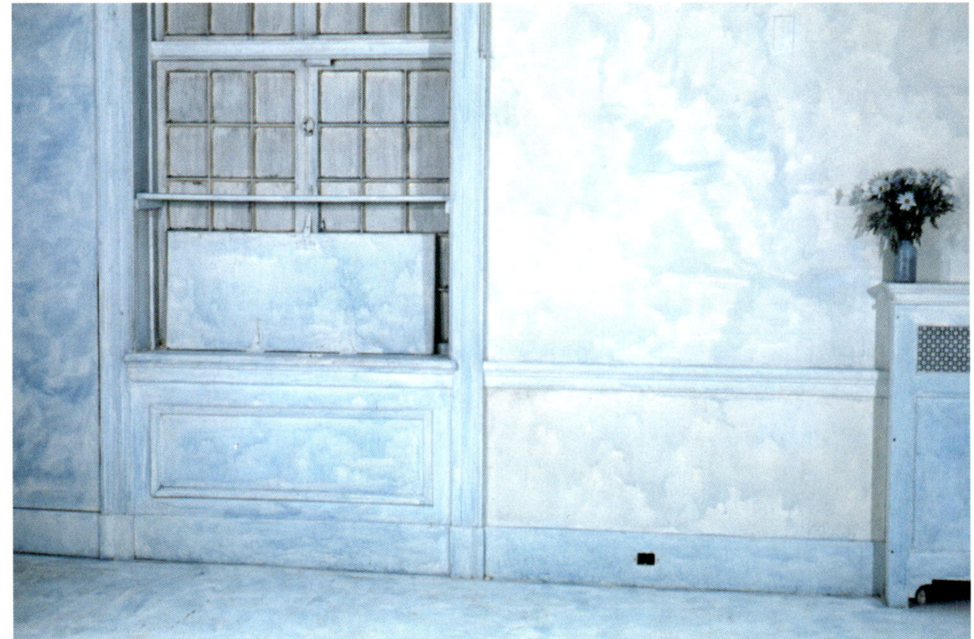

***Blue Room*, 1975**

and new libraries from which to draw her readings — did not mark a change in content, but rather an amplification of Holzer's themes of power, pain, hope, knowledge, conscience, love, trauma, and survival, and it has allowed her to explore more ambitious formal means to play the alpha-omega of her Goya-Matisse duality: the discomfort of actualities of precise content and the joy of metaphysical evocation.

How Holzer visually and spatially frames the word made public and orchestrates the tempo, experience, sites, and multisensory processes of reading makes for new visual forms, a new visceral participation on the part of her audiences, and new ways of understanding her works' embodied content. The taxonomy that follows sets out a contextual chronology and explores how she has succeeded in producing art of a double nature, shape-shifting language into matter as well as into immaterial, temporal presence.

THE PEDESTRIAN

Jenny Holzer's first pieces as a working artist were cheap stuff. Anonymously presented, these were posters wheat-pasted to walls in 1977, and were subject to degradation as well as amplification by weather and graffiti.[6] Modest in size, inexpensive to produce, and posted clandestinely, the *Truisms* (texts Holzer continued to write through 1979) took the form of lists that perhaps might have been sighted at a glance by a passerby. Written in multiple voices by Holzer, her lists incorporated contradictory phrasings and points of view, and suggested an anthology of found statements. "I presented the voices more or less simultaneously, and weighted evenly, to suggest that the thoughts were true to *somebody*. It seemed like a comprehensive and clean way to present belief systems, since I wasn't choosing. I wanted to avoid polarization. Then a young artist pointed out that contemplation is fine when there's no crisis, but when there *is* a crisis, you may have to come down on one side or another."[7]

Holzer has often credited the sources of her first texts to the "enormous reading list of serious and sometimes opaque books, everything from Marx to structuralism"[8] given to her by Ron Clark[9] while at the Whitney Independent Study Program, New York, during the 1976–77 academic year.[10] As she recalls, "I wanted to sort out what I was to do, or what anyone was to do, with that much dense and sometimes contradictory information. So I rewrote his library. I did it as a self-help maneuver, and posted the result — the *Truisms* — in the streets."[11] These multiplied — in length of text as well as in presentation — to form multicolored grids of wallpaper, presented indoors and out. Her one-line phrasings grew to the length of 100-word essays, some of them "inflammatory."

Holzer's posters were among the many inexpensive objects and street works made by the artists of Colab, or Collaborative Projects, of which Holzer was a member and within which she worked on a number of events, including the 1979 *Manifesto Show* that was organized with Colen Fitzgibbon at her storefront, 5 Bleecker Street. It was a concept that not only brought art into a daily realm but also into temporary exhibition spaces claimed in different neighborhoods, including the then-seedy Times Square and impoverished Lower East Side. Holzer set her *Truisms* to the body as well as to paper. Her T-shirts and caps were a more intimate if still public address (with echoes of commercial advertising as well as self-selected advertisements for the self), taking advantage of the pedestrian's body as signboard.

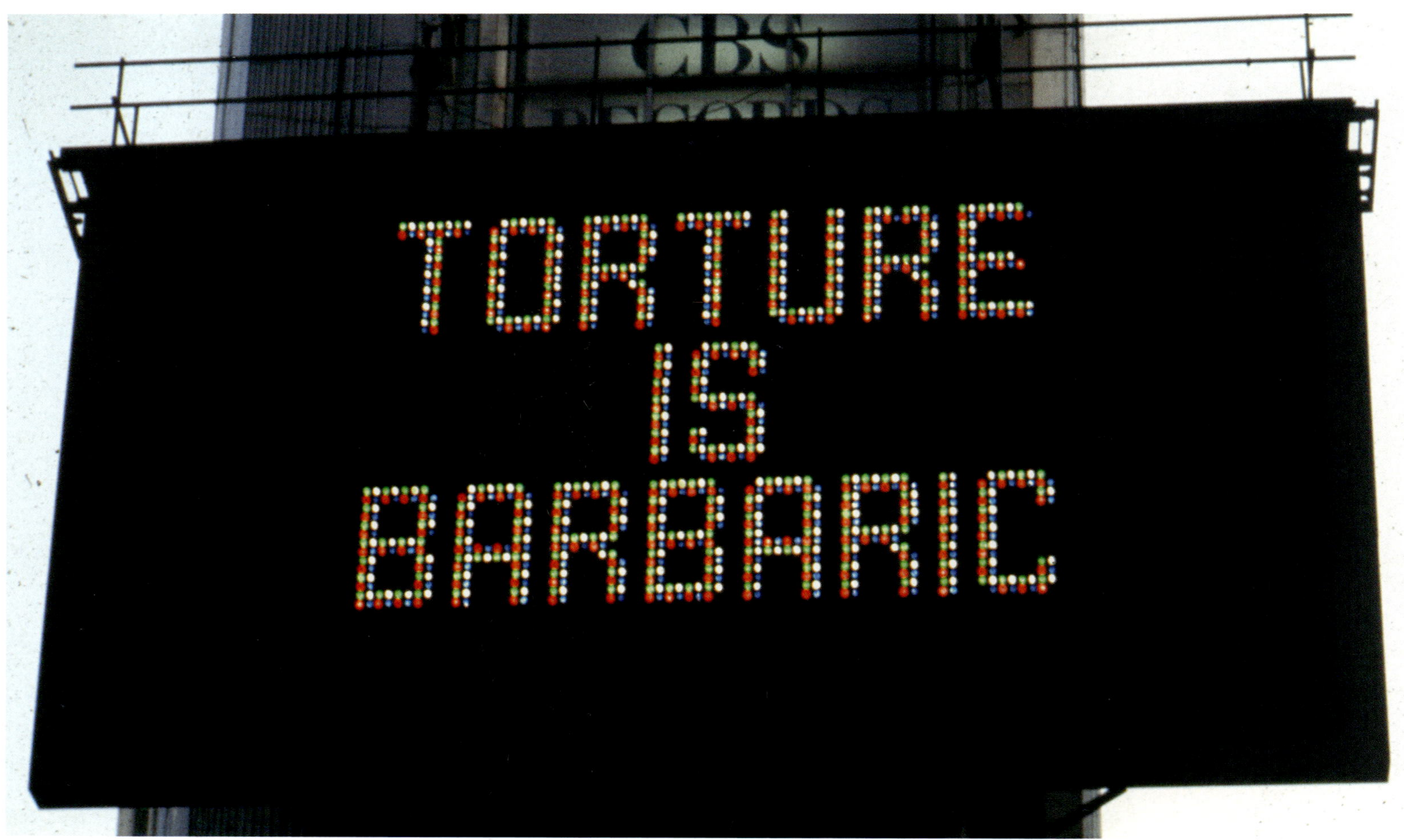

from *Truisms*, 1982

Holzer also sited her words on metal plaques that skewed the utility of these readily overlooked bits of information-architecture. The plaques looked strikingly similar to the street-side directories of a building's tenants next to which Holzer placed them, yet they offered something more like a street-wise concrete poem. They were in a sense camouflage, matching their neighbors, which had the effect of making their presence both more recessive and yet also more striking for the slant of information conveyed and the redirection of a pedestrian's attention. Unlike the earlier posters, which had the immediacy and temporality of flyers that could as likely have been sale announcements or plaints in search of a lost cat, the bronze plaques began to claim and subvert official-looking signs in service of other matters.

In 1982, Holzer's *Truisms* began to appear on small, rectangular LED signs, initially one color per sign in standard red, green, or yellow, then in larger sizes using all of the colors, before being crafted as architecturally responsive interventions — utilizing the structural columns of Dia's gallery space in 1989–90 to display her vertical signs, for example, or spiraling in one length up the parapet of New York's Guggenheim Museum in 1989–90.[12] At the Guggenheim, the formal effect kept the viewer both at a distance and within a changing experiential environment, for as Holzer says, "the sign pulled on you, and tugged harder when you walked against it. There was also an all-purpose dizzying, circling effect." It was something of the same disorienting "special effect" that first appeared in Holzer's *Blue Room* at RISD — what she has described as "perhaps the first Tilt-a-Whirl" — an immersion that increased by degrees in her Dia installation: "Dia worked on the body, especially when the room went all black for a little too long, and then all the signs came on at once, and this made you feel as if you were levitating. This was an important change made in the programming, once we had these signs installed." But the impulse to work with a given space and its particularities would soon lead Holzer to create environments with these LED signs that immersed the viewer in an inescapable totality of language and light.

THE TOASTER OVEN

Holzer conceived her work for the 1990 Venice Biennale, where she was the U.S. representative, within the perceived information — and disinformation — overload of the Reagan era and its aftermath. Her *Venice Installation* in the American Pavilion, which won the Golden Lion Award, began with texts set into the marble floor and into benches, and continued with a surround of floor-to-ceiling signs and their intense lighting. "My horizontal sign room with multiple texts in five languages flashed a glut of information. I wanted to signal the downside of the orgy of unexamined material and highlight assumptions about free-floating facts, pronouncements, and judgments. That's why I wrapped people with electronics in that room. It was known as the 'toaster oven.'"[13]

In its totality as an installation, the project referenced the specificity of historical Venice itself — the stones and the patterning were resonant of their use in the Doges' Palace, while the reflections in the highly polished marble were a nod toward the waters of Venice's lagoon. In scale, it was not unlike her prior installation at Dia, with its multiple signs. However, the Venice installation was far less dispersed than the Dia project and made for an atmosphere that turned up the volume of light as well as the stream of

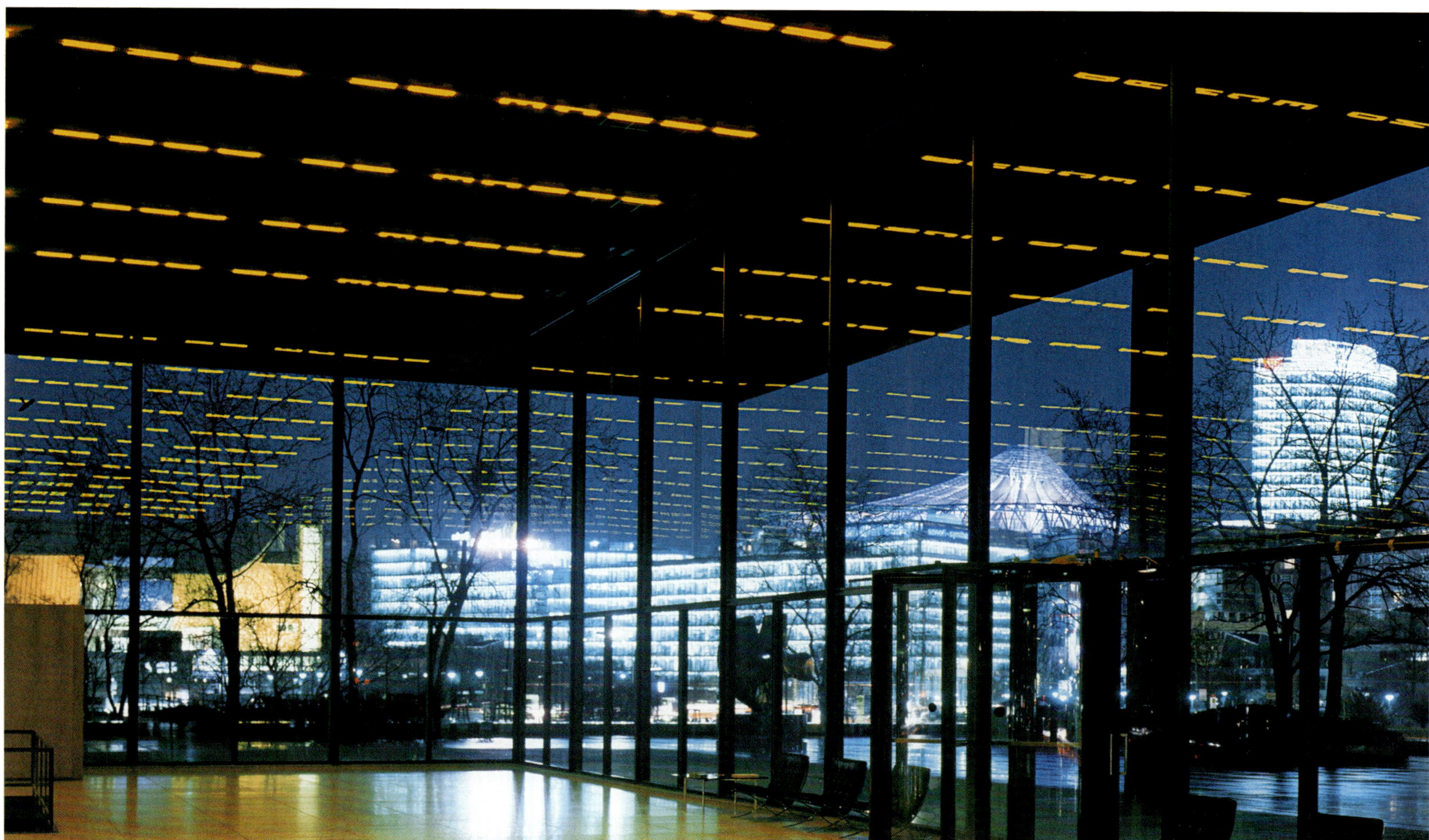

***Installation for Neue Nationalgalerie*, 2001**

seemingly endless messages, enveloping the viewer to such an extent as to create an almost no-way-out situation, an enticing, sensuous, palatial yet, at times, frightening surround that in fact critically changed the relation between Holzer's artwork and its audience. Holzer had erased the distance separating the reader and the text that still marked the experience of following her continuous spiral up the Guggenheim's parapet wall a year earlier; the Venice installation absorbed the visitor, now a participant, within its destabilizing attractions:

> I made a highly polished stone floor, so that in the room with too many electronic signs, you not only were overwhelmed with what was on the walls, but you saw writing fall into the floor. You were unsure about where you were in relation to the words—and uncertain about what you would do with all the information and the multiple languages. I think that the effect of the light on the body can stand in for some of the consequences of the content. That's another reason why I sometimes use aggressive light: it can represent what happens as a result of bad policy or bad faith or what have you.[14]

THE BODY POLITIC

Holzer's use of equivalent weights in her media to match her messages found an organic urgency in her *Lustmord* series (1993–95). Prompted by horrors of family violence and the rape-murder ("Lustmord") of war that is the work's title, this series of Holzer's texts was written on skin and then photographed, and was also printed on a card with a mix of blood and ink. The work was published in the November 1993 *Süddeutsche Zeitung Magazin.*[15] Holzer also engraved the *Lustmord* words on metal tags affixed to an array of human bones, creating a field of sculptural elements that starkly materialize the deaths referenced in her texts. These works, as literal embodiments of words on skin or tagged to bone, evoke Marshall McLuhan's probes of "language as an extension or uttering (outering) of all our senses at once."[16]

ROCK OF AGES

Sites for the body at rest, rather than attractions for the body in motion, Holzer's benches were first made in 1986. As durable public furniture and memorial markers, the first benches were shown in a chapel-like, almost funereal setting in a 1986 show at New York's Barbara Gladstone Gallery, oriented toward a single LED sign. Both sign and benches carried selections from Holzer's *Under a Rock* series. Its title, as Holzer says, derives from "things that need to crawl out from under a rock,"[17] and the images it conjures are brutal. One passage of death by rape reads: "CRACK THE PELVIS SO SHE LIES RIGHT. THIS IS A MISTAKE. WHEN SHE DIES YOU CANNOT REPEAT THE ACT. THE BONES WILL NOT GROW TOGETHER AGAIN AND THE PERSONALITY WILL NOT COME BACK. SHE IS GOING TO SINK DEEP INTO THE MOSS TO GET WHITE AND LIGHTER. SHE IS UNRESPONSIVE TO BEGGING AND SELF-ABSORBED." The writing of this text was inspired by a specific artwork, unusual for Holzer. As she told an interviewer in 1993, "That particular text came from a memory I have of a Käthe Kollwitz drawing of a woman, legs spread, lying in foliage in the forest. She had been raped and murdered. I wrote this text with that image in mind."[18]

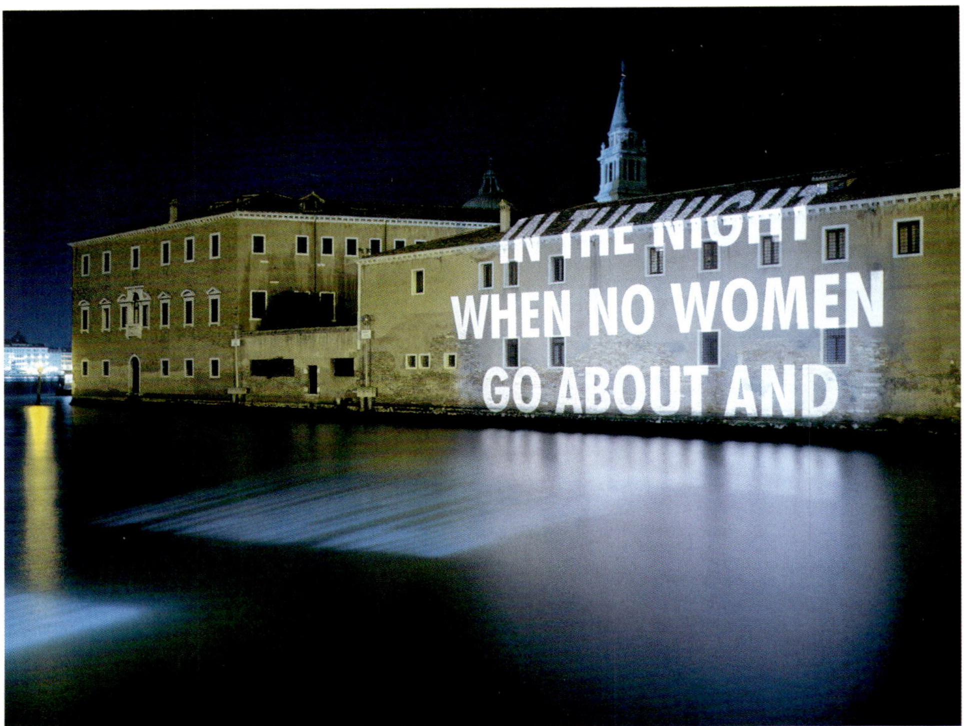

above: ***Xenon for Venice*, 1999**; below: ***The Venice Installation: First Antechamber*, 1990 (detail)**

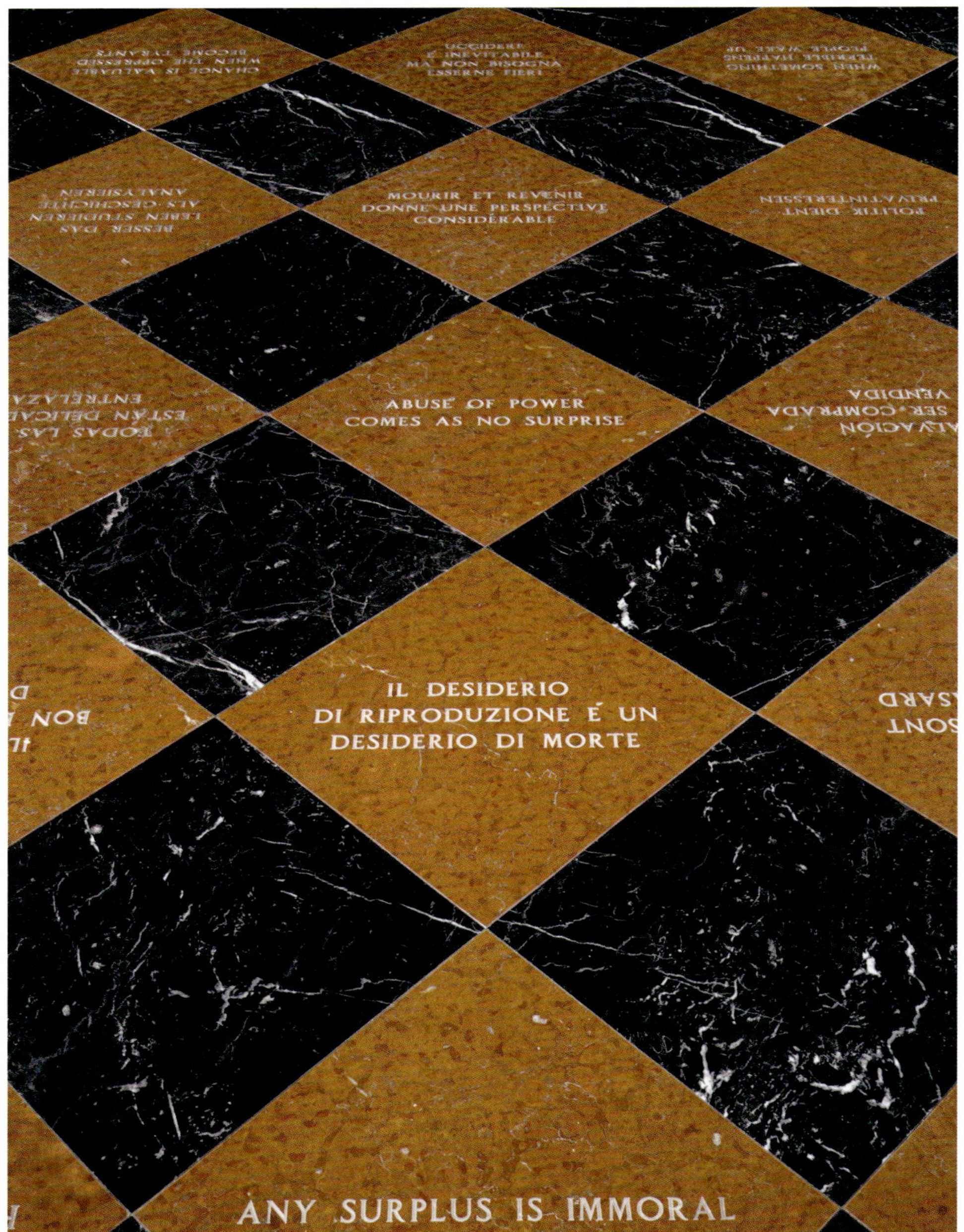

Holzer began to create stone sarcophagi in 1987. The first two were included in the 1987 *Documenta 8*, but came to prominence when 13 of them were used for her exhibition *Jenny Holzer: Laments* at the Dia Center for the Arts, New York, 1989. These were isolated in a room with ordinary lighting apart from the relatively dark gallery that housed the 13 vertical LED signs affixed to the building's columns. The sarcophagi bore Holzer's texts of death and dying, mournful in the extreme and the equivalent in text to the iconic containers on which they were incised. The work came at a time when, as Holzer recalls, two crises above all became her primary focus: her writings evoke death by AIDS and domestic violence. "*Laments* were intended to be the final remarks of dead people. It was as if the people had a last chance to say what they wish had been different in their lives, or to describe what happened to them, or to talk about what hurt them. I wanted to give these people who had died unnecessarily a chance to say what they couldn't say."[19]

Holzer's stone benches, by contrast, are more generally utilitarian, and while they might refer to cemetery furniture, they carry a more familiar use as garden seating, which has led to many and various public commissions over the years, often in combination with plantings and related sculptures. The benches have sometimes been carved with her own writings, and at other times have given voice to specific people as narrators evincing the history of a particular site. The beauty of these, for Holzer, is in the quality of the stone, its markings and coloration, the choice of typography, and in the hand-chiseled letters. The first of these ensembles, which included her first table as well, was a commission for the Stuart Collection on the campus of the University of California, San Diego, in 1992. *Green Table* took the form of a huge refectory or picnic table—20 feet long, with a stone top six feet wide and six inches thick—and surrounding benches, which together form an anthology of her own writings selected from her series *Truisms*, *Survival*, *Laments*, *Mother and Child, Inflammatory Essays*, and *Under a Rock*. The table's surface alone is carved with so much text that Holzer has referred to it as a "tattooed lady."[20]

She chose a serif font called Government ("If I can't be a government, I can look like one," she said)[21] and Prairie Green granite, "because it's dark and figured enough to absorb ketchup and still be lovely."[22] With a surface whose color seems to change depending on the play of natural light, it can appear black in some conditions or green in others. Here, for the first time, Holzer imagined a social space for her audience: "I made a place to sit, read books, talk, and eat, plus I supply some bite-sized chunks of ideology, confessions, accounts of awful real-world consequences, and a few laughs. What happens next in politics or in personal life is up to the students. I can be uncomfortable telling people what to do. Dictating usually doesn't work and is lousy. I am more able to say what people should not do, such as rape and murder."[23]

Holzer was soon asked to create memorials, and what she has called "anti-memorials," specific to their sites. *Black Garden* (1994) was commissioned by the town of Nordhorn, Germany, to mark the 50th anniversary of the end of World War II, for a site that had been a rallying ground for the National Socialist Party. Here Holzer deployed five sandstone benches that are incised with her *War* series, set within two gardens to create an environment that requires memory to be kept alive by its ongoing tending.

She planted rows of concentric "black" flora that range from deep purple to very dark reds to almost black, as well as a small white fragrant garden in honor of the murdered: members of the political opposition as well as the town's Jewish families. The contrast of a white garden invoking memory and hope in the face of the black garden's symbolism of the dark side of human actions remade a site that, as Holzer has said, was "an uncanny, deathly space."[24]

Holzer began to write her *War* texts in 1990, prompted by watching hours of CNN coverage of the Gulf conflict, and used them on electronic signs for installations in a museum and a church prior to incorporating them in the *Black Garden*'s benches.[25] Graphic, and not limited to any one war, the series invokes the horror of Goya's Black Paintings, particularly that of Saturn devouring his son in the section of *War* that reads: "HIS NECK STRAINS AND PIVOTS. HE BITES IN A CIRCLE AROUND HIM. HE CANNOT RAISE HIS ARMS BECAUSE HE IS PACKED IN MEN. THE THING THAT IS ALL OF THEM BEGINS TO SCREAM."

Holzer's *Erlauf Peace Monument* (1995) at the site of the German surrender at Erlauf, Austria, followed a year later and is in many ways related to *Black Garden*. A monument to peace rather than an "anti-memorial" to war, this public work incorporates an exclusively white garden and a different tone of writing as Holzer honors those:

> who gave milk
> who made beds
> who lived in the woods
> who ran to the river
> who died looking
> whose thoughts are missing.

The texts are set in pavers of Bethel White granite, which surround a base of the same material that supports a vertical searchlight, a beacon projecting its light a mile into the sky. For the first time, Holzer's field is both earth and sky, night and day. While her words remain literally grounded, within a year she would discover a way to merge language and vaporous light, in temporal changing forms played outdoors, and only at night.

CONSCIENCE FIREWORKS

In 1996, Holzer presented her first outdoor film projection as part of the *Biennale di Firenze: Il Tempo e la Moda,* working with a new apparatus and demonstrating what has become a typical adeptness at incorporating such technology in her work. "I found out that it existed and wanted to do something different from the electronic signs, with their Wall Street associations. The projections are more lovely and romantic looking. In Florence, we worked with the canoe club and projected the texts on the surface of the Arno and on buildings on the river bank opposite." She projected revisions of a project she had earlier created for an AIDS fundraiser, "Red Hot + Dance," which were seen in a video for the music that was being sold by the fundraising group, The Red Hot Organization. The texts, now titled *Arno,* are intimate reflections, summarized by Holzer as "I walk in... I see you... I watch you... I scan you... I wait for you... I tickle you... I tease you... I search you...."

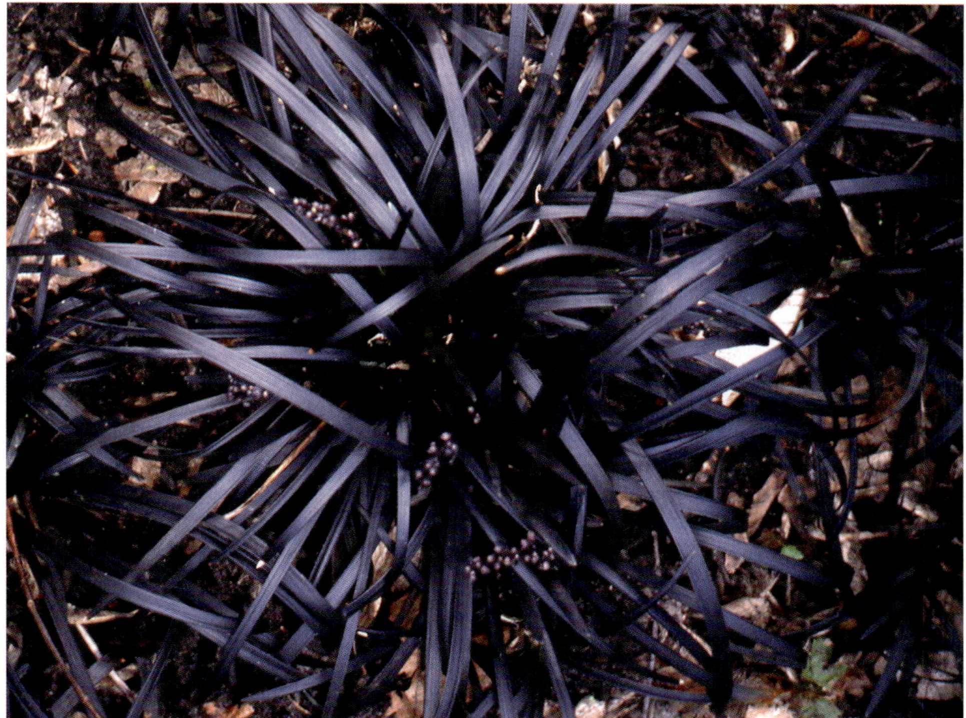

***Black Garden*, 1994 (detail)**

Originally referred to as "xenon" projections for the type of lamp used (derived from the Greek *xenos*, "strange"),[26] this film projection deploys 185-mm film and throws a bright, powerful light long distances. For these, Holzer supplied projection technicians with a digital file of her writing, which was then reproduced on the film stock. The extremely large film was run through a mechanical projector and controlled by a digital device, thus projecting the text as a slow-moving crawl. The choice to use traditional film rather than video was an aesthetic one for Holzer: "The film projectors are brighter than the digital equipment, and the quality of light more beautiful. The light passes through a mask, and is not chopped into digital."

Over the past dozen years, Holzer has exhibited her projections on supports as different as the crashing waves and shifting sands of the beaches of Rio de Janeiro, the exterior of the Helmut Lang shop in Paris, as well as on iconic buildings, such as I. M. Pei's Pyramide du Louvre, the New York Public Library, Rockefeller Center, and Castel Sant'Angelo in Rome, among many others. At the Gelman Library of The George Washington University, which houses the National Security Archive,[27] Holzer used a single projector to show selections of declassified government documents. At the Bobst Library of New York University, two projectors were employed. "At NYU, I split the documents so that on the right were policy documents, and on the left were first-person accounts, whether from detainees or soldiers: 'I saw . . . I did. . . This happened to me.'" The process was the same at both libraries: "Text transfers to film. Film scrolls very slowly on the façade. People ask if the documents are real."

In selecting which of her films (running about one hour, but looped to run continuously) to include for projection at a particular site, Holzer at times creates new anthologies of texts responsive to a site's particular history as well as to the possibilities for her "screen." A particularly literal and evocative choice informed her projection *For the Capitol* (2007) where the

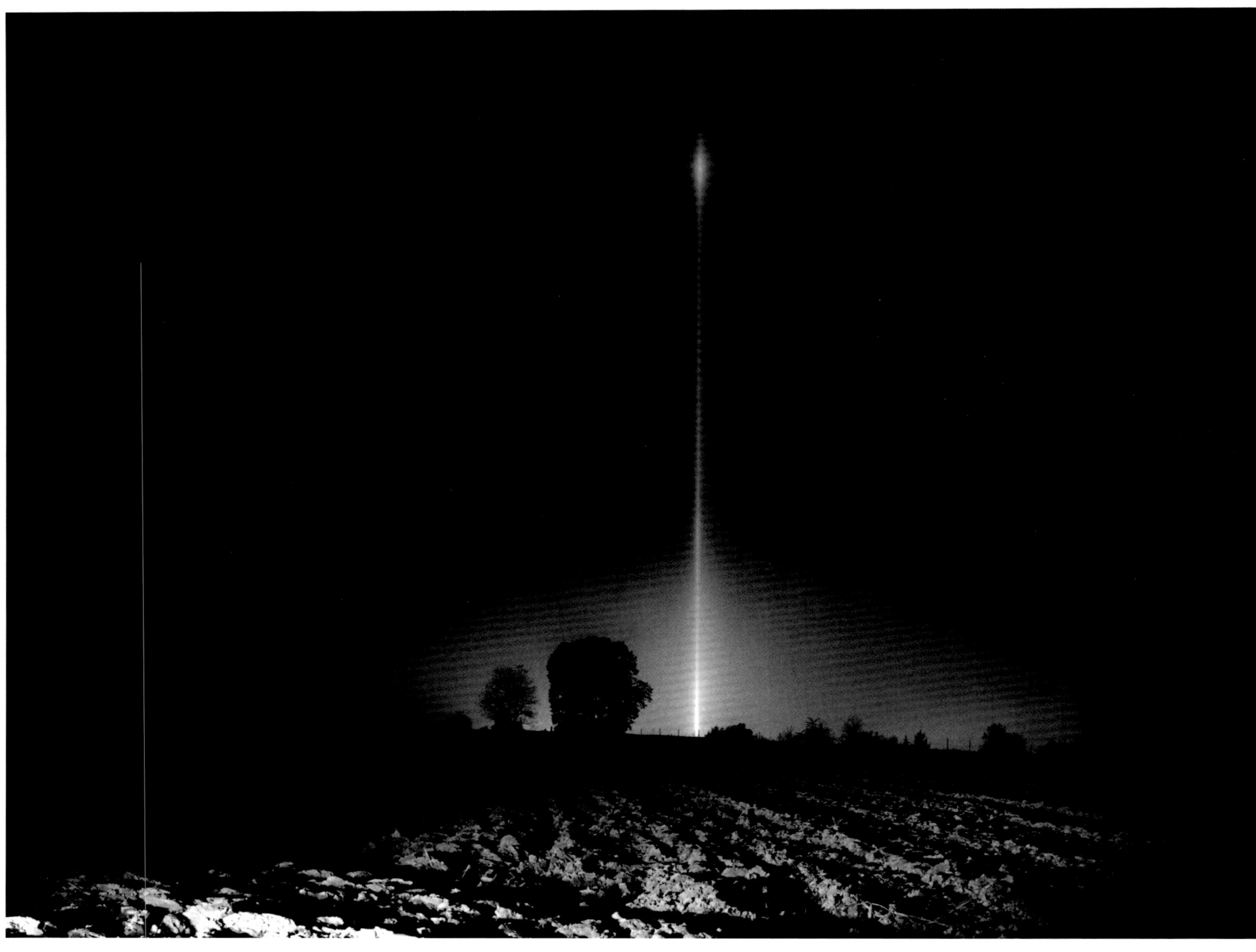

View of *Erlauf Peace Monument*, 1995

crawl of words was Holzer's simulcasting of quotations from John F. Kennedy and Theodore Roosevelt, projected from the outdoor terrace of the Kennedy Center in Washington, D.C., onto the Potomac River and Roosevelt Island. (There were two projectors at the Kennedy Center. The projector on the left ran the Roosevelt film; the projector on the right, the Kennedy.) This kind of echoing of place, of course, is also related to many of her commissions in other media, such as *For Pittsburgh* (2005), an enormous LED installation, her largest in the United States, which is sited along a pair of sweeping ascents that define the roofline of the David L. Lawrence Convention Center, and on which Holzer uses blue diodes to display the texts of novels that take place in Pittsburgh by Annie Dillard, John Edgar Wideman, and Thomas Bell,[28] or the Los Angeles garden of Holzer's *Blacklist* (1999), honoring The Hollywood Ten, who were blacklisted by the movie industry because of their refusal to testify, citing their First Amendment rights, when subpoenaed by the House Un-American Activities Committee in 1947.

Holzer's garden for *Blacklist* is surrounded by a circle of ten benches carved with the words of The Hollywood Ten, and critically these are placed within a larger context: the pavers of its paths give voice to the many others in the entertainment industry who spoke up against McCarthyism while also including the words of the investigating committee's members, serving as reminders of the vigilance ever necessary in the present.[29] Further, as Holzer said: "This garden would have you think how hate and fear can poison daily life. It is a monument to the First Amendment and a memorial to the creative artists and others who became victims of the Cold War. Blacklisting ended careers and ruined lives. It silenced public debate, undermined due process and freedom of thought, and weakened the elaborate protections of the minority that safeguard American liberty."[30]

The slow crawl of words of Holzer's light projections has often been noted as being related to the film credits at the end of a movie, the very credits The Hollywood Ten were denied (or else credited as pseudonyms, for those who managed to gain work sub rosa). Nor are Holzer's light projections unlike *son et lumière* shows at historic sites such as palaces and ruins, though Holzer's light projections forego musical accompaniment or separate narration. How it looks is indeed what it says, for her illuminated text-as-image is the narration.

As moving images projected at night, Holzer's works also recall the ambitions of Vladimir Tatlin's *Monument to the Third International* (1919), which was to beam broadcasts into the skies, and closer to home, the more

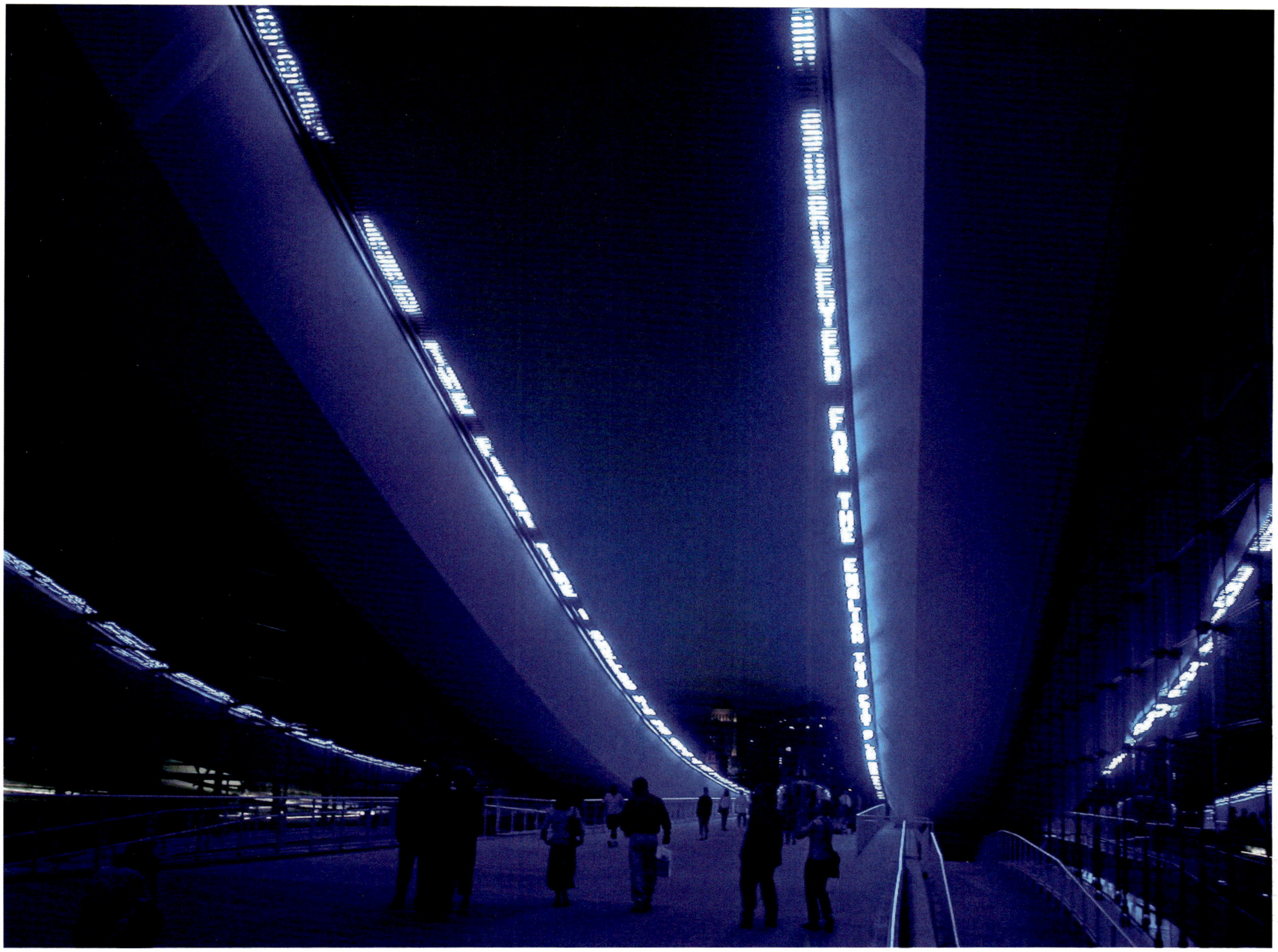

***For Pittsburgh*, 2005**

ad hoc collective experience of small communities assembling for a fireworks display. That Holzer has positioned her chosen texts as disembodied, luminous town criers makes for a changing theatrical spectacle moving slowly through space, one that serves also a need for communal, participatory events. Critic and poet Peter Schjeldahl aptly characterizes Holzer's film projections as "conscience fireworks," and writes as well of the mixed emotional response of individuals experiencing her "chastening and exciting" language in public: "It awakens what is abject in us to an awed joy."[31]

POETICS OF SPACE

The question of whether to use the same texts indoors and out has been one Holzer has faced for many years. "The text used to be identical whether it was shown out of doors or inside. The emphasis was on the public works. Then I would bring the artifacts from outside indoors, but I wasn't satisfied with them as official artwork."[32] This led her to a split practice, where there "are the public things, like the television spots. The subject matter tends to be the same, but what I'll do if I know it's going to be in a gallery or museum where people are willing to invest more time, is write longer, more complicated texts. On the street the text has to be a one-liner if I hope to catch someone's attention. The subjects are the same: war, sex, death. Premature death seems to be the recurring theme, but I approach it in different ways because of the different demands of the audience."[33] For her first light projections used indoors in 2006, the texts had not been used outdoors; for her second, the following year, she used the same texts both indoors and out.

Holzer slows the pace of her indoor projections, single lines moving at a crawl almost at the rate of breathing across the ceilings, floors, and walls of the gallery space as well as across any obstacles in their path, whether those be the audience or large islandlike pods for seating. The texts appear to deconstruct themselves as they distort and dissolve, splay into abstract marks and slip across the physical elements of the room and across the bodies of viewers who move through the space. The experiences of time as well as a fogged surround of changing light are paramount in grasping the language and its meanings. The immersion in light and languages turns reading into a physical presence, the experience almost a dreamlike state.

Holzer first brought her projections indoors, at Vienna's MAK in 2006, for a show titled *XX*, and she made the first U.S. presentation of such works at the Massachusetts Museum of Contemporary Art (Mass MoCA) in North Adams, Massachusetts, in 2007–8. In both shows she created opposing flows of text by using two projectors at the far ends of a long room, but Holzer's method of reading and, in fact, editing these works differed. For MAK, Holzer used two novels by Elfriede Jelinek — *Women as Lovers* and *Wonderful, Wonderful Times* — having been introduced to Jelinek's work by designer Helmut Lang, who had known the writer in Vienna. Before, Holzer had always used the complete text of other writers, whether whole novels, as was the case in *For Pittsburgh*, or sensitively edited anthologies, such as in *For 7 World Trade*. But here she abridged the Jelinek works. In the process, she continued to develop and refine a new way of reading, and editing, choosing different stresses for different passages to reshape the long texts for the slow, line-by-line reading of her audience. "Jelinek blessed the method as well as the result," says Holzer.[34] Jelinek wrote the artist: "Thank you, dear Jenny: wonderful wonderful work! you have done. I'm so glad I left it entirely to you." She goes on, sharing Holzer's deadpan humor: "It's very interesting for me to see the text 'butchered' by you. Very fine schnitzels and cutlets! I'm glad . . . kindest regards, Elfriede."[35]

For Mass MoCA, Holzer used the poetry of the Nobel Prize–winning Polish poet Wisława Szymborska for the dual projections within a 252-by-53-foot gallery. Szymborska in the Mass MoCA installation is, in a sense, a surrogate for Holzer; she is the poet that Holzer herself has never claimed to be, despite the appearance of some of her own writings as terse, evocative poems. As an anthologist and director of the filmed images of Szymborska's works, assuming the tasks of stage director and lighting designer, overseeing the scale, tempo, and placement of these changing elements, Holzer organized the flow of language by topics, some of which we expect of her, as in "Torture." Yet others came as a surprise, particularly "The Joy of Writing," perhaps an ironic reference both to the titles of popular cooking and sex books as well as to Matisse's *The Joy of Life* that seemed to imply another reason for her turn to the writings of others: Holzer has referred to the struggle of her own crafting of language as a recurring return to "writing jail."

In explaining her choice of Szymborska, Holzer has cited the work's deft combination of immediate relevance and timelessness. She recently said: "Szymborska writes on a number of subjects that are of interest to me. She has a poem about torture, about refugees. There's one about a terrorist. These are things on people's minds now. She writes about writing. She writes about being guilty. And then there's one about parting I like because it's a gentle release. Szymborska manages to speak to everything essential, and I think that's a good thing to proffer to people. Here is what's essential, written by a superb poet, floating by and on you."[36]

Holzer's engagement of the gallery space for these light installations invoked a history of experiential spaces such as El Lissitzky's *Proun* rooms of the early 1920s, which served as way stations for both painting and architecture, in addition to the psychological, literary, and visual projections of the Imagist poet H.D.'s "Writing on the Wall," and contemporary artists whose instructional language intended to result in images in space has been inspiration for Holzer, including that of Lawrence Weiner, "partly because it was language, but more so because it was about work that was immediate and available to people. That seemed worthy, particularly his early book *Statements,* where he gave instructions — a bunch of instructions and anyone can make the art." Especially important for Holzer are the instructions of Sol LeWitt as procedures for others to install his wall drawings. As she recently said, "I am reassured by order and ordering — I admired how LeWitt used systems as the foundation, and then made that mad and mysterious."[37]

Holzer's chosen words, fragmented at Mass MoCA by ceiling rafters or distorted into linear abstractions on the side walls, erupt a procedural system to create something of the mad and mysterious that Holzer attributes to LeWitt. They also create an experience of rapture that she once said she thought she had to leave behind when she began posting her *Truisms* in 1977, after a period, as she has said, when she "was bouncing back and forth between the Weiners and emotional floating things, like Rothko's." In her overwhelming presentations of text being formed and dematerializing, and the centrality of her audience who accumulate and absorb these fragments and recombine them into new understandings, Holzer has physically made present what Roland Barthes described as a characteristic of the "paradox of the reader":

> It is commonly admitted that to read is to decode: letters, words, meanings, structures, and this is incontestable; but by accumulating decodings (since reading is by rights infinite), by removing the safety catch of meaning, by putting reading into freewheeling (which is its structural vocation), the reader is caught up in a dialectical reversal: finally, he does not decode, he *overcodes;* he does not decipher, he produces, he accumulates languages, he lets himself be infinitely and tirelessly traversed by them: he is that traversal.[38]

SHAPELY, SELF-SUFFICIENT THINGS

If the indoor projections are experienced somatically, it is not just that we are bathed in the light of language but also that our readings of the text are experienced as if the interior mental projections of the sort we make always as we absorb text, focusing word by word, line by line, to internalize images and meanings, were made manifest. In Holzer's most recent sculptures, which she refers to as "rib pieces" or "rib cage" pieces, the body itself is invoked in different ways, and in contrast to the division of text into fragments of the light projections, these depend on multiplication for the clarity of their longer, faster-paced moving phrases, and for the ambient, controlled spill of light they emanate. Holzer began to create these sculptures, made up of multiple curved LED signs, with diodes of different colors, "around five or six years ago," as she says, "when I realized, boy, was I not a sculptor; I wanted to see if I even could approach that. I tried to make self-sufficient pieces that didn't, for example, rely on a shapely building on which to project. I thought I'd make shapely things all by myself."

The first of these sculptures incorporated poems by Henri Cole, whom she had met at the American Academy in Berlin in 2001. As she recalls, "The odd ducks gravitated to one another, and I was sick of writing. I was so relieved to be able to show his poems." Holzer first projected Cole's texts in 2003 at the Peggy Guggenheim Foundation in Venice, before using them for sculpture. *Rib Cage* (2004), exhibited at Yvon Lambert Gallery in Paris that year, "had a poem by Henri called 'Beach Walk,' a hard poem, a perfect one. Hard enough to make you slit your throat on the spot." Its illuminations of passing LED letterforms shape a situation that beckons the viewer to remain within a performative space (by the glow of its white diodes on the front of the bands), while also defining a sculptural space within its bounds, for the same text plays (almost unseen to the viewer) in red and white diodes on the back of the bands to create a glowing pink column of light within that also plays onto the floor and ceiling. Holzer integrates other Cole poems into the angular tilts of her electronic signage *Looming* (2004), which includes the poems "Gravity and Center," "Bowl of Lilacs," "Self-Portrait with Hornets," "Poppies," and "The Lost Bee," and in the zigzag bars of *Purple Cross* (2004), whose red and blue diodes illuminate the poem "Blur" and create an aura in its wake that bathes the reader in a perceptual shift of red, blue, and fields of purple.

Holzer's new independent "shapely" sculptures have both an intimacy and grandeur, and create almost force fields around and within the situations they define, transforming the contemporary gallery's "white cube" into a sensorium. In her most recent variants, such as *Monument* (2008), she has taken her serial repetition of ribs and a new palette to a baroque complexity of colors and programming, while at the same time cycling back, as she says, to "the basic kit" of her earliest texts, using for this piece her *Truisms* and *Inflammatory Essays*.[39] Created for exhibition in Moscow, *Monument* scales a 20-foot wall, using 22 half-circle LED signs for a tunnel of light in shocking pinks, reds, purples, and oranges that bedazzles, raising the fearsome heat of her Venice Biennale "toaster oven" to an even edgier barrage and choosing a palette just in the balance between bubblegum tawdry and Schiaparelli glamour, while also evoking in its title Tatlin's revolutionary tower.

SECRETS AND THE PAINTED WORD

"I came to language because I wanted to be explicit about things, but didn't want to be a social realist painter. I had been an abstract painter and that was the painting that I loved, and that I could do. It's not that I thought that one was better than the other, but for some reason I couldn't become a figurative painter. I wanted to be explicit about things, and it became clear that the only other way for me to do it was to use language. People can understand you when you say or write something."[40] Her abstract works as a graduate student at RISD had been paintings on walls, canvases that displayed single lines of text, painted and sometimes knotted fabric left in long lines on a beach, as well as bread crumbs distributed in lines and geometric shapes outdoors so as to have them vanish over time when pigeons ate them. By contrast, Holzer's recent paintings, begun in 2005, find their sources in language.

These new paintings were begun, as she says, "about three years ago, in the middle of the war—this last one. The paintings came after *Wired* magazine asked me to imagine something new for the Google start page. I said I wanted to see secrets, a different secret every time I logged on. I went looking for something not commonly known, and found a letter from Enron's Ken Lay to then-Governor Bush thanking him for a gift of art, a Western-style work. The Enron letter was in thesmokingun.com—a frisky, cheerful site. Then I searched more widely for former secrets, and came to the National

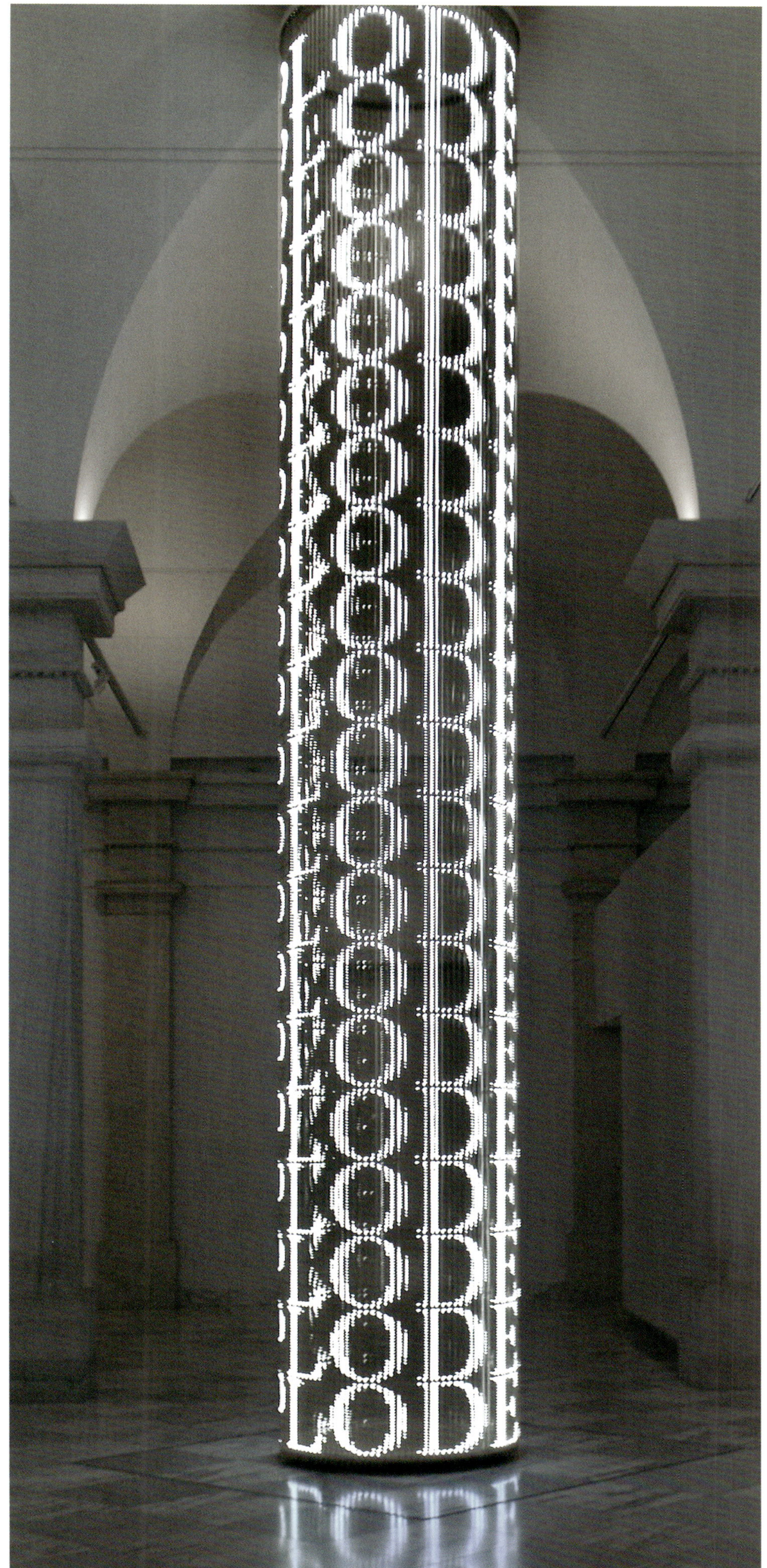

***For SAAM*, 2007**

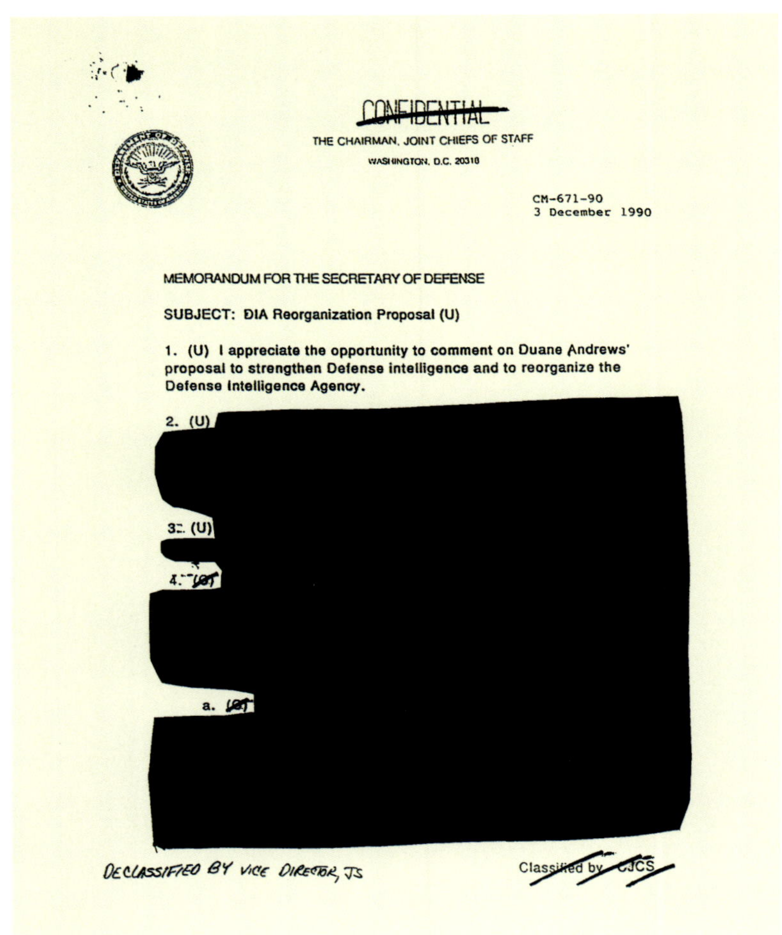

CONFIDENTIAL

THE CHAIRMAN, JOINT CHIEFS OF STAFF
WASHINGTON, D.C. 20318

CM-671-90
3 December 1990

MEMORANDUM FOR THE SECRETARY OF DEFENSE

SUBJECT: DIA Reorganization Proposal (U)

1. (U) I appreciate the opportunity to comment on Duane Andrews' proposal to strengthen Defense intelligence and to reorganize the Defense Intelligence Agency.

2. (U)

3. (U)

4. (C)

a. (C)

DECLASSIFIED BY VICE DIRECTOR, JS

Classified by CJCS

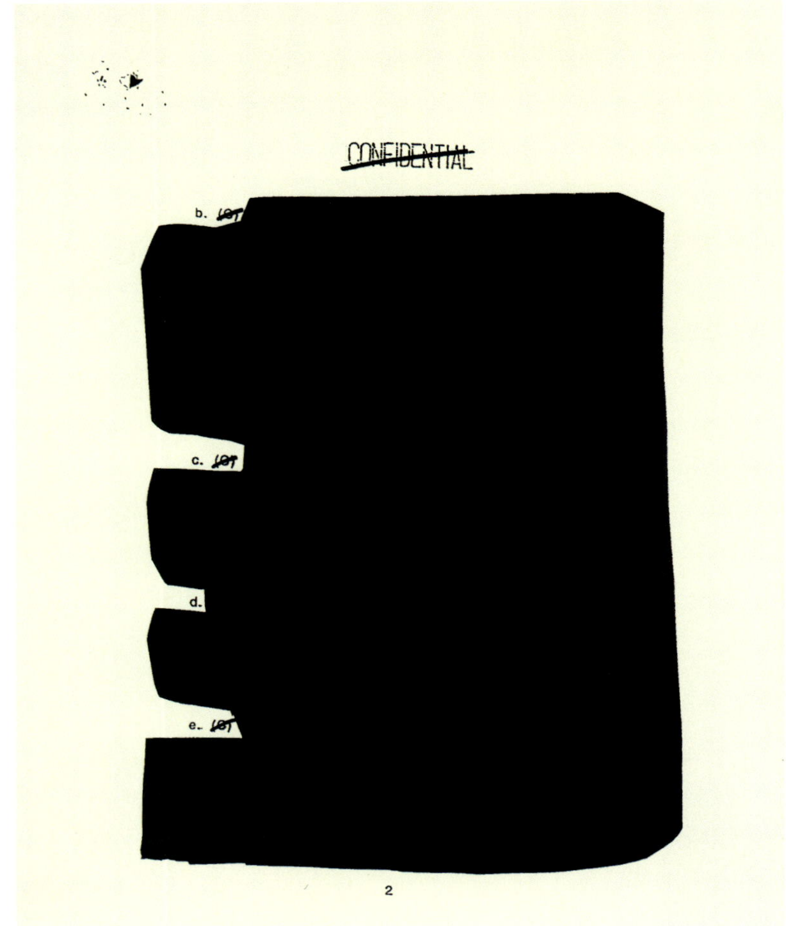

CONFIDENTIAL

b. (C)

c. (C)

d.

e. (C)

2

***COLIN POWELL** GREEN WHITE*, **2006**

Security Archive, the ACLU, and the FBI site. I concentrated on documents about the Middle East, and when I found something good I'd paint it. But when I located interesting pages about Alice Neel, I'd paint those, too. Alice Neel had an FBI file because she was red. She was followed for some time."

Though Holzer "did not use the Enron–Bush thing" for any of the paintings, it was, as she says, "the launch." Some of the first in this series of paintings were based on FBI e-mails from Guantanamo in which "the FBI guys and women were aghast at how DOD [Department of Defense] personnel were handling the interrogations and were angry that they dressed as FBI, so that when information about torture came out, there would be deniability." That Holzer used paintings to make public these texts was a critical turn in her practice, for she had first used the texts in her 2004 *Truth Before Power* show in Bregenz, where they were programmed in LEDs and also displayed as light projections. Holzer explains her decision to return to painting after some 30 years: "Because people study and preserve paintings and take them seriously, whereas the information wasn't always noticed or taken seriously. It's feeble, but that was my logic."

One of the earliest of these paintings was based on a document called "Wish List"—an e-mail from a U.S. Army captain to interrogators in Iraq requesting that they come up with a "wish list" of "innovative interrogation techniques." Such techniques proposed in the chain of e-mails include confinement in close quarters, sleep deprivation, white noise, and "a litany of harsher fear-up approaches . . . fear of dogs and snakes appear to work nicely." Holzer offers, "One gung-ho guy wrote, 'The gloves are coming off gentlemen regarding these detainees (redaction) has made it clear that we want these individuals broken'; while another answered, 'We are American soldiers, heirs of a long tradition of staying on the high ground. We need to stay there.'"

In their flatness and superimposed image, Holzer's paintings may recall the layering of silk-screen images on Warhol's overall fields and, similarly, his implied off-handed, disinterested stance. They invoke as well the procedural fabrication of works by Process and Minimal artists and Holzer's own prior use of expert advice and assistance, for she does not paint these canvases herself. She works with a painter following a practice in which she has worked with professional stone masons for the lettering on her benches and sarcophagi; projectionists for her outdoor light projections and, more recently, indoor projections; and electronics engineers and various other technicians for her LED signs and web pages. "I didn't paint them," Holzer offers. "I was lucky enough to be introduced to an artist, Ben Snead, who graduated from RISD with a master's degree in painting. To make the backgrounds, we look at books about great painters, Goya books, for example. We sample skies in his black paintings. We take an inch and make that the whole ground." Working with a painter, and using a template for scale, Holzer's process partakes somewhat of the instructions of Minimalists to fabricate their works, but differs in the exchange between artist and fabricator. Holzer uses an appropriate literary reference to convey this partnership: "I give colors and the level of 'smeariness,' and he translates."

Though each is unique, there "was a desire to repeat certain" of her subjects: "If I really like a document, or if I can't figure out what emotional qualities should attach to it, I'll screen it in and on different colors—black on white is different from black on awful purple. I go beautiful or ugly

~~CONFIDENTIAL~~

1. (C)

5. (C)

6. (C)

3

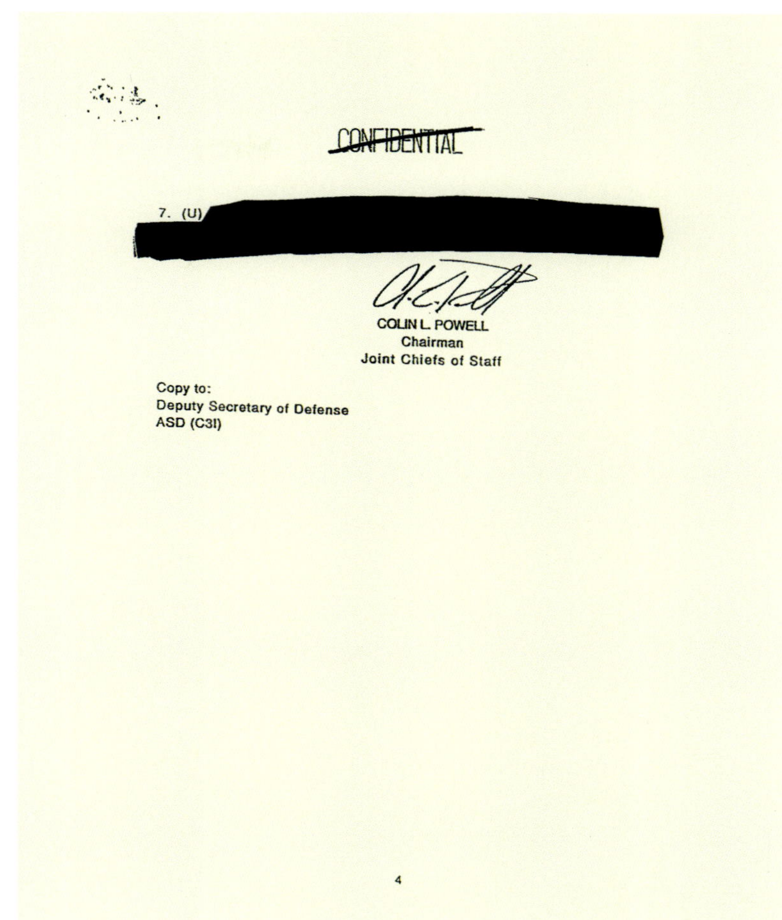

~~CONFIDENTIAL~~

7. (U)

COLIN L. POWELL
Chairman
Joint Chiefs of Staff

Copy to:
Deputy Secretary of Defense
ASD (C3I)

4

depending on which seems appropriate. Black on white seems factual. Other documents are hazy about what happened, and I'll go to emotional color choices and surfaces. And as with the *Inflammatory Essays*, I'll use a color at a time to distinguish one text from another."

Using "high quality oils" on linen, Holzer works the evidence in direct, explicit ways, as she says, "in contrast to the president's repeated denial of torture." The horrific nature of some of these documents, all in the public record, prompts Holzer to question investigative reporting itself: "Press, where are you? Where were you?" An excerpt from an autopsy report reads: "According to the investigative report provided by U.S. Army CID [Criminal Investigation Command], the decedent was shackled to the top of a doorframe with a gag in his mouth at the time he lost consciousness and became pulseless. The severe blunt force injuries, the hanging position, and the obstruction of the oral cavity with a gag contributed to this individual's death." From an FBI file: "These discussions were prompted by the recognition that members of the Defense Intelligence Agency's (DIA) Defense HUMINT Services (DHS) were being encouraged at times to use aggressive interrogation tactics in GTMO which are of questionable effectiveness and subject to uncertain interpretation based on law and regulation. Not only are these tactics at odds with legally permissible interviewing techniques used by U.S. law enforcement agencies in the United States, but they are being employed by personnel in GTMO who appear to have little, if any, experience eliciting information for judicial purposes. The continued use of these techniques has the potential of negatively impacting future interviews by FBI agents as they attempt to gather intelligence and prepare cases for prosecution."

For a time, Holzer fixed on a series of maps that were used to plan the invasion of Iraq. "I needed to get out of some of the manic terror the maps occasioned — I made some 35 map paintings, and I screened a series of works using handprints of detainees who died in detention and of soldiers who were charged with detainee abuse." The handprint paintings, especially seen in series, are perhaps the most shocking in both their content and in their abstraction. In each stark black-and-white translation, and cumulatively in series, Holzer offers a systematic portrayal of torture — a concerted, repeated, authorized, undeniable pattern of offense, and not individual rogue episodes. As the artist says, "These are redacted, and redacted by many people. In most cases the black partially covers the handprints — so that the prints can't be identified. Some are almost completely blackened, some have lines through them so the hands look like skeletons. Some seem cartoony, others appear sinister." Holzer's portrayal of the handprint in black (an echo of the ink used to take these in the first place) on white fields, not only emphasizes the factuality of the images, but coupled with her enlargement of them, makes the emotional and actual import of these subjects unavoidable, almost unbearable.

Holzer speaks of the reaction to these paintings when exhibited: "The hands are startling to some. A few were shown in Venice [in 2007]. People find them sad. The prints from the detainees are post-mortem, and it is ghastly to take a dead man's hands and yank them down to make prints. That's why those handprints are distorted." In response to the paintings of maps documenting the planned invasion of Iraq: "Some people think the maps are fake. That's also been the experience when we project various documents outdoors. Who would want to think they're real? For example, the words on the maps were: 'Protect,' 'Exploit'. . . 'Seize North oil. Seize South oil'. . . 'Defeat,' 'Destroy,' 'Degrade,' 'Suppress.'"

In choosing no longer to write her own texts, Holzer has invited the lyrical, more joyous aspects of a chosen poet's voice to enter the body of her work, and by using the tone of these poets' words, to find amplifications and illuminations on subjects that have been her concern. In her use of government documents, she has at the same time extended her field of view to include passionate, political reporting. Through these works, Holzer has, in fact, published earlier and more extensively than many journalists' accounts. While the media were broadcasting officials' public denials of torture and their equivocations before Congress on the question of what constitutes criminal treatment of detainees, Holzer was bringing to light, sometimes quite literally, those explicit texts that show a government incriminating itself. In the course of researching these secrets, Holzer has also found materials relating to other figures, familiar in the world of the arts and entertainment, that cumulatively paint a picture of a history of invasions of privacy, including Rock Hudson, Marion Anderson, George Orwell, and Nat King Cole as well as the above-mentioned Alice Neel. Holzer has already painted some of these redacted documents. Others remain to be executed.

In Holzer's use of previously classified documents and whole series of them, the artist often incorporates truths that are stranger and more horrific than she herself voiced in her own writings; in those policy documents that chart the course of war and which Holzer incorporates into her work as she found them, the narratives and instructions are so specific as to seem surreal. When using the declassified redacted documents that are almost fully blacked out, she has found ready-made abstractions. Their irregular black fields call to mind Richard Serra's wall drawings, while at the same time their "presence" marks not only the absence of information but also serves as stark evidence of authority's will to silence and stifle dissent. One becomes only more curious, for example, about what General Colin Powell may have reported in the multi-page document, serially blackened, that Holzer has painted. In her paintings, using totalities of elements of found image/texts, she has accomplished in content and form, as an artist and anthologizer of language, something that Susan Sontag defined in her text "The Conscience of Words": "Information will never replace illumination. But something that sounds like, except that it's better than, information — I mean the condition of being informed; I mean concrete, specific, detailed, historically dense, first-hand knowledge — is the indispensable prerequisite for a writer to express opinions in public."[41] These are the qualities of language in these documents, whose writers express opinions to each other, and now, via the Freedom of Information Act and Holzer's paintings, in public.

As of 2008, the declassified documents that Holzer has been including in her paintings for the past three years are being reported in the press and in congressional hearings, but as the artist says, she is "not quite done with the painting." In part, she says, this is because "it's wonderful to roll around in color, a long-delayed, long-repressed impulse. I don't know whether I'll continue with it. I thought maybe I'd go back and paint key documents from the Vietnam era, or trace the history of interrogation tactics. There are really interesting documents about what is gentlemanly and logical to do during interrogation. It seemed there used to be limits, for ethical, practical, and legal reasons. The process is still worth doing. Still, I like changing. I've been wanting to do a cell phone project, may be I could get that — secret docs for people on the phone."

Holzer speaks of using "intelligent animatronics" that can writhe and wriggle and also respond to the movements of people nearby. As for whether she will return to writing her own texts, Holzer says for now her writing is limited to "e-mails only, although I got three-quarters of the way through a country-western chick song the other day. The opening line is, 'You know that boy you think is yours.' I can do more art if I don't try to write. I can try what I'm better at, to make things look right. And I can have more and better content if I'm choosing rather than generating it. It's practical and a relief to work this way. Even joyous at times."

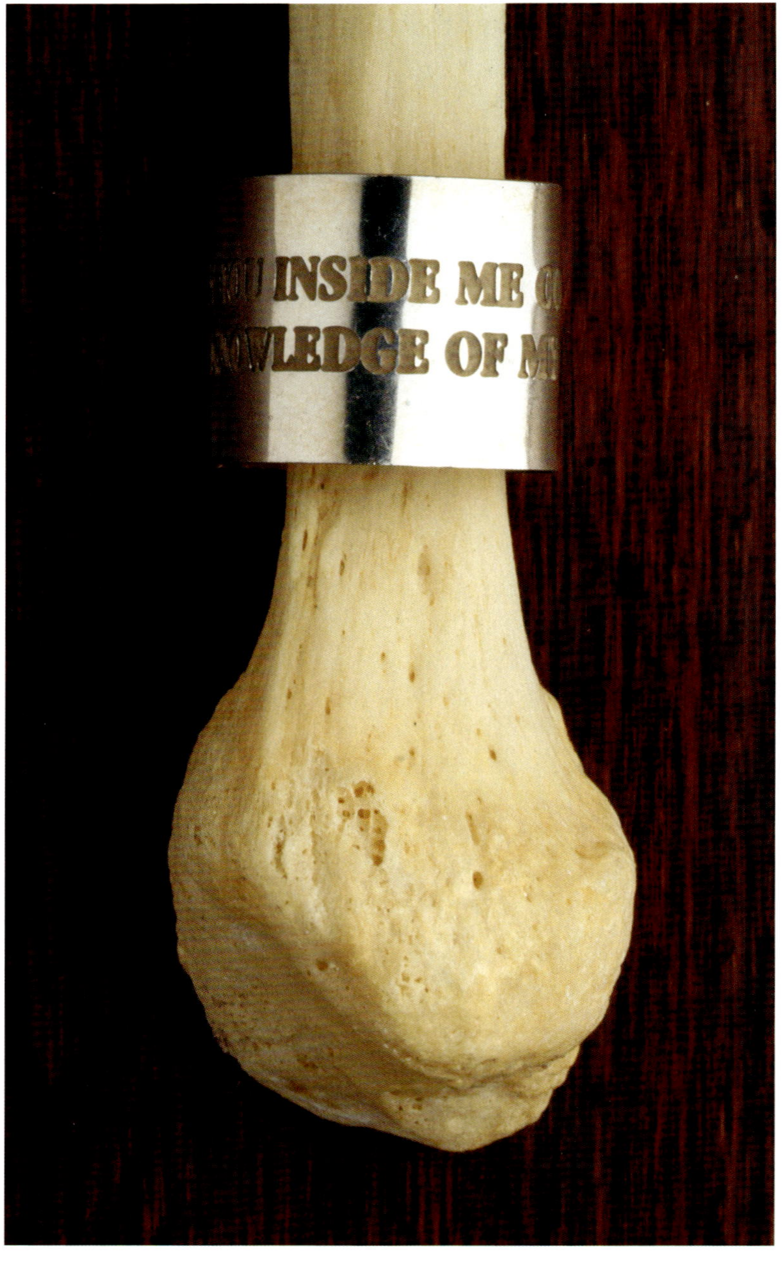

***Lustmord*, 1996 (detail)**

NOTES

1 Unless otherwise noted, all Jenny Holzer quotations are from conversations with the author between October 2007 and May 2008.

2 Holzer's next versions of the "ribs/cage" LED rungs, *Bar, Stave, True Ribs,* and *Thorax,* all created in 2008, include, respectively, declassified government documents programmed with autopsies; materials regarding the prison at Guantanamo Bay; various files concerning alleged atrocities in the Middle East; and a case regarding a civilian murder in Iraq.

3 Holzer made her first sarcophagi in 1987, and the first two were exhibited in *Documenta 8,* Museum Fridericianum, Kassel, Germany, from June 12 through September 20, 1987. The first stone benches were made in 1986 for the series *Under a Rock.*

4 Initially the poetry of Israel's Yehuda Amichai (the first in a projection), in 2001, and the United States's Henri Cole (the first in an electronic sculpture), in 2004, and later that of Poland's Wisława Szymborska and Adam Zagajewski, Palestine's Mahmoud Darwish, Iraq's Fadhil Al-Azzawi, as well as extensive thematic anthologies that include the prose and poetry of New York stories (including the entirety of E. B. White's *Here is New York*); the "Pittsburgh" novels of Annie Dillard, John Edgar Wideman, and Thomas Bell; in addition to the many different series of declassified government documents, sometimes interweaving as well selections of her own earlier writings.

5 Roland Barthes, "Writing Reading," in *The Rustle of Language,* trans. Richard Howard (Berkeley: University of California Press, 1989), 30.

6 Holzer occasionally also used her *Survival* series for stickers affixed to lampposts.

7 Steven Henry Madoff, "Jenny Holzer Talks to Steven Henry Madoff," in "'80s Then," *Artforum* 41, no. 8 (April 2003), 82.

8 Ibid.

9 Ron Clark, director of the Whitney Independent Study Program (ISP) since 1981, wrote in an e-mail to the author (May 23, 2008): "Jenny was in the Program during the 1976–77 academic year, from the beginning of September through the end of May. My title at that time was Senior Instructor and I was in charge of the Studio component of the ISP while David Hupert was in charge of the Museum Studies Program. At that time, we had once-a-week seminars with professional artists, critics, and art historians. Throughout the seventies, the artists leading seminars were prominent members of the minimalist and conceptualist movements (for instance, Donald Judd, Dan Flavin, Robert Morris, Carl Andre, Richard Serra, Vito Acconci, Joseph Kosuth, Frank Stella and Brice Marden,) and also filmmakers (Michael Snow, Hollis Frampton) and dancers and musicians (Yvonne Rainer, Trisha Brown, Joan Jonas and Phil Glass). In 1981, I began our weekly theory seminar on a formal basis. Prior to that, we mostly had informal discussions relating to critical, cultural and social theory on a more or less ad hoc basis. Jenny would have been part of those informal discussions. The reading list that she often refers to was one that I prepared and distributed to the students every year. The list at that time would have included structuralism and semiotics (Roland Barthes), Frankfurt School (Walter Benjamin, Theodor Adorno, Herbert Marcuse), structural Marxism (Louis Althusser) and feminism (Laura Mulvey)."

10 Holzer gained credits from the Whitney program that applied to her last year of graduate school at the Rhode Island School of Design (RISD). She had previously studied liberal arts at Duke University, Durham, North Carolina (1968–70); drawing, painting, and liberal arts at the University of Chicago (1970–71); and painting and printmaking at Ohio University, Athens (1972–73, BFA).

11 Madoff, "Jenny Holzer Talks to Steven Henry Madoff," 82.

12 Holzer's "single" lengths of signs were later used at dramatic, extended size, responsive also to particular sites, such as the almost 43-foot-high rectangular, vertically oriented LED piece that she installed in the room devoted to her work at the Guggenheim Bilbao, or the 668-foot signage for the roof of Pittsburgh's David L. Lawrence Convention Center in her 2005 commission *For Pittsburgh.*

13 Madoff, "Jenny Holzer Talks to Steven Henry Madoff," 83.

14 John Yau and Shelley Jackson, "An Interview with Jenny Holzer," online journal of the Poetry Foundation. Available at: www.poetryfoundation.org/features/feature.onpoetry.html?id=178606 (accessed July 17, 2008).

15 Jenny Holzer, "Lustmord," *Süddeutsche Zeitung Magazin* (Nov. 19, 1993), 1–31.

16 Marshall McLuhan, "The Spoken Word," in *Understanding Media: The Extensions of Man* (Cambridge, MA: MIT Press, 1994), 80.

17 Patrick J. B. Flynn, "Jenny Holzer—Artist—Interview," *The Progressive* (April 1993). Available online at: http://findarticles.com/p/articles/mi_m1295/is_n4_v57/ai_13561338?tag=artBody;col1 (accessed July 10, 2008).

18 Ibid.

19 Ibid.

20 Joan Simon, "Jenny Holzer Interview," in *Landmarks: Sculpture Commissions for the Stuart Collection at the University of California, San Diego*, ed. Mary Livingstone Beebe, James Stuart DeSilva, Robert Storr (New York: Rizzoli, 2001), 208.

21 Ibid., 210.

22 Ibid.

23 Ibid., 211.

24 Joan Simon, "Joan Simon in Conversation with Jenny Holzer," in David Joselit, Joan Simon, Renata Salecl, *Jenny Holzer* (London: Phaidon, 1998), 32.

25 As Holzer said, "Vertical signs with *War* made the stairs of the Kunsthalle Basel impassable [1992]. The signs went to Saint Peter's Church in Cologne [1993]." Simon, "Joan Simon in Conversation with Jenny Holzer," 28.

26 While the technology for Holzer's light projections remains the same as from the outset, the specific "xenon" lamp is no longer employed.

27 An independent, non-governmental research institute and library located at The George Washington University, the archive collects and publishes declassified documents obtained through the Freedom of Information Act. It also serves as a repository of government records on a wide range of topics pertaining to the national security of the United States and to the country's foreign, intelligence, and economic policies. http://www.gwu.edu/~nsarchiv/nsa/the_archive.html

28 The Pittsburgh novels included are: *An American Childhood* by Annie Dillard; *NYC; Sent for You Yesterday*, *Hiding Place,* and *Damballah* by John Edgar Wideman; and *Out of This Furnace* by Thomas Bell.

29 "The First Amendment/Blacklist Project committee was formed by faculty members of the Filmic Writing Program in the School of Cinema-Television at the University of Southern California in Los Angeles at the suggestion of an undergraduate student, Drew Weinbrenner, and in response to a recognition that many future filmmakers knew little or nothing of this governmental infringement on professional creativity and personal civil liberties." The planting design was created by Professor Achva Benzinberg Stein, FASLA. Fisher Museum of Art at USC, "Jenny Holzer: Blacklist," http://uscfishermuseumofart.org/index.php?page=collections&action=blacklist (accessed July 10, 2008).

30 Ibid.

31 Peter Schjeldahl, "Jenny Holzer: Conscience Fireworks," in Peter Schjeldahl, Beatrix Ruf, and Joan Simon, *Jenny Holzer: Xenon* (Küsnacht, Switzerland: Ink•Tree Editions, 2001), 118.

32 Flynn, "Jenny Holzer—Artist—Interview."

33 Ibid.

34 For works using the texts of other writers, Holzer routinely obtains permission to incorporate the writing in these new media.

35 Elfriede Jelinek, e-mail to Jenny Holzer, March 2006.

36 Stacey Kors, "At Mass MoCA, Jenny Holzer Lights up a Room," *Boston Globe* (Nov. 23, 2007). Available online at: http://www.boston.com/ae/theater_arts/articles/2007/11/23/at_mass_moca_jenny_holzer_lights_up_a_room/(accessed July 10, 2008).

37 The relationship between LeWitt's mark-making and Holzer's writing on the walls with light projections is particularly sensed in the large galleries of Mass MoCA, where Holzer's exhibition, in Building 5, is next door to Building 7, which will house 40 years of LeWitt's wall drawings, to remain on view for 25 years. The in-progress installation was visited by the artist and author. Mass MoCA has timed the opening of the LeWitt to overlap with the closing weekend of the Holzer (the LeWitt officially opens Nov. 16, 2008), and for a short period a door will connect the two, allowing visitors entering from the former to view the latter from a balcony.

38 Barthes, "On Reading," 42.

39 As an ongoing part of her practice, Holzer fluidly circulates texts through many of her different support structures. Her *Truisms*, for example, may be seen in light, in stone, on paper, in film projection, and on cloth or other objects. Among recent examples: on selected rocks within the 1,800-meter-long stone wall of *Wanås Wall* (2002); via the 25 curved LED signs of *Blue Curve* (2007); the tilted verticals of *Blue Purple Tilt* (2007); and on 13 of the 22 LED signs of *Monument* (2008). Similarly, her declassified government documents have been anchored in three dimensions for LED sculptures, in two dimensions for paintings, and in immaterial light for her projections.

40 Flynn, "Jenny Holzer—Artist—Interview."

41 Susan Sontag, "The Conscience of Words," in *At the Same Time: Essays and Speeches,* ed. Paolo Dilonardo and Anne Jump, foreword by David Rieff (New York: Farrar Straus Giroux, 2007), 154.

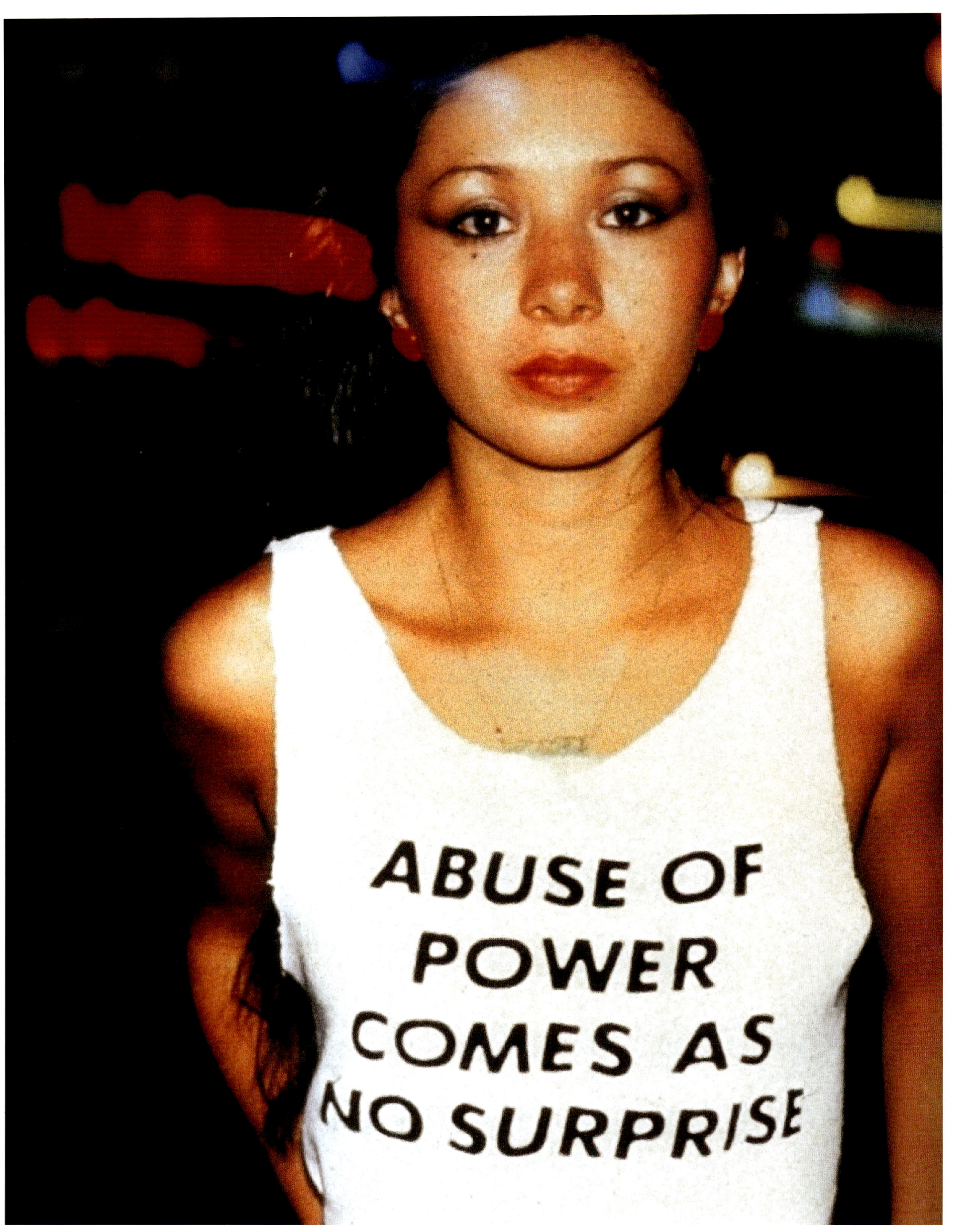
ABUSE OF
POWER
COMES AS
NO SURPRISE

PROTECT PROTECT: THE SOCIALLY USEFUL ART OF JENNY HOLZER

ELIZABETH A. T. SMITH

Jenny Holzer asks us to respond to a world where good and evil coexist as love and hate do in the soul.

— Henri Cole[1]

IN HER ESSAY "Against Interpretation," first published in 1961, writer Susan Sontag persuasively argued in favor of an art criticism that "dissolves considerations of content into those of form."[2] These ideas, which had considerable impact on art history and theory, continue to have currency in that today such considerations of form and content are rarely separated in discussions about art. Through her staunch commitment to the central role of language in art and her unique, inimitable approach to presenting it in various visual manifestations and contexts, Jenny Holzer intertwines form and content to produce a potent tension between the realms of feeling and knowledge. Yet the unceasing presence of social and political ideas throughout 30 years of her work reveals the depth of her engagement with subject matter that is timely and topical in its direct, unflinching consideration of world events and their human impact. This essay will therefore focus on the sociopolitical dimension of Holzer's work — a persistent component of her practice that is foregrounded in her most recent works, which form the basis of this exhibition.

Holzer has engaged with socially and politically charged ideas throughout her career from the vantage point of the socially useful.[3] She has consistently emphasized the artwork as a carrier of ideas that stimulate a passive viewer to become an active questioner by inviting reflection on intentions, meaning, and authorship. Poet Henri Cole aptly pinpoints how Holzer's language-based work operates to offer "the experience of reading, where self-forgetfulness brings about recognition of the self."[4] This characteristic spans her entire body of work — from text pieces begun in the late 1970s to LED works programmed with text that have been ongoing since the early 1980s, to the more recent light projection pieces she has realized on building exteriors since the mid-1990s and in interiors since 2006, and her newest silk-screen paintings that present text and images culled from declassified U.S. government documents.

Labeling Holzer as a political artist oversimplifies her practice of presenting our culture's range of voices and values; nonetheless, her work is deeply political in the way it raises questions and catalyzes thinking about the role of individuals in society and the relationship between the public and private realms. Power and vulnerability, violence and tenderness, moral struggle and depravity — all manners of contradictory motivations — are chronicled in her work as interwoven impulses. The method in which she reveals our society's and our collective psyche's deeply embedded actions, emotions, and intellectual constructs offers a mirror of ourselves that spans the complexities of human experience.

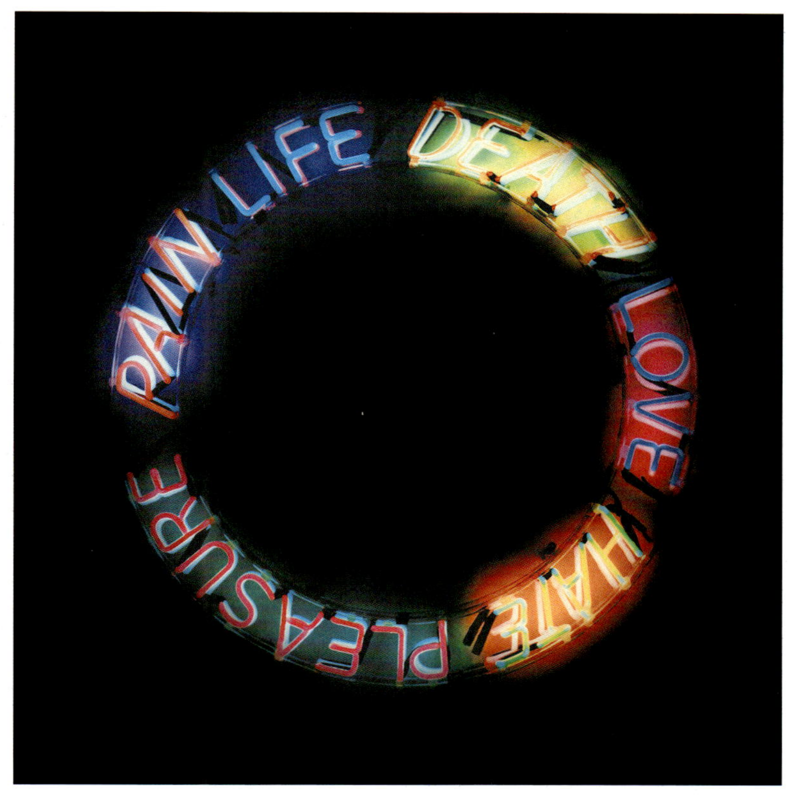

opposite: **from *Truisms*, 1983**
above: **Bruce Nauman, *Life, Death, Love, Hate, Pleasure, Pain*, 1983**

"From a political standpoint, I was drawn to writing because it was possible to be very explicit about things," Holzer has commented.[5] An extensive literature exists on Holzer's early work and the formation of her text-based series of the late 1970s and early 1980s, such as *Truisms* (1977–79), *Living* (1980–82), and *Survival* (1983–85), each fraught with contradictory meanings, and *Inflammatory Essays* (1979–82), decidedly more incendiary and polemical in tone. Analyzing the statements comprising the series *Truisms,* critic Hal Foster suggests that their revelation of multiple beliefs and biases uncovers the idea of truth as arbitrary as the individual voices become "lost in a plurality of public voices."[6] Speaking further to the social utility of these ostensibly neutral and non-partisan texts, Foster deems them "conflicted and cogent by turns . . . verbal anarchy in the street."[7] Resonating with that of the early 20th-century Dadaists — the first model for Holzer's work between art and politics — this sensibility has continued to animate her subsequent activity. The absurdity, chaos, and aimlessness of the Dada movement, along with its frequent confrontations with and mediations on the political reality of the time, were important starting points for Holzer; its example continues to be significant in her current responsiveness to the disastrous consequences of war as a key subject in her work.

During a period when many of Holzer's contemporaries saw themselves as cultural activists directly linked to the political activism of the New Left, Holzer began her explorations of the power of language and its presence in nonart contexts, first while a student in the Whitney Independent Study Program and later as a member and active participant in the group Collaborative Projects, known as Colab, from 1978 to 1985. The importance of working collectively at this time was, for Holzer as for many other artists, a crucial way to experiment with techniques of direct address and the public impact of highly charged subject matter. In 1979, she and artist Colen Fitzgibbon organized the *Manifesto Show* in the latter's downtown Manhattan storefront; it included work by both artists and ordinary citizens — "anyone with something to say" who wished to present passionate commentary. Describing the show, Holzer recalls, "There were manifestos in the window; printed tirades on the right-hand side of the room; visual manifestos — things that looked more like art — on the left; a platform for shouting in the middle; and we blasted speeches from a loudspeaker outside."[8] The activist function of art at this time and its relationship to ideas about protest were informed by the anti-war, anti-establishment emphasis of the 1960s and early 1970s; to American artists of Holzer's generation, issues of urgency spanned racism, sexism, homophobia, the impact of gentrification, the consequences of gross economic disparity, and the specter of nuclear war as vital social problems in need of creative, committed forms of address. Engagement with these issues stimulated the formation of other artists' collaboratives such as Group Material and Gran Fury, which produced important bodies of politically charged work, often presented in nonart contexts to achieve the greatest public impact.

In 1982, Holzer's work first began to reach a mass audience when she displayed selections from *Truisms* on the Spectacolor signboard in New York's Times Square, as part of a project sponsored by the Public Art Fund to situate artists' work in public spaces. Here and in other highly visible contexts, the ideologically polymorphous overtones of Holzer's messages were heightened, providing a broad yet trenchant social commentary. Her 1984 project *Sign on a Truck* — a project developed in anticipation of the U.S. presidential election, containing live comments by artists and passersby combined with prerecorded and live interviews with others that highlighted their conflicting opinions — presented a kind of democracy in action intended to reveal a survey of public opinion. The work also included pieces and images by such artists as Claes Oldenburg, Keith Haring, Barbara Kruger, Vito Acconci, and others. Influenced by the experimental mix of entertainment values, politics, and aesthetic purpose in artist Nam June Paik's 1973 video *Global Groove,*[9] the participatory experience of *Sign on a Truck* predated later mainstream formats like those employed on CNN's series *Talk Back Live* and other mediated efforts to present a plurality of public opinion. In this and in her many other language-based works presented in the LED signboard format, Holzer's use of strategies borrowed directly from news media or from the sign systems of the urban landscape as material for art succeeded in challenging assumptions about authorship and authority. This decidedly political approach was an important manifestation of the interrogatory techniques also being developed by a number of Holzer's contemporaries that significantly shaped the direction of art after modernism.

"My work takes you in and out of advocacy, through bad sex, murder, paralysis, poor government, lunacy, and aimlessness," Holzer commented in 1990.[10] Always seeking to avoid didacticism, her work has consistently been characterized by its slippage in and out of the realm of the overtly political. Spanning and commingling the universal and the topical — from early works to later series including *Under a Rock* (1986), *Laments* (1989), and *Mother and Child* (1990) — the politics of Holzer's work are often revealed in terms of bodily and sensory references conveyed through the interaction of text and the form within which she embeds language. This practice creates intriguing parallels to that of such artists as Leon Golub or Kara Walker, who have largely employed images to portray the consequences of criminal or dehumanizing actions and attitudes that are often state-sanctioned. A sense of moral outrage inhabits all of their work, yet in 2003 Holzer reflected, "Maybe it's wishful to imagine that my work has political or social value . . . other parts of my work have more to do with expressionism and cruelty than with pious utility."[11] Golub has also referenced a paradoxical attraction to violence as an underpinning of his work alongside its premise of exposing humanity's dark side, an impulse shared by Holzer that forcefully complicates her work's political resonance.

Holzer's recent projections, LED pieces, and silk-screened paintings center on the experience of war and U.S. involvement in the Middle East over more than 50 years, beginning with events predating the first Gulf War. War is yet another lens through which Holzer probes violence, hope, despair, tragedy, quiet reflection, and pain, conveyed through text and images from existing sources, carefully chosen to spotlight these conditions and their roots in social and political conflict. Having ceased composing her own texts in 2001 and now relying on the writings of others — from poets to politicians, from the anonymous voices of bureaucrats and functionaries to those of individual soldiers and their loved ones — the tenor of Holzer's socially useful commentary is newly inflected. Yet the disjunction between belief and feeling that writer Nancy Princenthal noted in Holzer's earlier work persists in her recent production, for example in the dialogue she orchestrates among declassified documents and literature or poetry, or in the introspective nature of texts chosen for projection in monumental outdoor settings where they are at once bold and ephemeral.

In 2006, Holzer first exhibited her redaction paintings. These silk-screened works in black and white or various colors contain texts ranging from impersonal memos and bureaucratic documents to first-person accounts of atrocities, offering differences of opinion and revealing ethical dilemmas, with passages blacked out, or redacted, by censors.[12] These letters, e-mails, memos, and official reports were culled from the National Security Archive (NSA) at The George Washington University in Washington, D.C., as well as the American Civil Liberties Union (ACLU) website.[13] Segueing back and forth across nearly 30 years of documents and transcripts, from the early 1980s to the present, Holzer's selections of texts unmask a dizzying spectrum of facts, interpretations, opinions, and analyses that zigzag from the minutiae of the quotidian to the platitudes of policy statements to autopsy reports. Describing Holzer's intent, David Breslin comments, "The work tries to reveal what slips through the cracks when a particular ideology or power controls how information is framed and disseminated."[14] Like the layered strata of an archaeological dig, these texts construct a vivid portrait of U.S. involvement in the Gulf region over an extended period as far back as the Cold War era, shedding light and providing insights while free of any overlay of didacticism. For the viewer, the statements within these texts underscore the disorienting nature of the morass of war and highlight the impossibility of a consistent, authoritarian viewpoint.

Although the paintings resemble aspects of Holzer's earlier *Inflammatory Essays,* their reliance on recent historical fact in the form of primary documents differentiates them, as does their incorporation of imagery and their status as painting, a departure for Holzer, who had not used this medium since her student years. An indelible portrayal of individual vulnerability and powerlessness, as well as violence and cruelty, emanates from a group of paintings of redacted documents that contain handprints accompanied by minimal text, two of which were first presented at New York's Cheim & Read gallery in 2006, followed a year later by the exhibition of two more at the Venice Biennale. A subsequent installation in 2008 at the Monika Sprüth Philomene Magers gallery in London showed a similar series of paintings, these based on the handprints of American soldiers accused of crimes in Iraq. The paintings point to the difficulty of a fixed reading or determination of culpability and speak more generally to overarching themes of violence and victimization, power and powerlessness, that result from the mechanics of war. The subject of torture, a topic that Holzer has said she considers as central to her art as death, dying, martyrdom, murder, slaughter, rape, and more, emerges powerfully and poignantly from these images without the necessity of language.[15] As critic Cathy Lebowitz has written: "By choosing to make paintings, Holzer inserts these works into a long tradition of political pictures, from those of Géricault and Goya to Picasso and George Grosz. Two notable contemporary examples are Andy Warhol's Death and Disaster works of the early 1960s (particularly the Race Riot paintings) and Gerhard Richter's Baader-Meinhof cycle (1988) . . . Like Richter, she purposefully selects her subject matter as a calculated political act and, it could be said, as a means of facilitating historical memory."[16]

Such analogies to history painting persist in Holzer's ongoing treatment of the text and imagery found in declassified documents as subject matter for an increasingly bold and incisive commentary on war. A group of 2007 paintings of maps of Iraq, emblazoned with words delineating various phases of U.S. military planning for invasion and variously colored in bruise-like purples and grays, makes a beautiful and chilling visual and verbal statement. The images and texts within these works are taken directly from a PowerPoint presentation given by the U.S. military's Central Command to the White House to strategize the stages of the Iraq invasion. Their titles — phrases such as PROTECT PROTECT and SHAPE THE BATTLESPACE — are drawn verbatim from the documents. These "found" texts resonate strongly with Holzer's previous use of such forcefully declarative phrases in earlier works, where they also succeed in underscoring the danger of positions of certainty imposed and enforced by structures of power.

With their factual, purposeful evidence of governmental workings, Holzer's recent works — whether paintings, LED displays, or other media — chronicle a dismaying and often bewildering chain of events and interpretations, exposing complexities and uncertainties. For instance, *Thorax* (2008), an LED work programmed with accounts from official documents of the shooting of an Iraqi noncombatant by U.S. forces, reveals the interplay of emotions, actions, and anguished dilemmas in legal processes and technicalities that calls to mind the tortured scenarios of Franz Kafka or the multivalent realities presented in Akira Kurosawa's film *Rashomon.* These transcriptions provide an astonishing window into the workings of the U.S. military at war — a situation of enormous difficulty, complexity, and pathos, in which the repeated, multiple variations on questions and answers take on the voice of the chorus in a Greek tragedy.

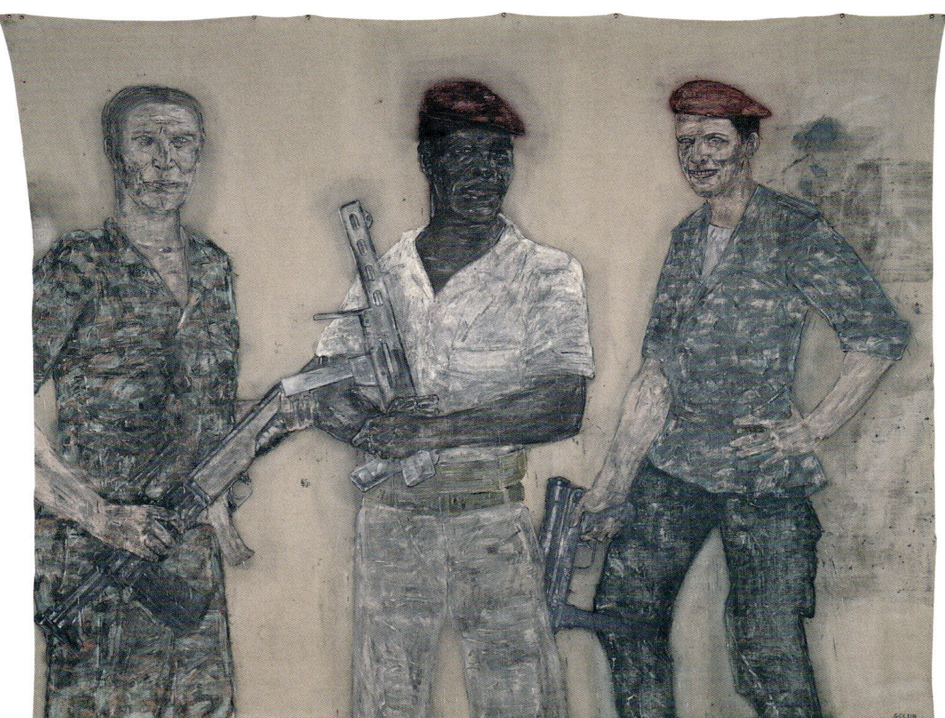

Leon Golub, *Mercenaries I,* 1979

Holzer's first use of declassified U.S. government documents occurred in LED pieces and a projection for the 2004 exhibition *Truth Before Power* at the Kunsthaus Bregenz in Austria. The title of the exhibition came from a text by CIA intelligence expert Sherman Kent titled "Estimates and Influence." Kent's work shares affinities with much of Holzer's own thinking about how meaning, intentions, and authorship are variable constructions, and it illuminates how those in power can shape not only the gathering and the interpretation of facts, but also the policies and actions that result.[17] Predating the Bregenz exhibition was a 1999 commission for the interior of the Reichstag in Berlin, Holzer's first attempt at making official state information accessible and visible. Consisting of a large, vertical LED sign programmed with the text of speeches over time in this symbolic seat of government as well as in other German parliaments dating from the 19th century, this permanently installed work spotlights the country's shifting politics by giving voice to history. In 1999, Holzer employed a similar methodology in the work *Blacklist,* permanently installed on the campus of the University of Southern California in Los Angeles, where stone benches and pavers bearing texts in the form of direct quotes from individuals blacklisted as well as some from those who supported the anti-Communist agenda during the

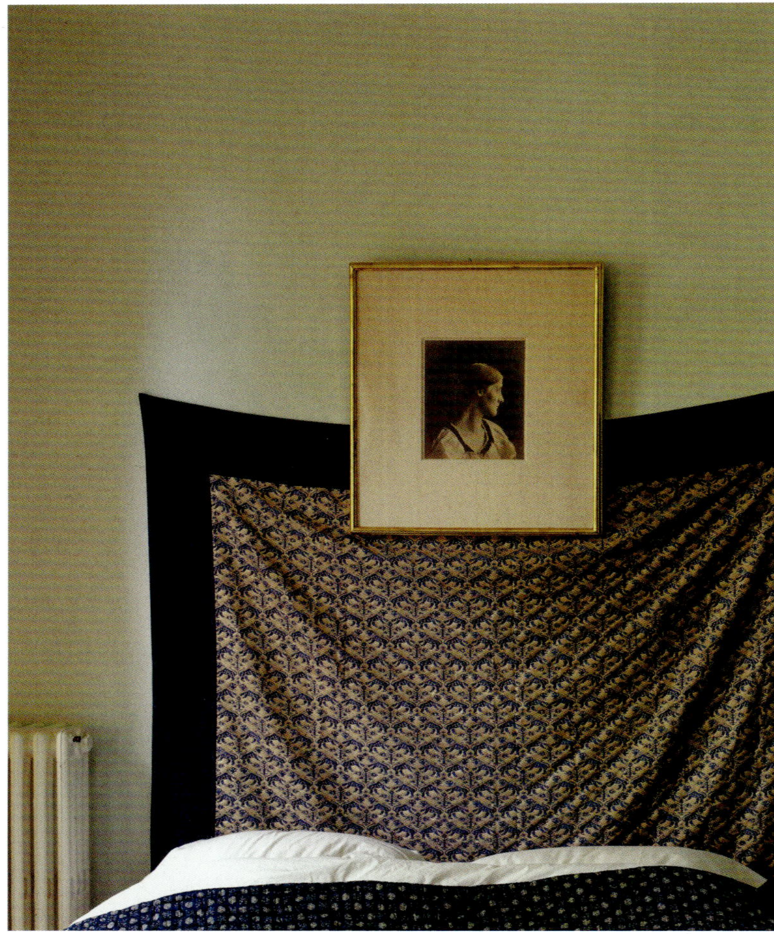
Louise Lawler, *War is Terror,* 2001/2003

McCarthy era of the late 1940s and early 1950s speak directly to the suppression of civil liberties during that chapter of American history.

Since 1996, Holzer has been presenting large-scale outdoor light projections of text in public spaces in Europe and, since 2004, in various U.S. contexts. Monumental, ephemeral, cerebral, and emotionally resonant, the light projections move at a slower, more elegiac pace than the rapid motion of the LEDs; they scroll across the entire space of a façade or a room with text that demands our more meditative absorption. Most often, Holzer uses poetry or literature, but she occasionally relies on her own writings or incorporates examples of declassified documents. In the latter case, the act of publicly revealing once-secret material demonstrates the "argument the government has with itself,"[18] as Thomas Blanton, director of the NSA, has said, fashioned by Holzer as a kind of "constructive, loving, and patriotic" criticism.[19] The selection of verse by such poets as Wisława Szymborska complicates the relationship between fact and fiction in yet another way of referencing and obscuring the polarities between private and public, the personal and the social.

Engagement with war as a subject has been present in Holzer's thinking over many years, overtly referenced in works and series such as *War* (1992), texts she began writing during the Gulf War; *Black Garden,* a 1994 "anti-memorial" in Nordhorn, Germany; and *Erlauf Peace Monument* (1995) in Erlauf, Austria. *Lustmord* (1993–95) is a series of writings centering on physical violation and the murder of women, recounted from three perspectives—witness, perpetrator, and victim; it was triggered by events during the wars in the former Yugoslavia. This jarring text, alternately graphic and enigmatic, recounts the horror of wartime mutilation, violence, and death. Its insistence on bodily sensation signaled Holzer's shift in emphasis toward a more emphatic engagement with the physical and the psychological that is strong in her current work. Holzer had the *Lustmord* texts handwritten on human skin and then photographed. The texts were also printed on cards in ink mixed with human blood. Both of these were then incorporated into a section of the *Süddeutsche Zeitung Magazin* (November 19, 1993), which had invited Holzer to contribute a new artwork. She went on to incorporate objects that embody the anguish and terror of the events.[20] Using a found, worn wooden table, Holzer systematically arranged a selection of human bones, some of which are ringed with silver bands etched with *Lustmord* texts.

Her commitment to the subject of women as victims of violence and "targets of war"[21] is also a long-standing manifestation of conscience that stems from a feminist-inflected spirit of social critique. Art historian David Joselit notes the efficacy of Holzer's use of language drawn from patriarchal, authoritarian sources as indicative of its roots in feminism, and Holzer herself readily acknowledges the importance of the first and second waves of feminism to her own work and that of her peers.[22] She comments, "By the '80s it was pleasantly routine for women to make art and for people to look at it—even to watch for it . . . Courtesy of the women's movement, '80s women were encouraged and able to thrive."[23] The strength and influence of women artists at this juncture has been eloquently demonstrated as a defining feature of the art of the late 1970s and early 1980s, when Holzer and her contemporaries Barbara Kruger, Louise Lawler, Cindy Sherman, and others came of age—a period that Kruger has described as important for "a number of artists working today develop[ing] an awareness of the mechanics of power and dispersal that predated the election of Ronald Reagan."[24] Deconstructing and reimagining strategies of authorship, these artists—many of them women—produced highly important bodies of work, the social politics of which centered on complexity, ambiguity, and difference.[25]

Provocative connections, as well as distinctions, exist between the work of Holzer and Kruger in their approach to politics and social critique. Wary of the categorization of their work as "political," both are among the foremost artists of our time to expand the notion of politics in their work from a narrowly defined terrain to a much broader spectrum of human actions, motivations, and relationships. According to art historian Jeanne Siegel, Kruger, who employs techniques borrowed from advertising to explode cultural and social myths, has stated that she "tries to critically engage issues frequently not dealt with in so-called 'political' work: that is, the terrain of gender and representation."[26] Kruger asserts, "There's a politic in every conversation we have, every deal we close, every face we kiss."[27] Holzer's use of language and images tends toward more contradictory positions: "I find that writing is more effective if it's not dogmatic and if it's not immediately or not entirely identifiable as propaganda."[28]

For Holzer, Lawler's approach to uncovering the politics of a situation through her ostensibly neutral images, quietly yet sharply revealing socially charged, class-based, or other interpretively fluid circumstances, shares important affinities with her own thinking. Calling into question authorship and authority, Lawler's photographic work, in a similar way to Holzer's, revolves around stimulating reflection or posing questions that

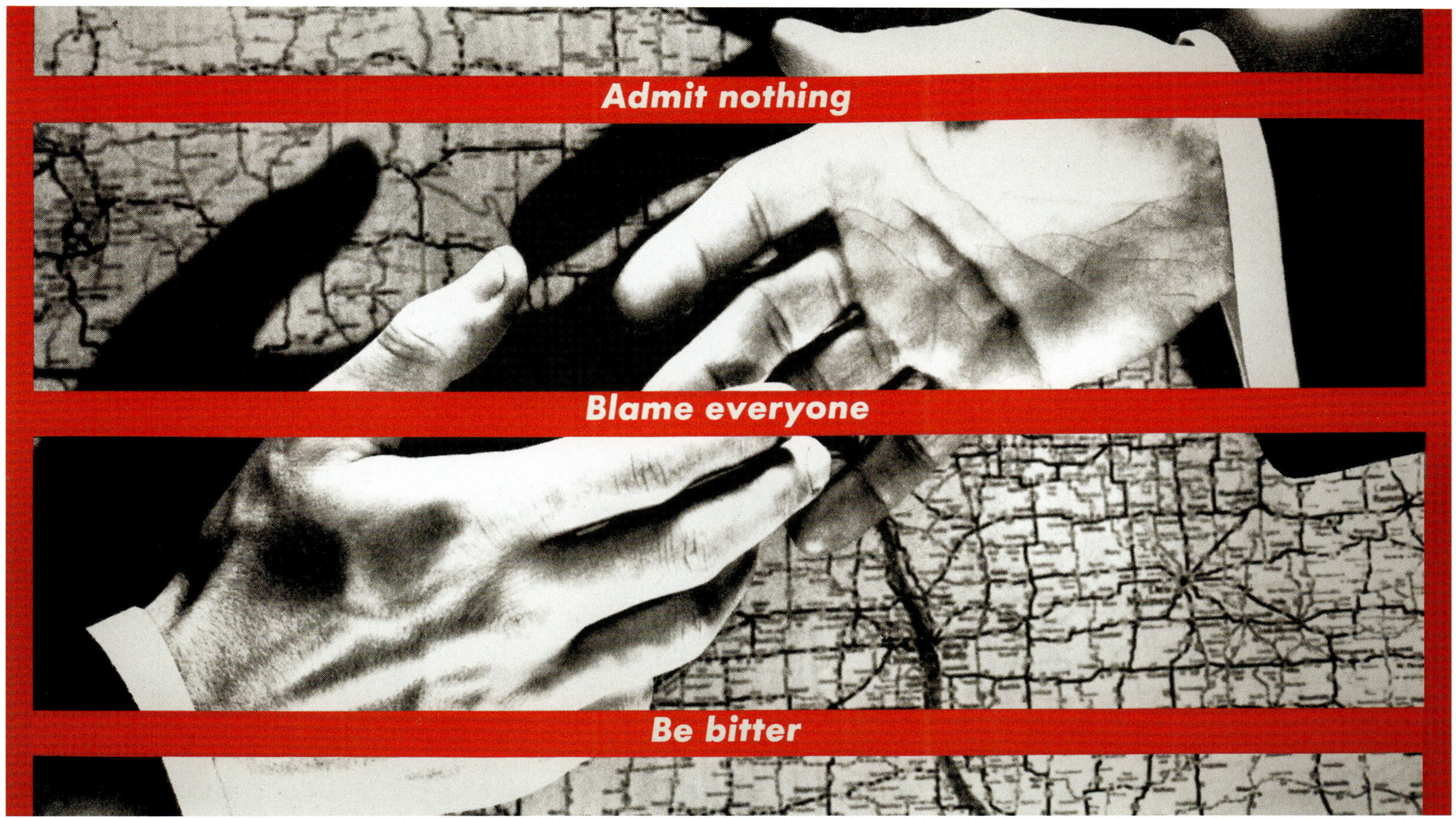

Barbara Kruger, *Untitled* (*Admit nothing/Blame everyone/Be bitter*), 1987

might lead to action. Holzer comments on the importance of Lawler's work and its relevance to her own concerns, especially those recent examples that directly engage the impact of war and politics, such as Lawler's photograph *War is Terror* (2001/2003), in which a poignant domesticity is revealed. The work of artist Christian Boltanski also resonates with aspects of Holzer's thinking in terms of the balance he seeks between opposing emotional states and the ambiguous references and refusal of fixed meaning in his *Monuments* series. Despite the fact that both Lawler's and Boltanski's work are primarily image-based, their practices reveal affinities with the spirit and sensibility of Holzer's in ways that are both understated and obvious. Furthermore, alongside the importance to Holzer of artists such as Donald Judd, Sol LeWitt, and Bruce Nauman as formative influences, women artists of the generation of Nancy Spero, Louise Bourgeois, and Alice Neel were also precursors for Holzer and her contemporaries; Holzer cites Spero, especially, as a source of inspiration because she always kept women's bodies at the forefront of her work.[29]

Throughout its various inflections and directions over time, social critique and a commitment to the political has always been central to Holzer's art. Whether offered with humor and absurdity or with wrenching despair, her work can perhaps best be associated with an art of protest in its continuous engagement with difficult, sobering, and sometimes ghastly subject matter: from war and other forms of violence to rage, grief, injustice, and deprivation. Its spirit of protest, however, is predicated on absurdity as much as on outrage, wherein a profound tension is maintained between attraction and repulsion, goodness and violence, ethical behavior and baseness. The motivations behind her art that Holzer has articulated at various times throughout her career are fluid but remarkably consistent in that she has said that she wants to make a socially useful art. More recently she stated, "I do make work that focuses on unnecessary cruelty, in the hope that people will recoil."[30]

Art's changing relationship to politics has been a persistent phenomenon throughout the past century. From movements spanning the Dadaists' anarchic responses to the tension of World War I and the revolutionary aspirations of the Russian avant-garde and Mexican muralists from the late 1910s through the 1930s, to the anti-establishment, socially progressive ideals of the Situationists in the late 1960s and the culture wars of the late 1980s and throughout the 1990s, artists have infused their work with social and political content that aims to inspire and influence the public and challenge the status quo. This seemingly cyclical tendency of artists' impassioned engagement with politically charged content, ebbing and flowing in response to larger social and cultural forces, has reemerged in the first decade of the 21st century in response to the complexities and uncertainties of the post–9/11 era and the pervasive escalation of violent conflict and tension worldwide. At the time of this writing, on the eve of the 2008 U.S. presidential election, public dissatisfaction with the human and economic costs of war and an increasing desire for discourse on matters of national and global significance — not only war, but also race, gender, civil liberties, and growing economic disparity — reverberate strongly with the attitudes of many artists, signaling a renewed mandate for art and social utility.[31] This mandate has, in addition, stimulated the resurgence of collective practices in a manner that recalls those of earlier decades.

Holzer's past and present work stands to prefigure that of a new generation of artists whose engagement with the politics of the world around

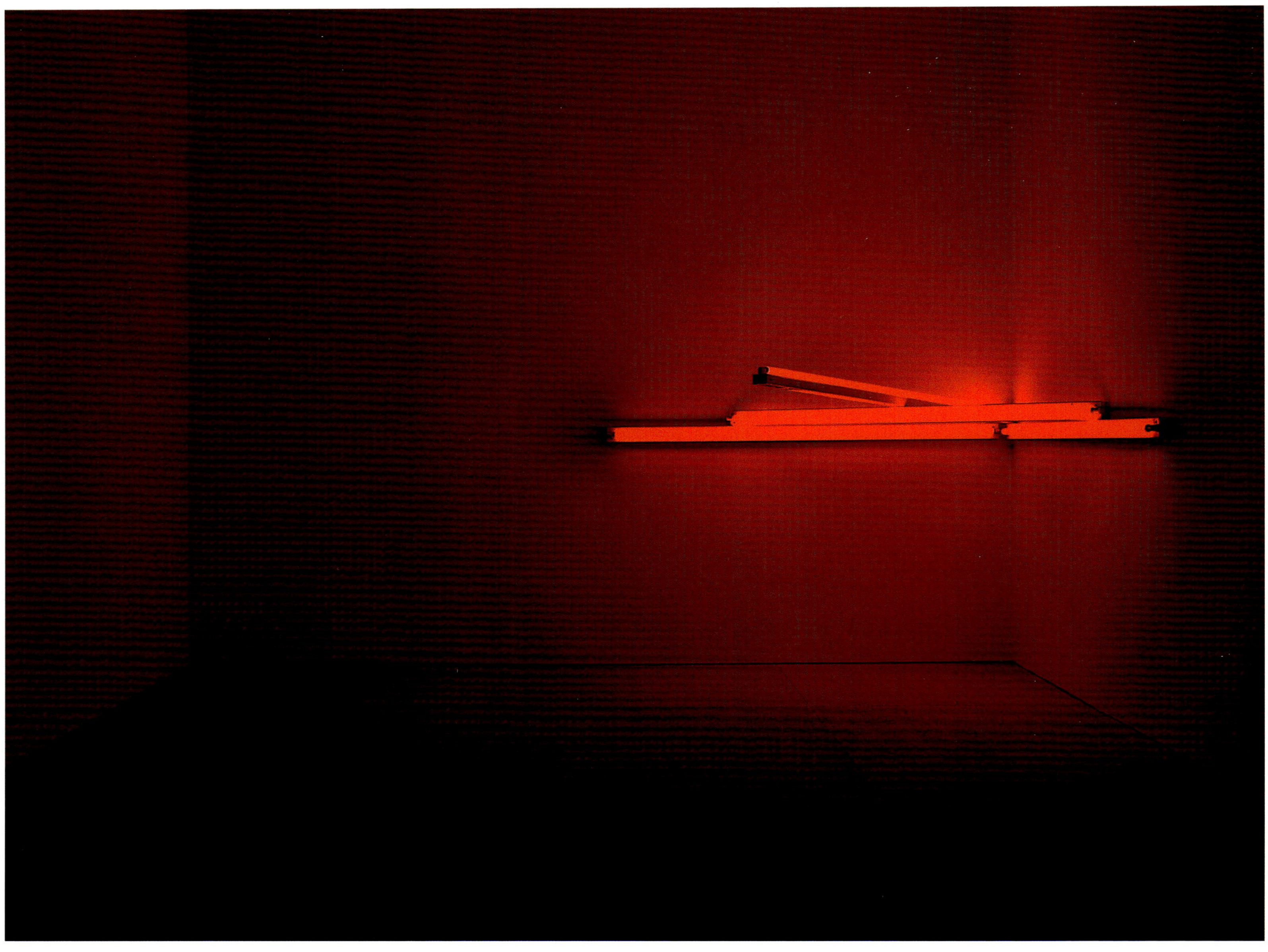

Dan Flavin, *monument 4 those who have been killed in ambush (to P.K. who reminded me about death)*, 1966

them reveals itself in the making of a complex, multivalent art that operates on the level of affect and emotion and, as described by art historian T. J. Demos, "unleashes unconscious processes and imaginative scenarios."[32] In current discourse surrounding new definitions, intentions, and efficacy of political art as distinct from that of practices in the 1960s and 1970s, artists, historians, and critics call for a reframing and rethinking of "activist art" or "political art" to encompass the importance of the psychic and subjective. An insistence on revealing uncertainties, rather than truths, emerges again and again in recent literature on and discussions about what constitutes the political dimension of art. These attitudes take their cues directly from the example of Holzer, whose work, as Joselit has noted, "has long been distinguished by its introduction of passionate and politicized speech into traditions of Conceptual and installation art."[33] Tania Bruguera, Paul Chan, Jeremy Deller, Sam Durant, Sharon Hayes, and Mark Wallinger are just a few of the notable figures within this younger generation of artists whose work builds on Holzer's legacy and on that of other artists ranging from Golub and Hans Haacke to Kruger, Adrian Piper, and others who have consistently, over long careers, engaged with the various aspects of the political in their work. About the importance of Holzer's work to his own practice, Durant comments that as a young art student, "It was a revelation to find artists using both text and the forms of signage. Holzer's work was especially significant because of its more direct address and explicitly politicized messages . . . and the multiple ways she circulated the texts . . . Holzer has consistently been an important example for me . . . Hers is a courageous stance. It joins with many other American artists in creating a culture of resistance."[34]

Theorist Jacques Rancière's definition of what constitutes a critical or political art resonates aptly with how Jenny Holzer's work communicates meaning to the viewer: as a "negotiation . . . [that] borrows from the zones of indiscernibility of art and life the connections that provoke political intelligibility. And it borrows from the separateness of artworks the sense of sensory strangeness that enhances political energies. The main procedure of critical or political art consists thus in setting out the encounter and possibly the clash between heterogeneous elements."[35] Rancière further comments, "The dream of a suitable political work of art is in fact the dream of disrupting the relationship between the visible, the sayable, and the thinkable."[36] His ideas about the nature of relationships between aesthetics and politics, extensively elaborated in a body of recent writings which have had a high degree of currency among a younger generation of politically engaged artists, seem to coincide with Holzer's emphasis on making sensate the messages inherent in her chosen texts, reinforcing and amplifying their meaning as an experience that only art can offer. With statements like "PROTECT ME FROM WHAT I WANT" and "MEN DON'T PROTECT YOU ANY MORE" (*Survival,* 1983–85) and "PROTECT PROTECT" from the map paintings, and guided by her commitment to provoking knowledge and feeling, Holzer complicates the idea of the socially useful in an art that is equal parts social critique, anarchy, absurdity, and emotional resonance. Responding to questions in a 2001 interview by Henri Cole, Holzer's comments reveal her quietly optimistic yet knowing stance on the purpose and function of the political in art:

> Cole: Can a socially responsible artist effect change?
> Holzer: Conceivably; it depends on whether one is competent, lucky, and change is about to happen anyway.
> Cole: Do you think an artist living in an atmosphere of conformity or obedience to authority can be thought provoking?
> Holzer: It is the time to try especially hard. When art or writing functions, it raises ideas and has them felt, and this knowledge and feeling may be the basis for decent action.[37]

NOTES

1 Henri Cole, "Jenny Holzer in Berlin," in *Jenny Holzer* (Berlin: Neue Nationalgalerie, Staatliche Museen zu Berlin Preussischer Kulturbesitz, 2001), 101.
2 Susan Sontag, "Against Interpretation," in *Against Interpretation and Other Essays* (New York: Anchor Books, 1990), 12.
3 Holzer has frequently mentioned the idea of social utility as an impetus behind her work.
4 Cole, "Jenny Holzer in Berlin," 101.
5 Jeanne Siegel, "Jenny Holzer's Language Games," in *Artwords 2: Discourse on the Early 80s,* ed. Jeanne Siegel (Ann Arbor, MI: UMI Research Press, 1988), 288. Originally published in *Arts Magazine* 60, no. 4 (December 1985), 64.
6 Hal Foster, "Subversive Signs," *Art in America* 70, no. 10 (November 1982), 91.
7 Ibid., 88.
8 Steven Henry Madoff, "Jenny Holzer Talks to Steven Henry Madoff," *Artforum* 41, no. 8 (April 2003), 82. Other participants in Colab, a loosely organized group of about 50 young artists who approached art as a medium for radical communication and social change, included John and Charlie Ahearn, Jane Dickson, Mike Glier, Tom Otterness, Kiki Smith, and Robin Winters. See also Jeffrey Deitch, "Report from Times Square," *Art in America* 68, no. 7 (September 1980), 60.
9 David Ross, "Nam June Paik's Videotapes," in *Nam June Paik* (New York: Whitney Museum of American Art, 1982), 107.
10 Michael Auping, "Interview with Jenny Holzer," in *Jenny Holzer* (New York: Universe, 1992), 110, as quoted in Nancy Princenthal, "Jenny Holzer: Language Lessons," in Eleanor Heartney, et al., *After the Revolution: Women Who Transformed Contemporary Art* (New York: Prestel, 2007), 144.
11 Madoff, "Jenny Holzer Talks to Steven Henry Madoff," 83.
12 The paintings were shown at the Cheim & Read gallery in New York from May 12 through June 17, 2006, simultaneous to a display at Yvon Lambert New York of photographs of Holzer's exterior projections. This dual presentation mirrored the components of her subsequent exhibitions, where factual and fictive coexist in a relationship of mutual interdependence.
13 Both the NSA and ACLU employ the Freedom of Information Act, the law enacted by Congress in 1966 that established a process to make federal agency records available to the public, in order to declassify and release governmental information.
14 David Breslin, e-mail message to author, May 21, 2008.
15 Amei Wallach, "New 'Truisms' in Words and Light," *New York Times* (Sept. 28, 2005). Available online at: http://www.nytimes.com/2005/09/28/arts/design/28holz.html?scp=1&sq=amei+wallach+jenny+holzer&st=nyt (accessed June 10, 2008).
16 Cathy Lebowitz, "Protect Us from What We Don't Know," *Art in America* 4, no. 9 (October 2006), 162–3.
17 Sherman Kent, "Estimates and Influence," reprinted in *Jenny Holzer: Truth Before Power* (Bregenz, Austria: Kunsthaus Bregenz, 2004), 99. Kent's text was an important stimulus for Holzer's engagement with declassified documents in the years following the events of 9/11.
18 Wallach, "New 'Truisms' in Words and Light."
19 Ibid.
20 Joan Simon, "No Ladders; Snakes: Jenny Holzer's *Lustmord,*" Parkett 40/41, 1994, 79–87. The piece offers an insightful analysis of the *Lustmord* project.
21 Nicola Kuhn, "Warum muss die Kunst schmerzen, Frau Holzer?" *Tagesspiegel* (Berlin) (Feb. 1, 2000). Available online at: http://www.tagesspiegel.de/kultur/;art772,1904156?_FRAME=33&_FORMAT (accessed June 10, 2008). Original German: "als Angriffsziele des Krieges."
22 Holzer, e-mail message to author, April 28, 2008.
23 Madoff, "Jenny Holzer Talks to Steven Henry Madoff," 83.
24 Siegel, "Jenny Holzer's Language Games," 301.
25 Ann Goldstein has written extensively on this idea, most recently in "In the Company of Others," in *Twice Untitled and Other Pictures (looking back)*, by Louise Lawler with Helen Molesworth, ed. (Columbus, OH: Wexner Center for the Arts, Ohio State University, 2006), and in other sources including *A Forest of Signs: Art in the Crisis of Representation* (Los Angeles: The Museum of Contemporary Art, Los Angeles, 1989).
26 Siegel, "Jenny Holzer's Language Games," 307.
27 Ibid.
28 Ibid., 293.
29 Holzer in a live chat session on the ada website on May 23, 1995 for the project "Please change beliefs." Transcription available at: http://adaweb.walkerart.org/context/artists/holzer/holzero.html (accessed June 10, 2008). While during the past couple of decades writers have downplayed the feminist dimension of Holzer's work despite its insistent emphasis on the experience of women in such series as *Mother and Child* and *Lustmord,* a reemergence and reframing of feminist discourse can be noted in projects such as the 2008 "Women in the City" series of publicly sited works by Holzer, Kruger, Sherman, and Lawler in Los Angeles. See www.westofrome.org.
30 Holzer interviewed at the website for Art:21, http://www.pbs.org/art21/artists/holzer/clip1.html (accessed June 10, 2008).
31 Two significant recent publications on this issue include *Who Cares* (New York: Creative Time Books, 2006), transcriptions of a series of artists' forums organized by New York–based Creative Time beginning in 2001 to give voice to artists' concerns about their roles as contributors to social dialogue and discourse, and the winter 2008 issue of the journal *October,* which also treats the theme of artists' political engagement in the post–9/11 world with contributions by a wide range of historians, theorists, and artists. Another useful text that situates such developments in historical context is the anthology *Art and Social Change: A Critical Reader,* ed. Will Bradley and Charles Esche (London: Tate Publishing, 2007).
32 T. J. Demos, response to questionnaire, *October* 123 (Winter 2008), 35.
33 David Joselit, "Voices, Bodies, and Spaces: The Art of Jenny Holzer," in *Jenny Holzer* (London: Phaidon Press, 1998), 42.
34 Sam Durant, e-mail message to author, May 22, 2008. Tania Bruguera has also commented specifically on the impact of coming to know Holzer's work as a young artist in Cuba. Numerous non-American artists of this same generation whose work is also politically and socially charged are also interesting to consider in light of their works' relationship to or distinctions from the examples of Holzer and her contemporaries, artists such as Liam Gillick, Thomas Hirschhorn, Jota Castro, and the collective Claire Fontaine.
35 Jacques Rancière, "Aesthetics and Politics: Rethinking Some Links" (lecture, University of California, Berkeley, Sept. 30, 2002).
36 Jacques Rancière, *The Politics of Aesthetics* (London: Continuum, 2004), 63. First published as *Le partage du sensible: Esthétique et politique* (Paris: Fabrique, 2000).
37 Henri Cole, "Jenny Holzer in Conversation with Henri Cole," in *Jenny Holzer* (Berlin: Neue Nationalgalerie, Staatliche Museen zu Berlin Preussischer Kulturbesitz, 2001), 116.

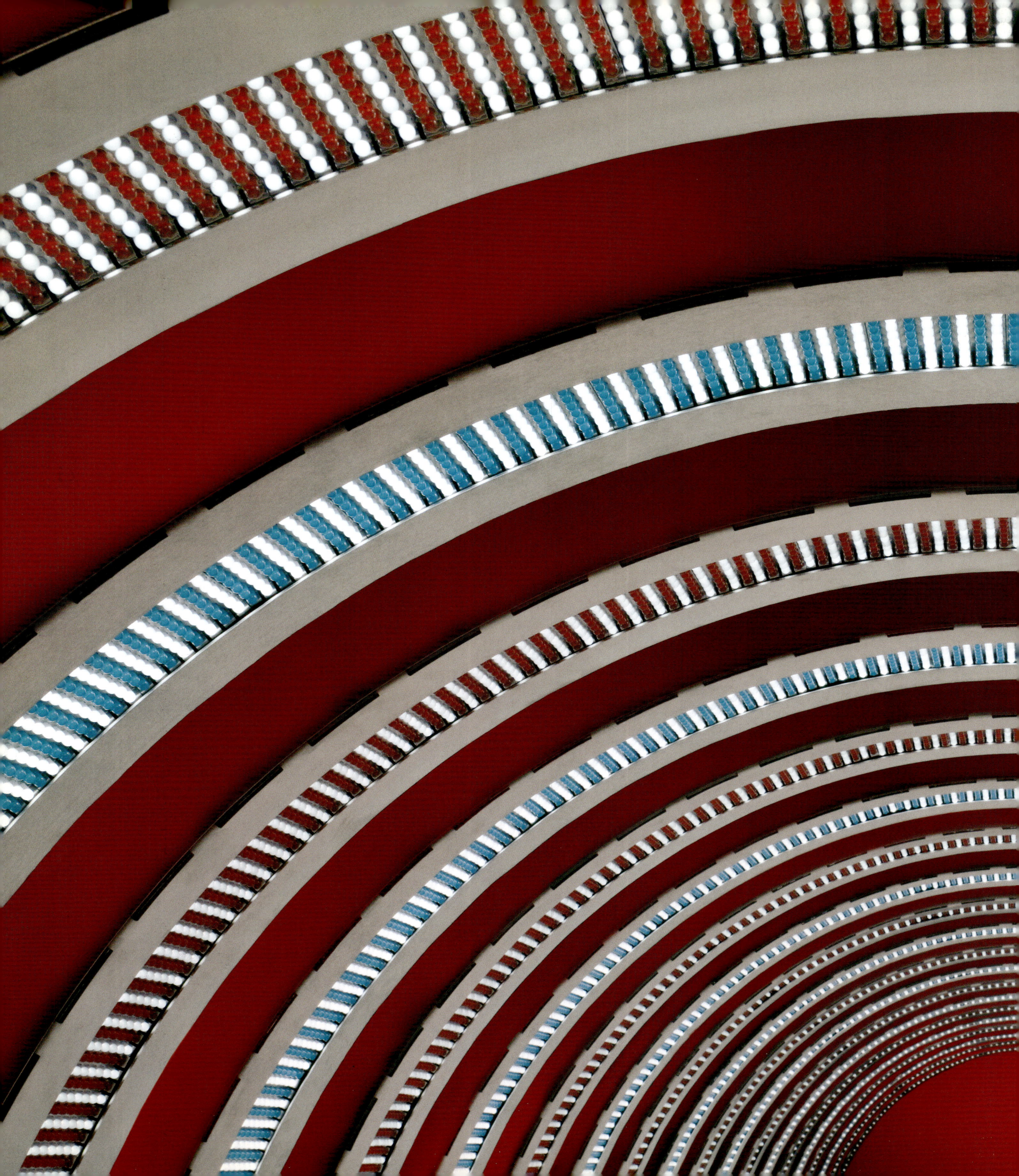

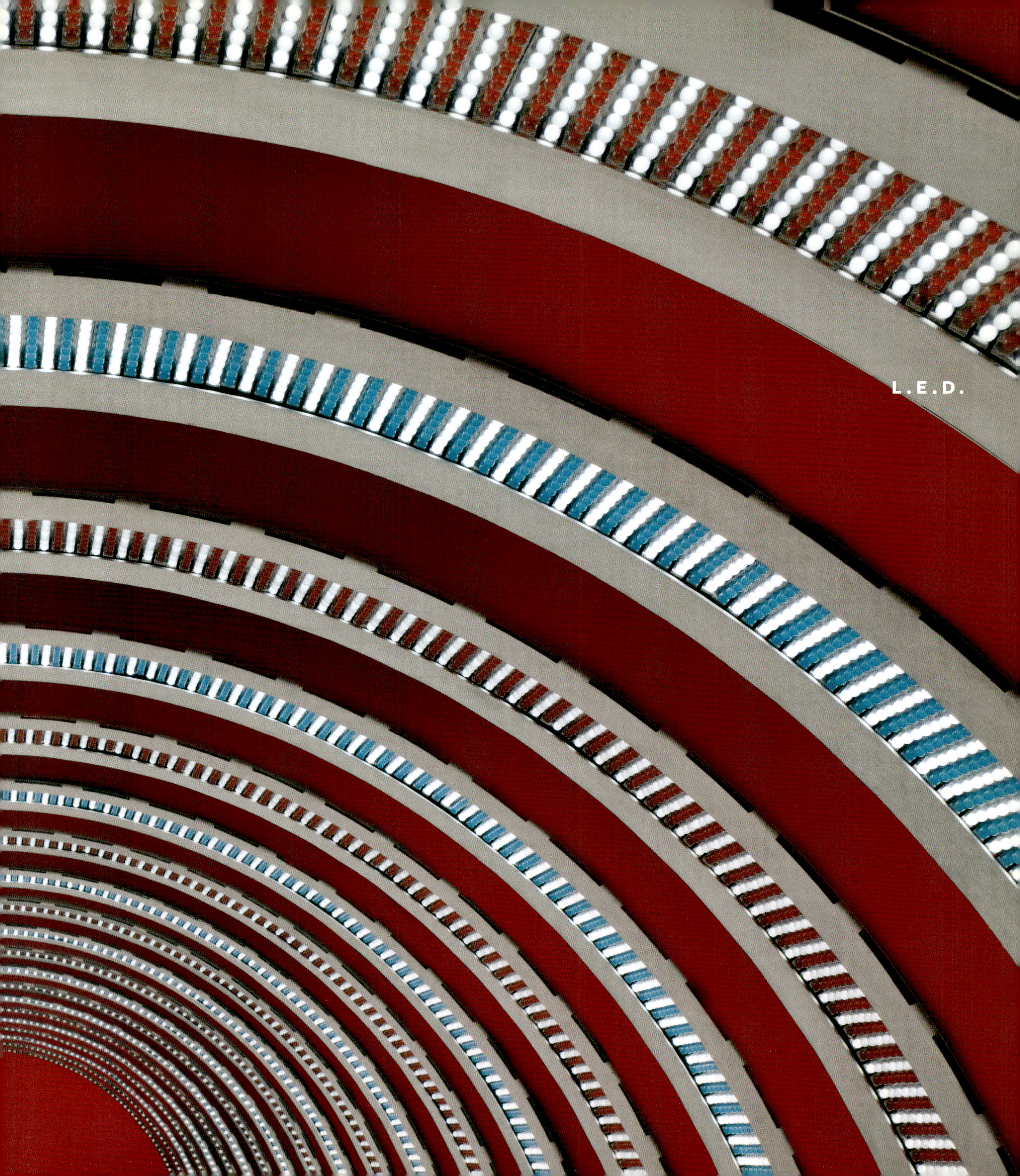
L.E.D.

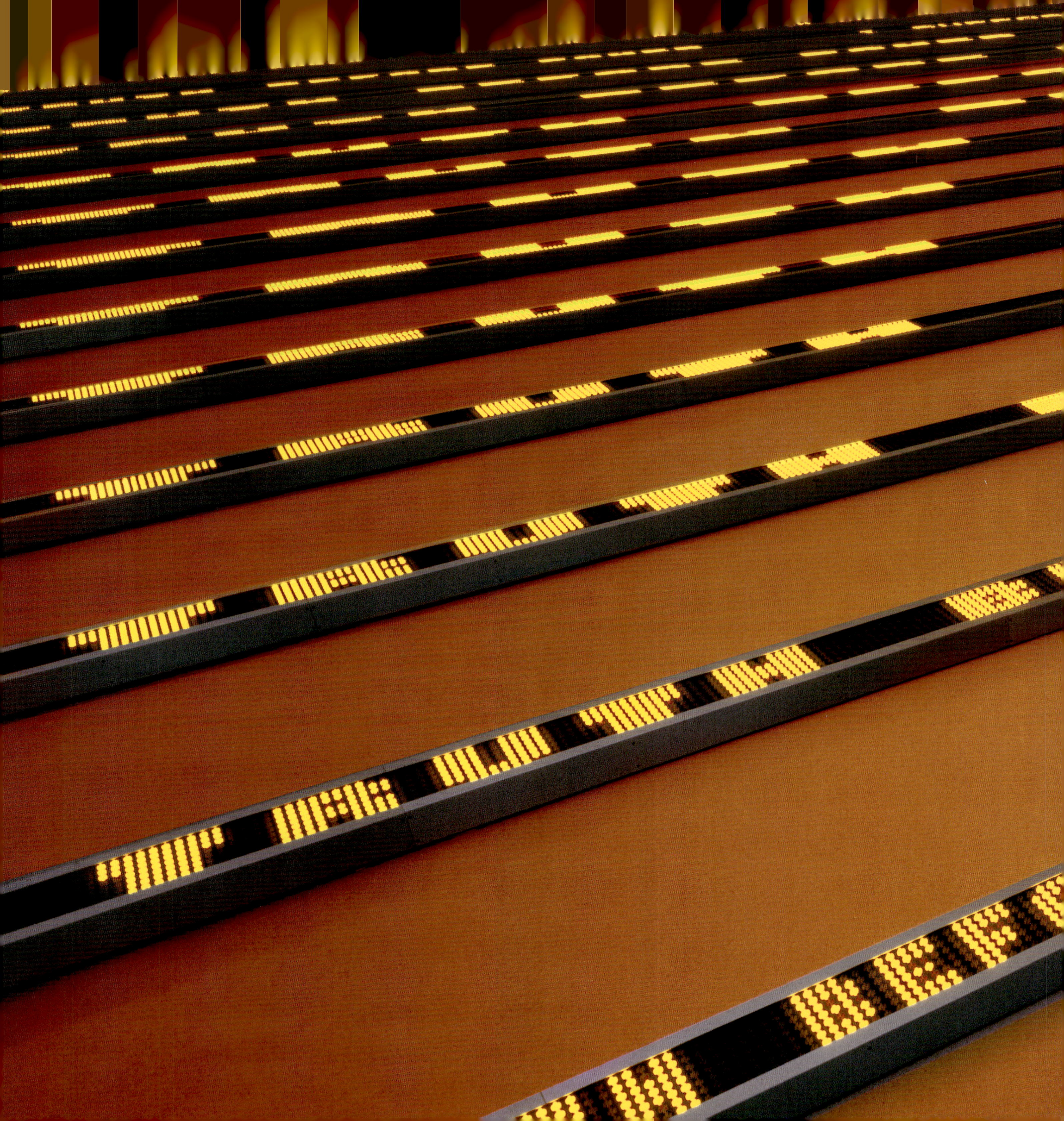

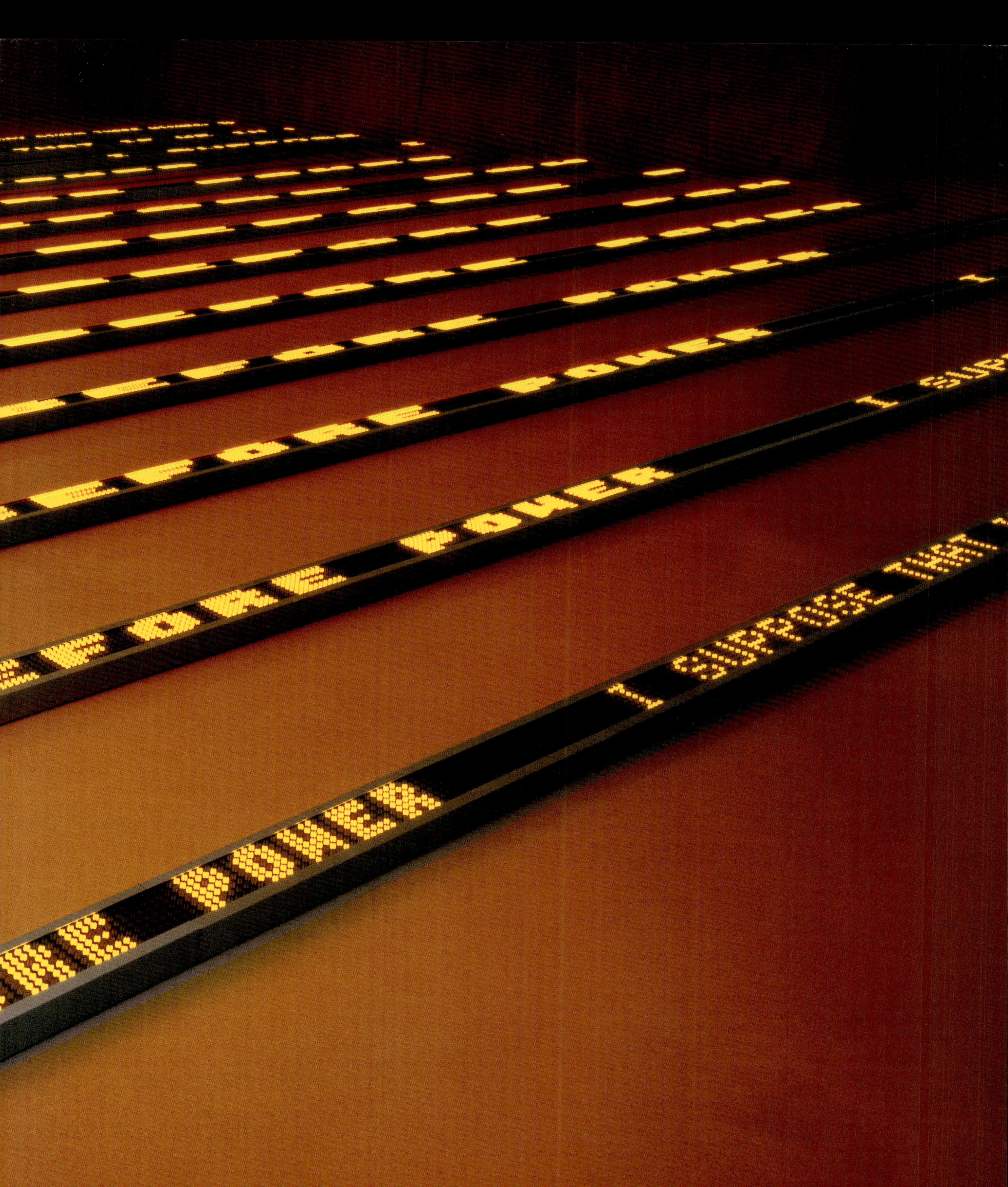
I SUPPOSE THAT
POWER

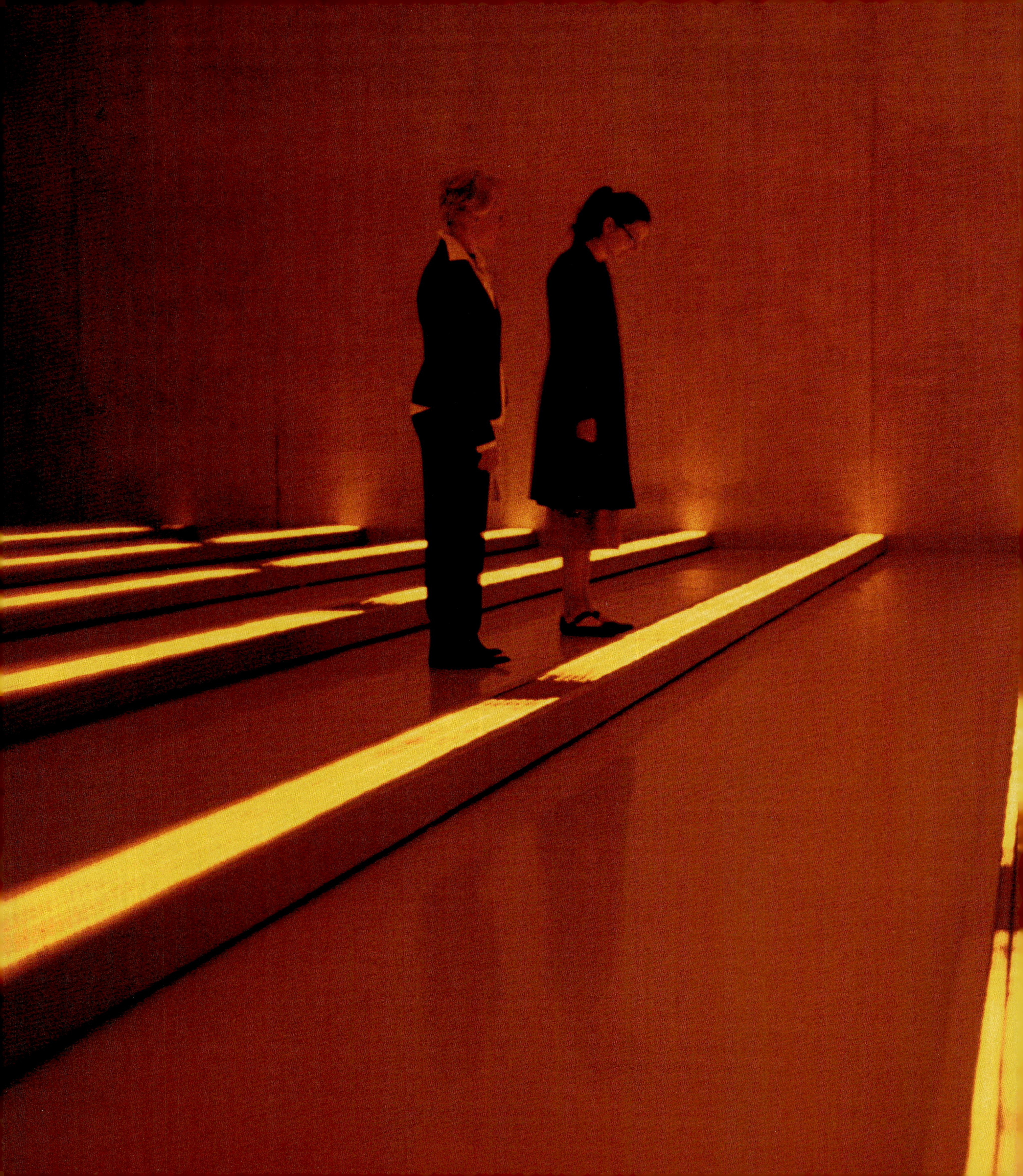

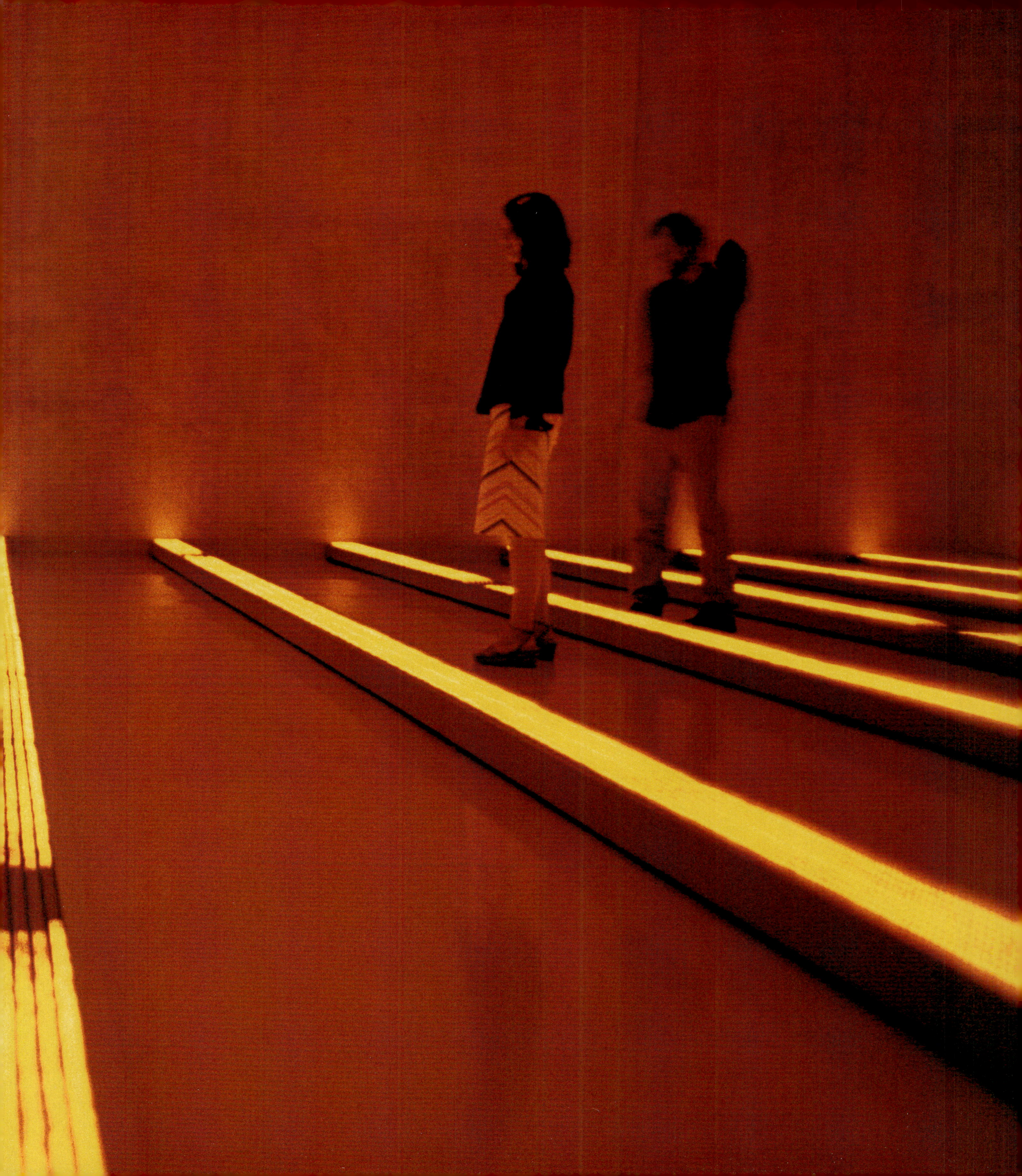

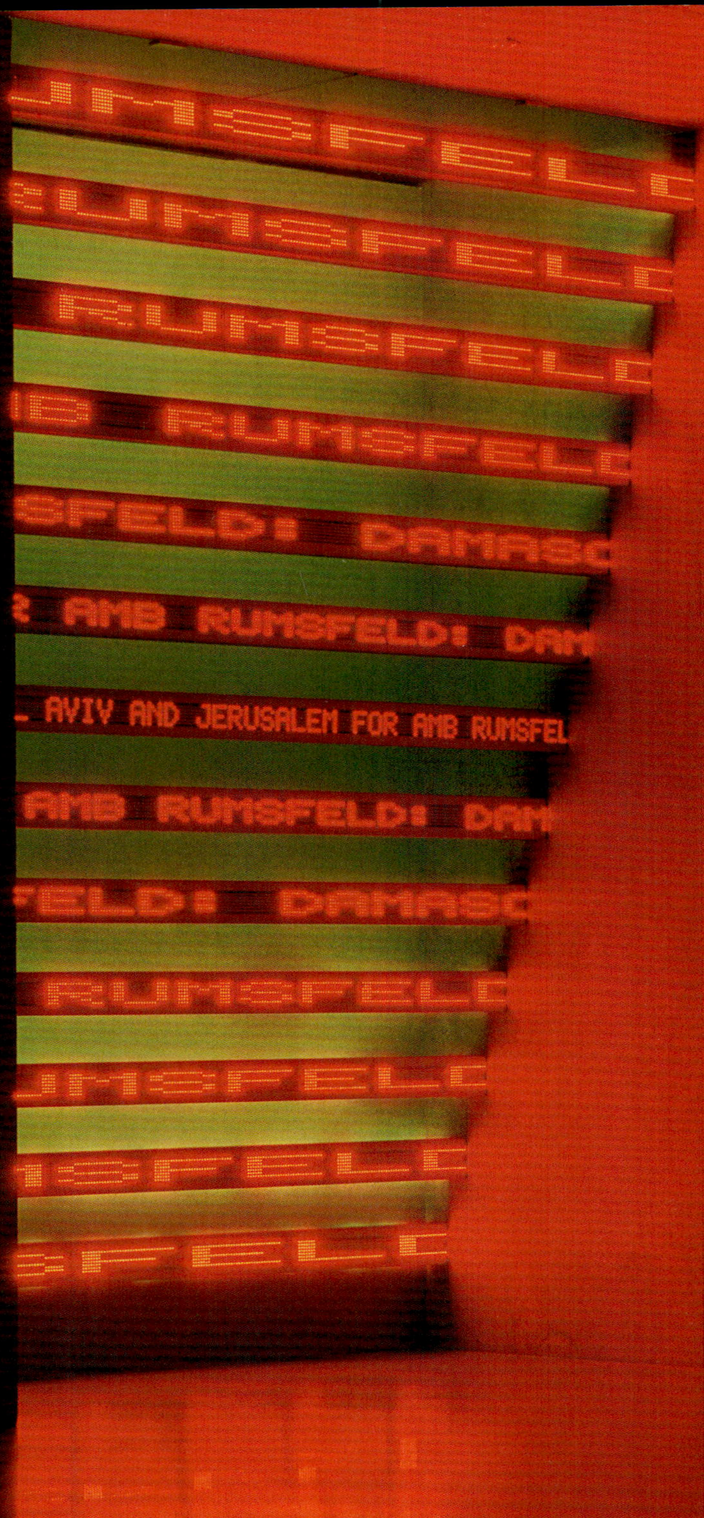

SFELD: DAMASC
AMB RUMSFELD: DAM
AVIV AND JERUSALEM FOR AMB RUMSFEL
AMB RUMSFELD: DAM
FELD: DAMASC

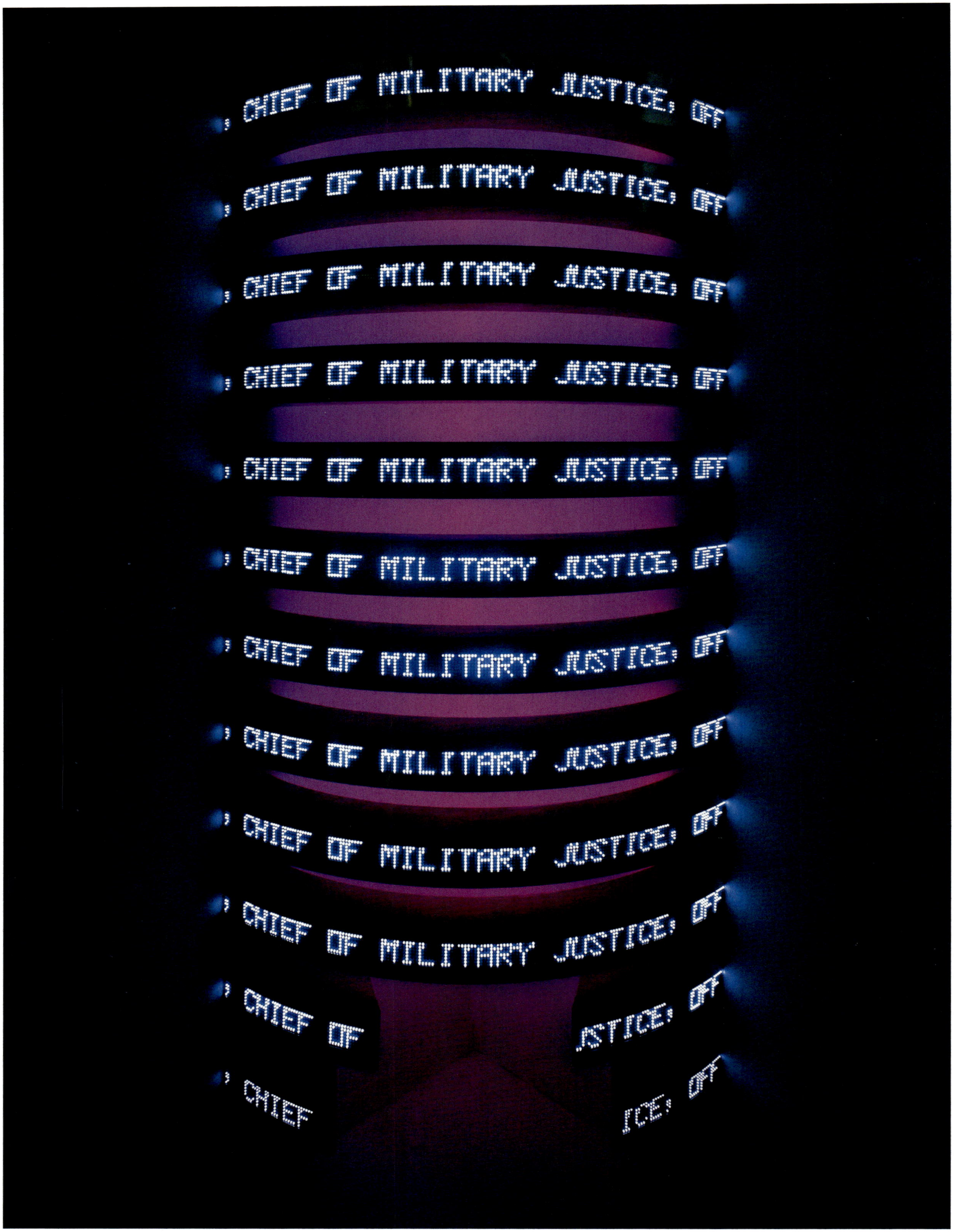

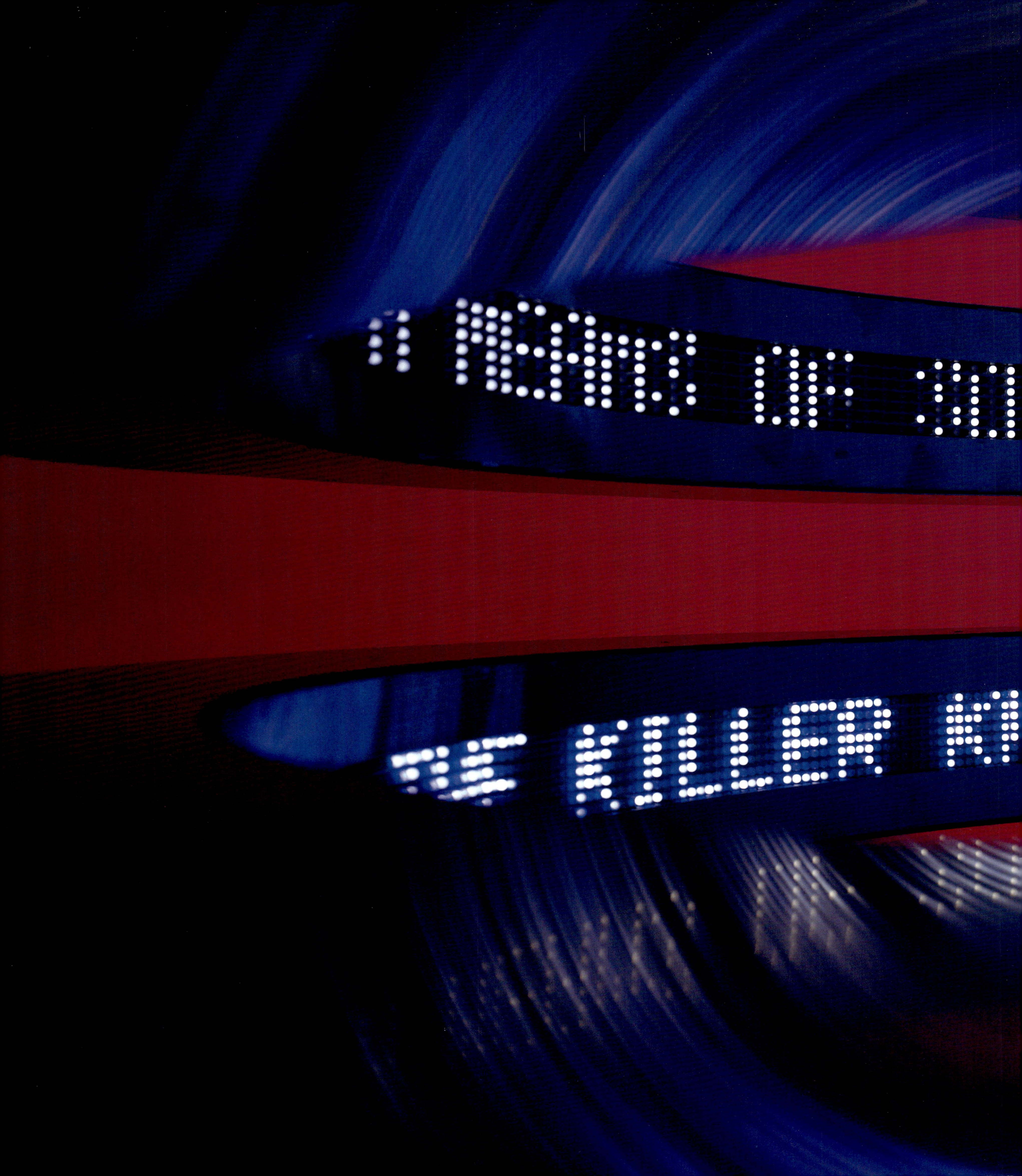
KILLER

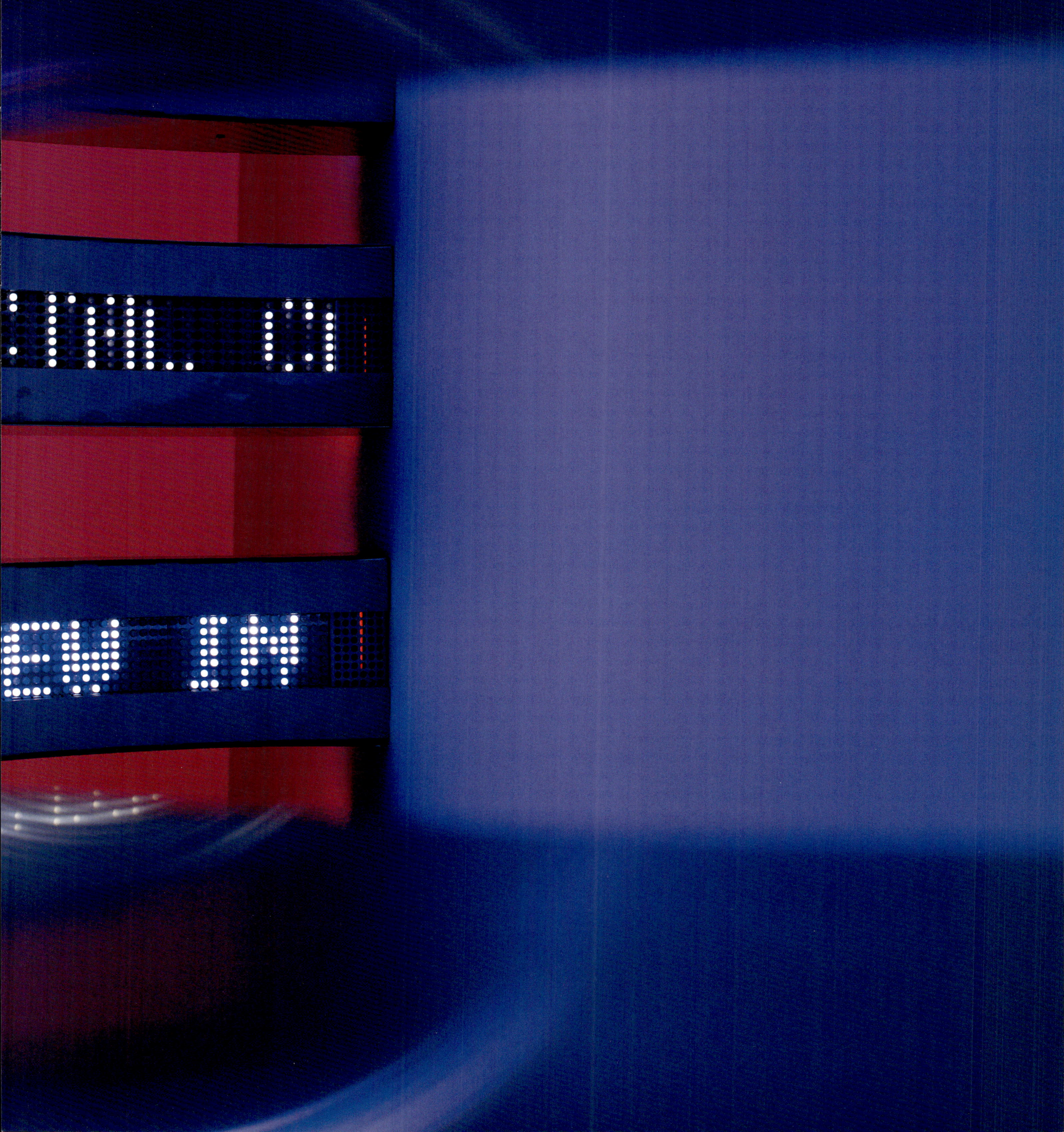

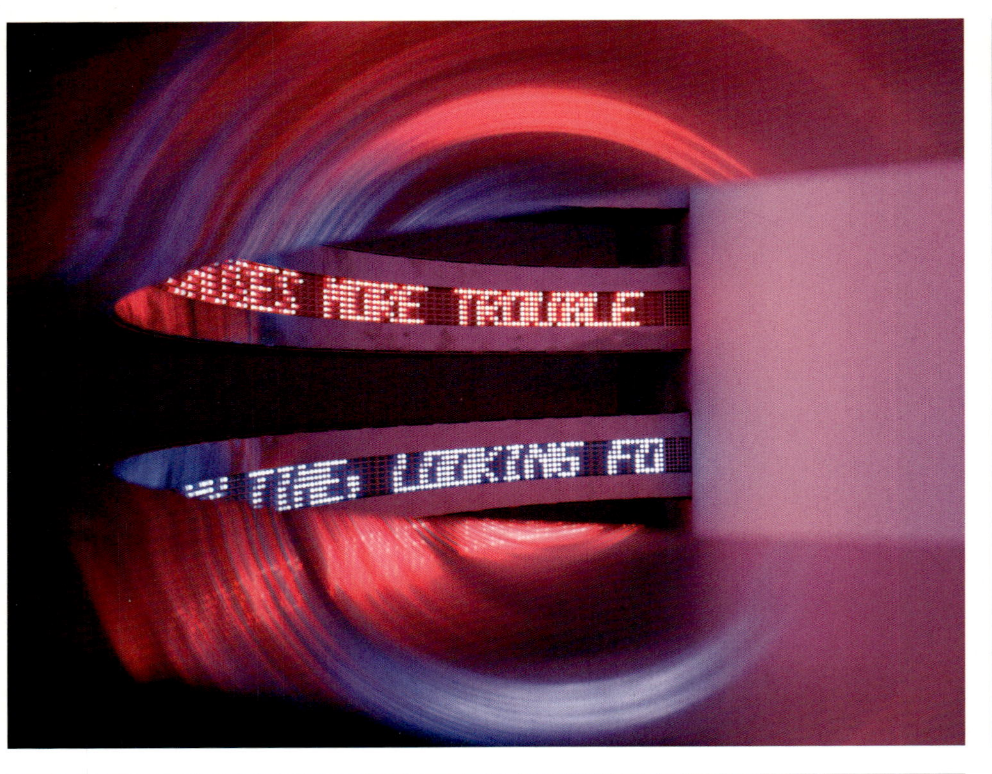
MORE TROUBLE
LOOKING FO

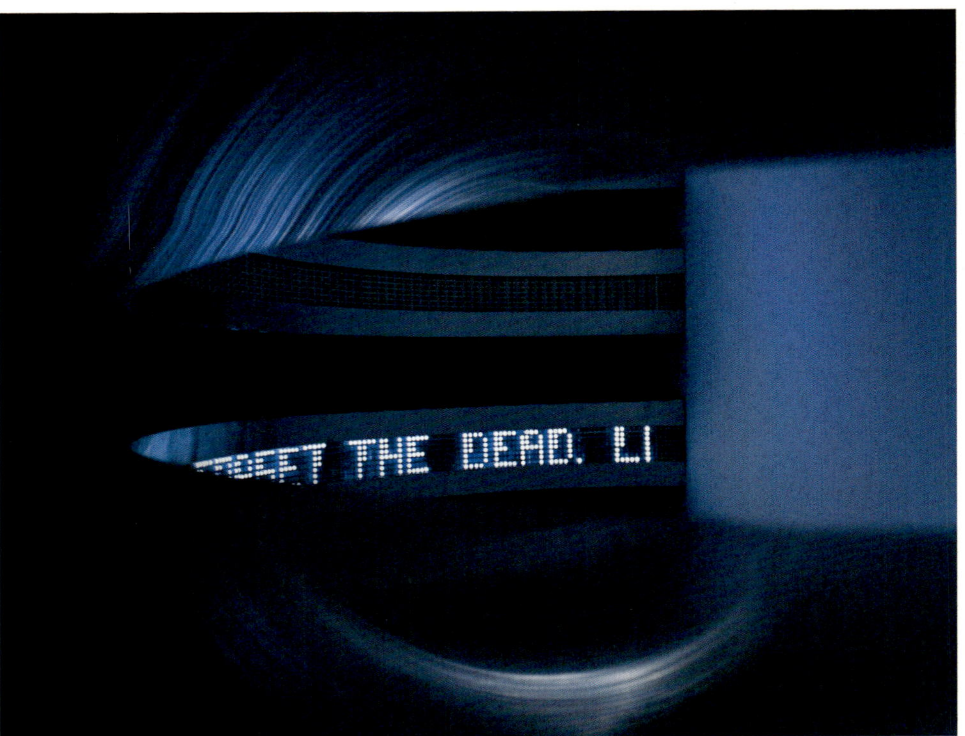
THE DEAD. LI

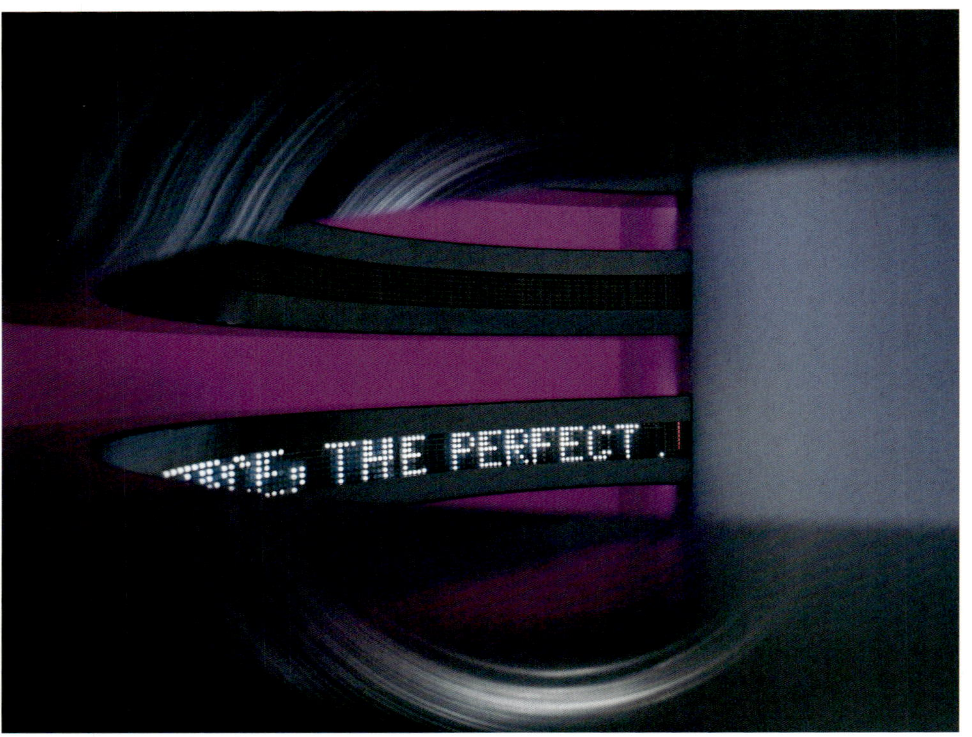
THE PERFECT

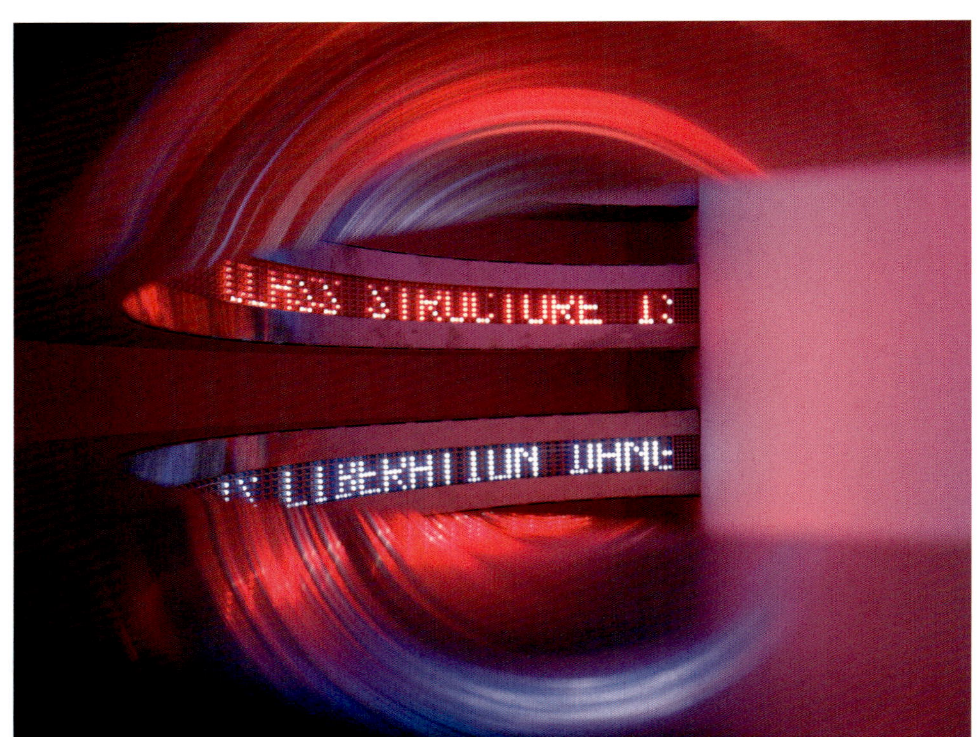
STRUCTURE

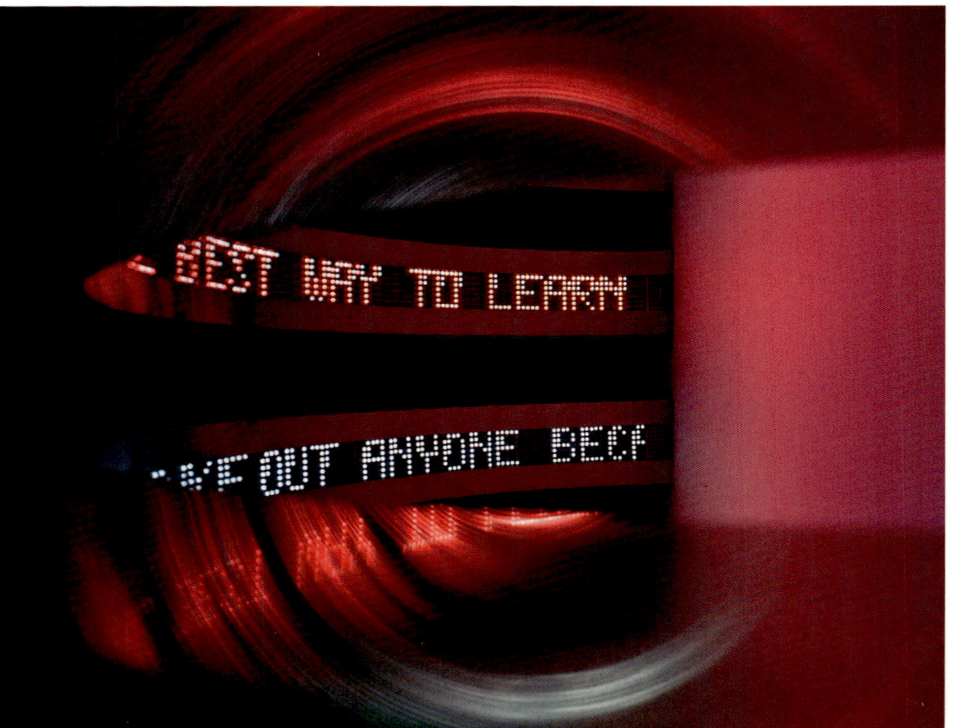
BEST WAY TO LEARN
OUT ANYONE

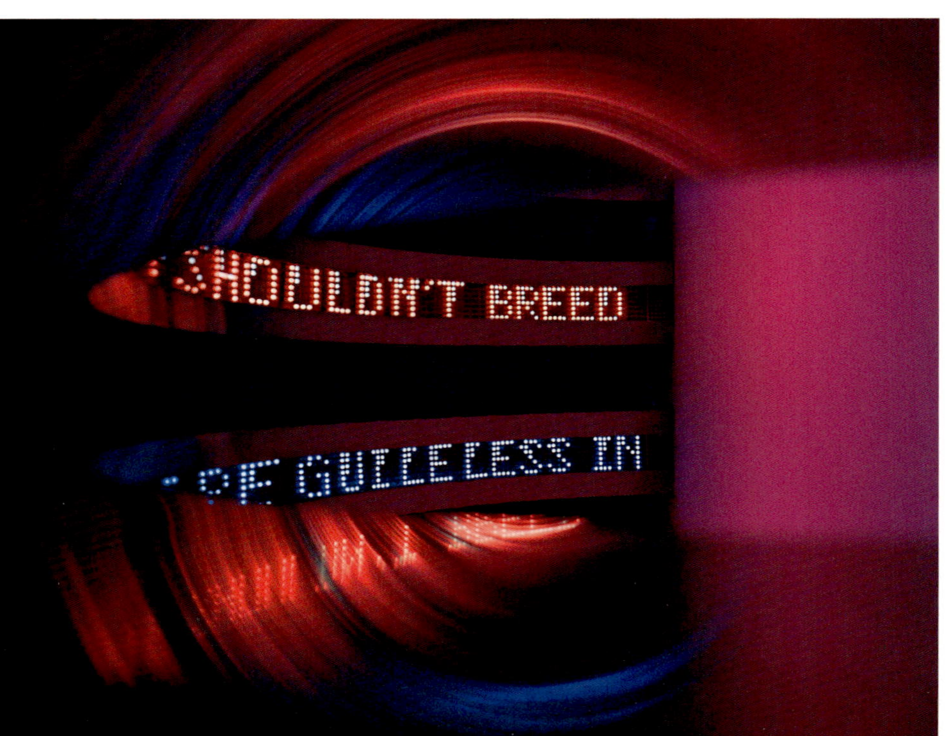
SHOULDN'T BREED
GUILELESS IN

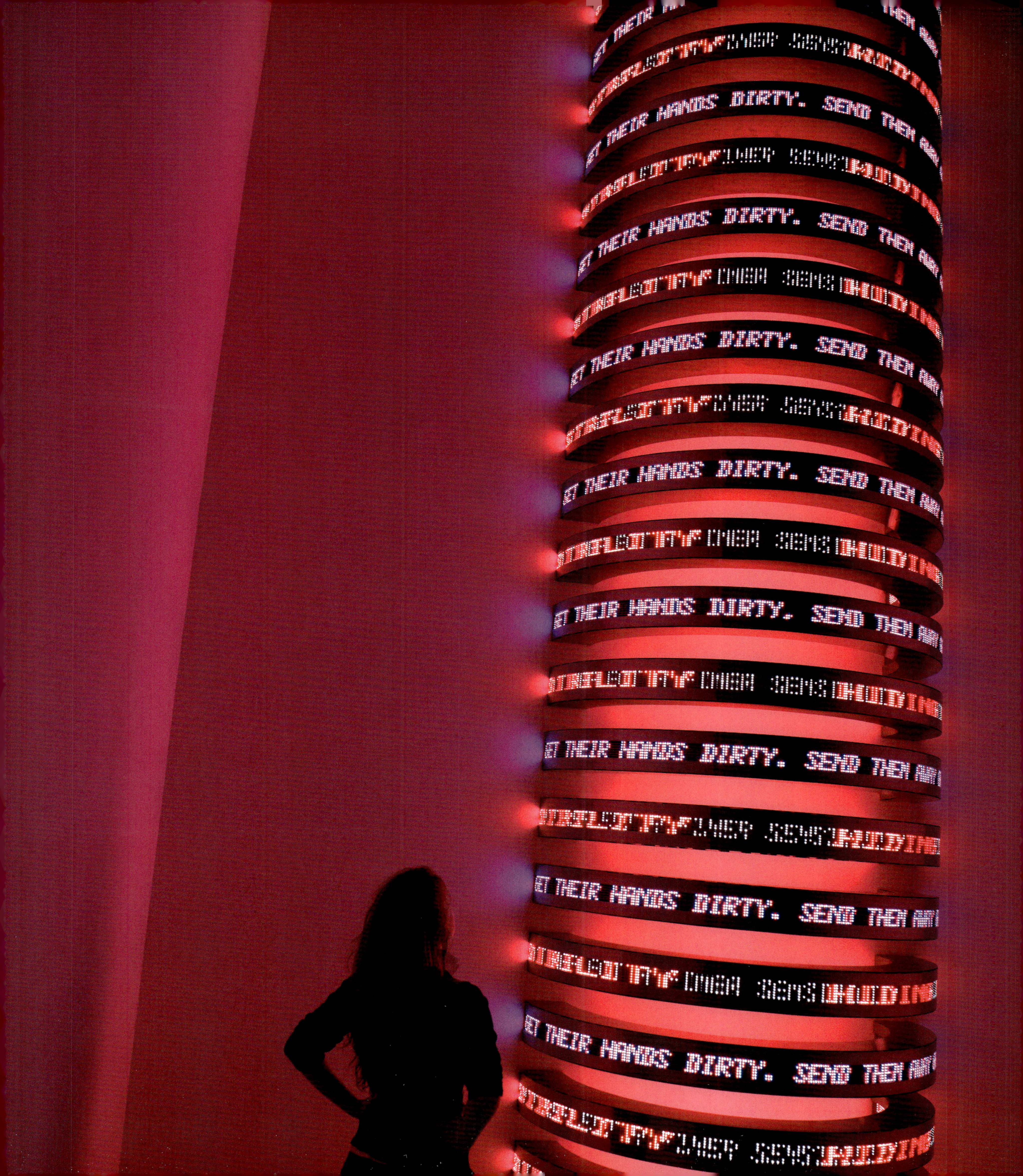
THEIR HANDS DIRTY. SEND THEM

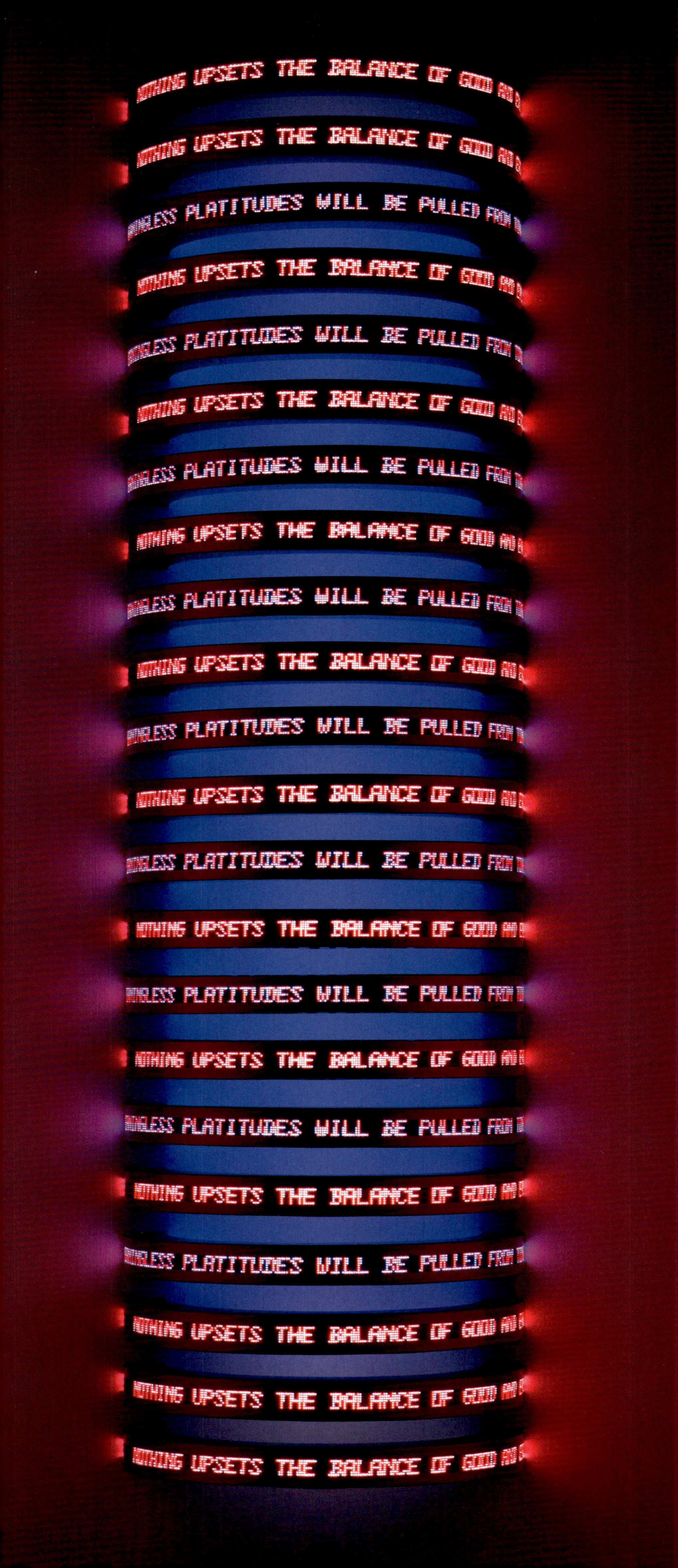

NOTHING UPSETS THE BALANCE OF GOOD AND

PLATITUDES WILL BE PULLED FROM

MONEY CREATES TASTE

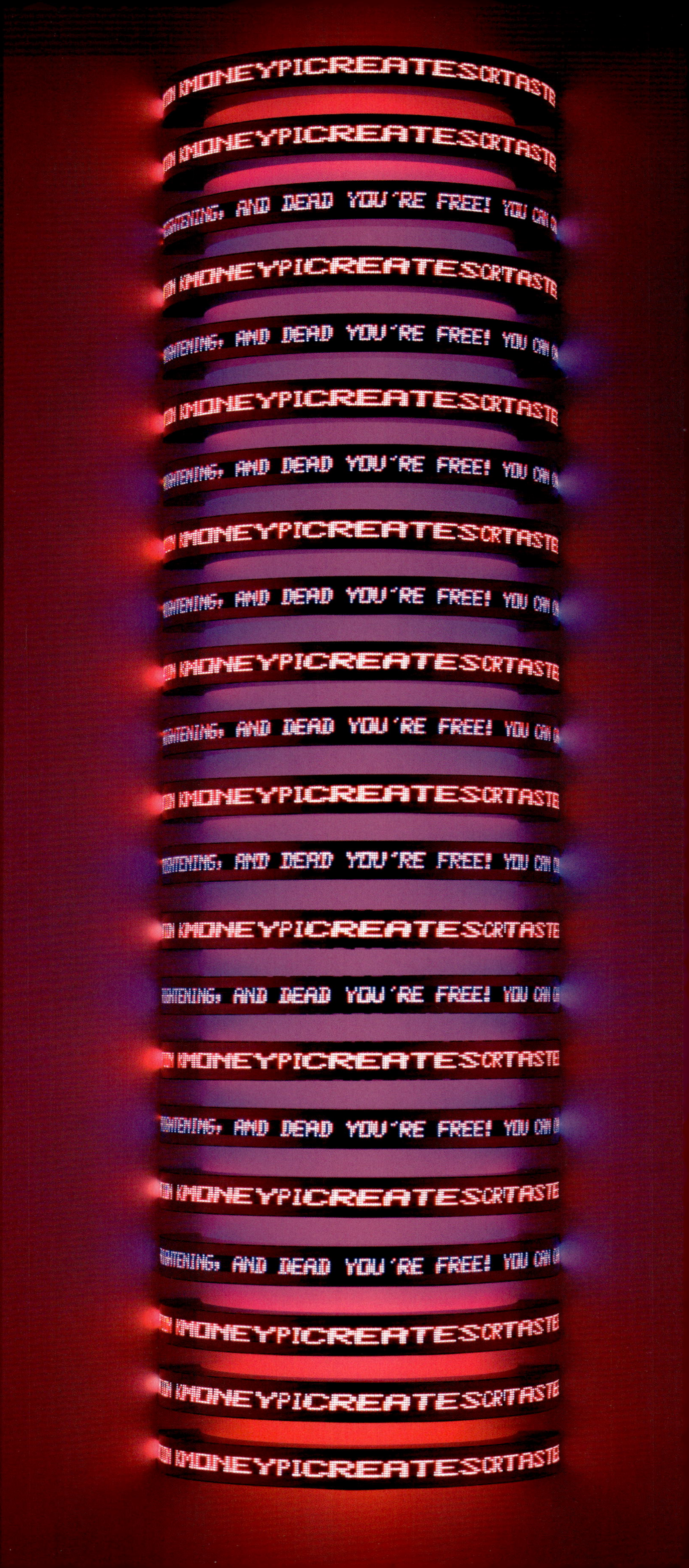

AND DEAD YOU'RE FREE! YOU CAN

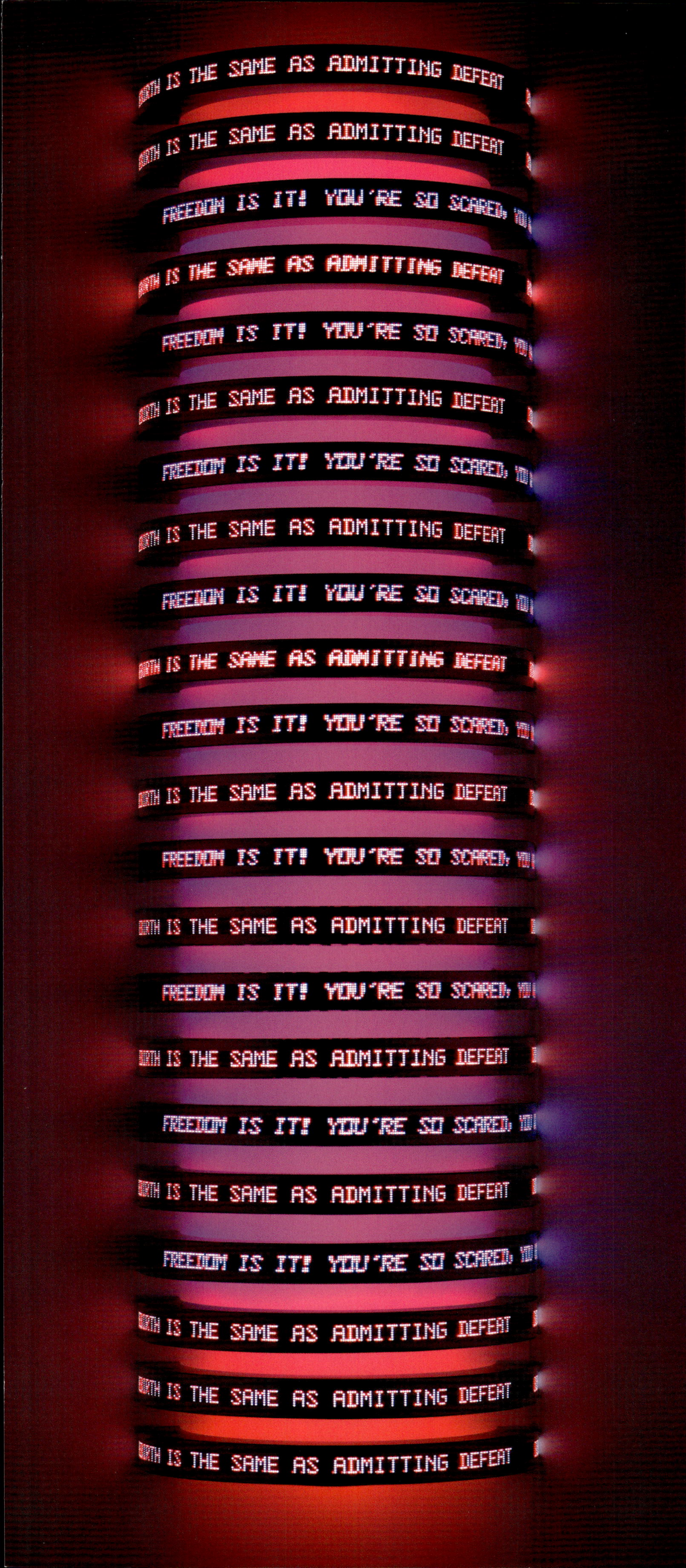

IS THE SAME AS ADMITTING DEFEAT
FREEDOM IS IT! YOU'RE SO SCARED, 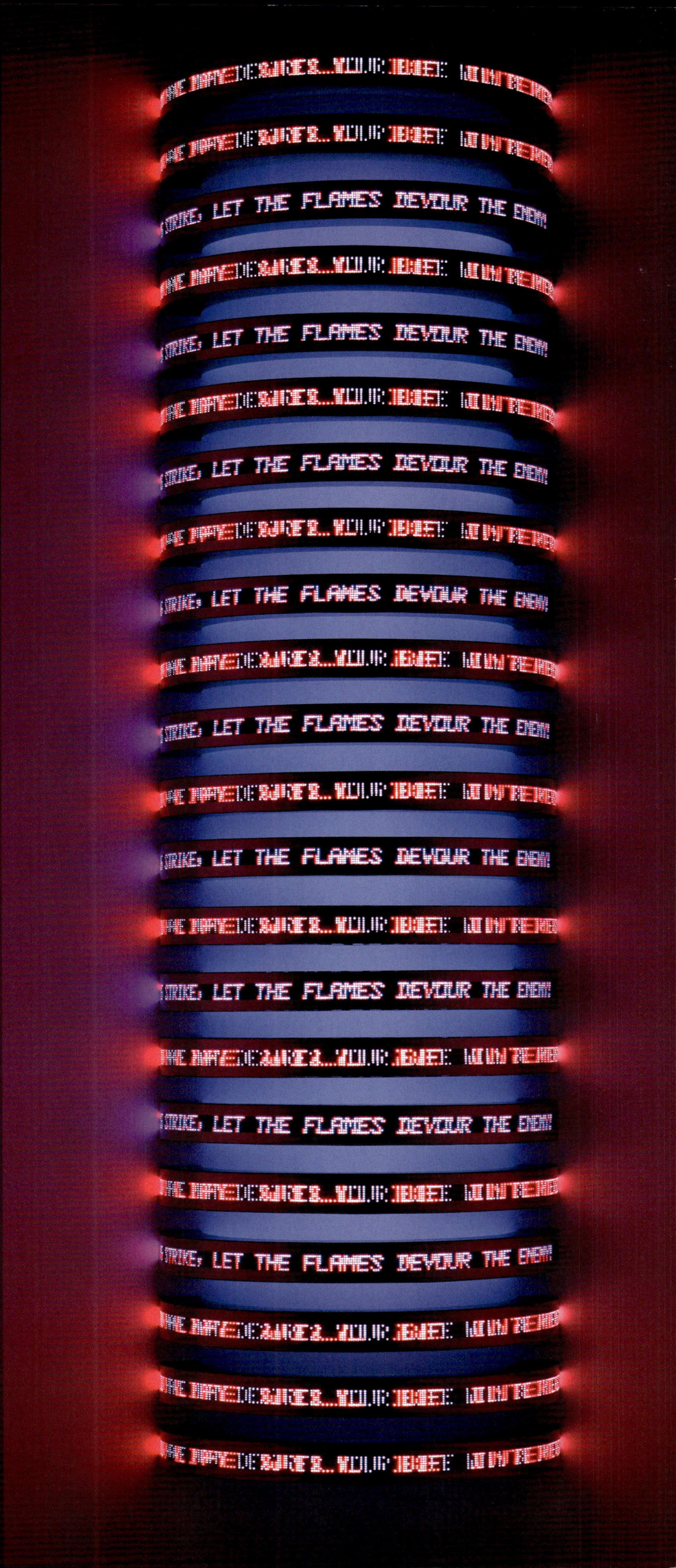
STRIKE; LET THE FLAMES DEVOUR THE ENEMY

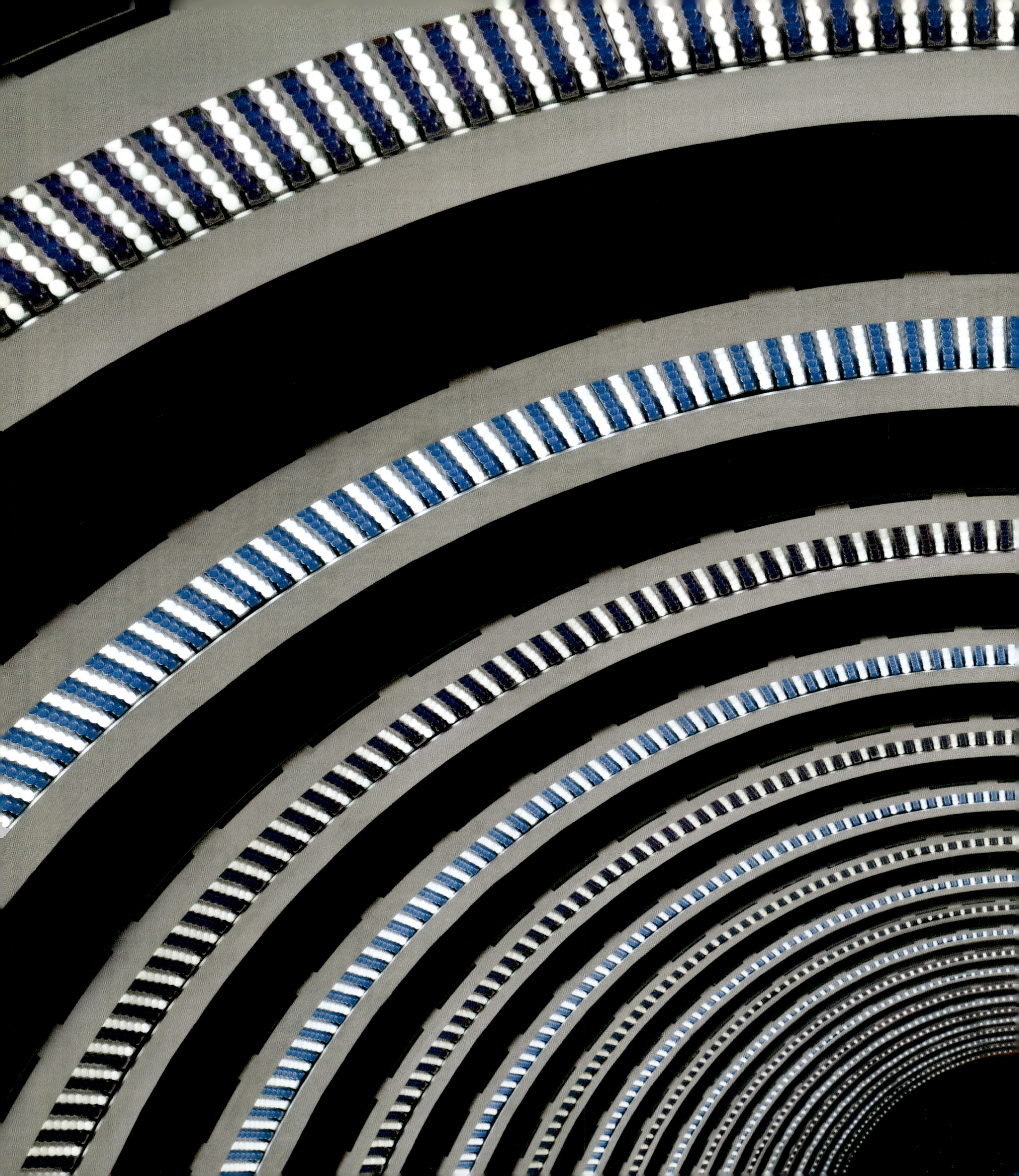

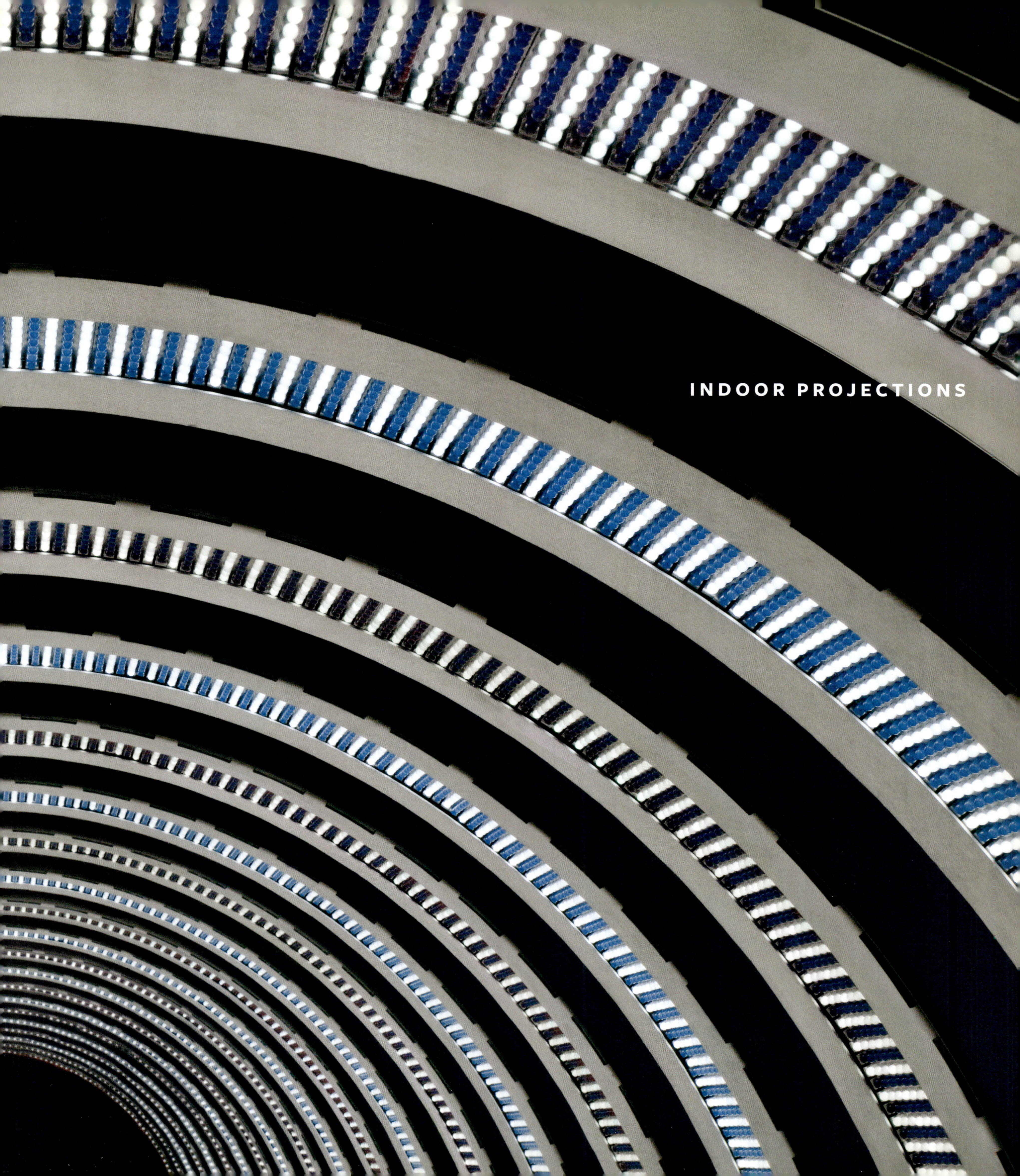

INDOOR PROJECTIONS

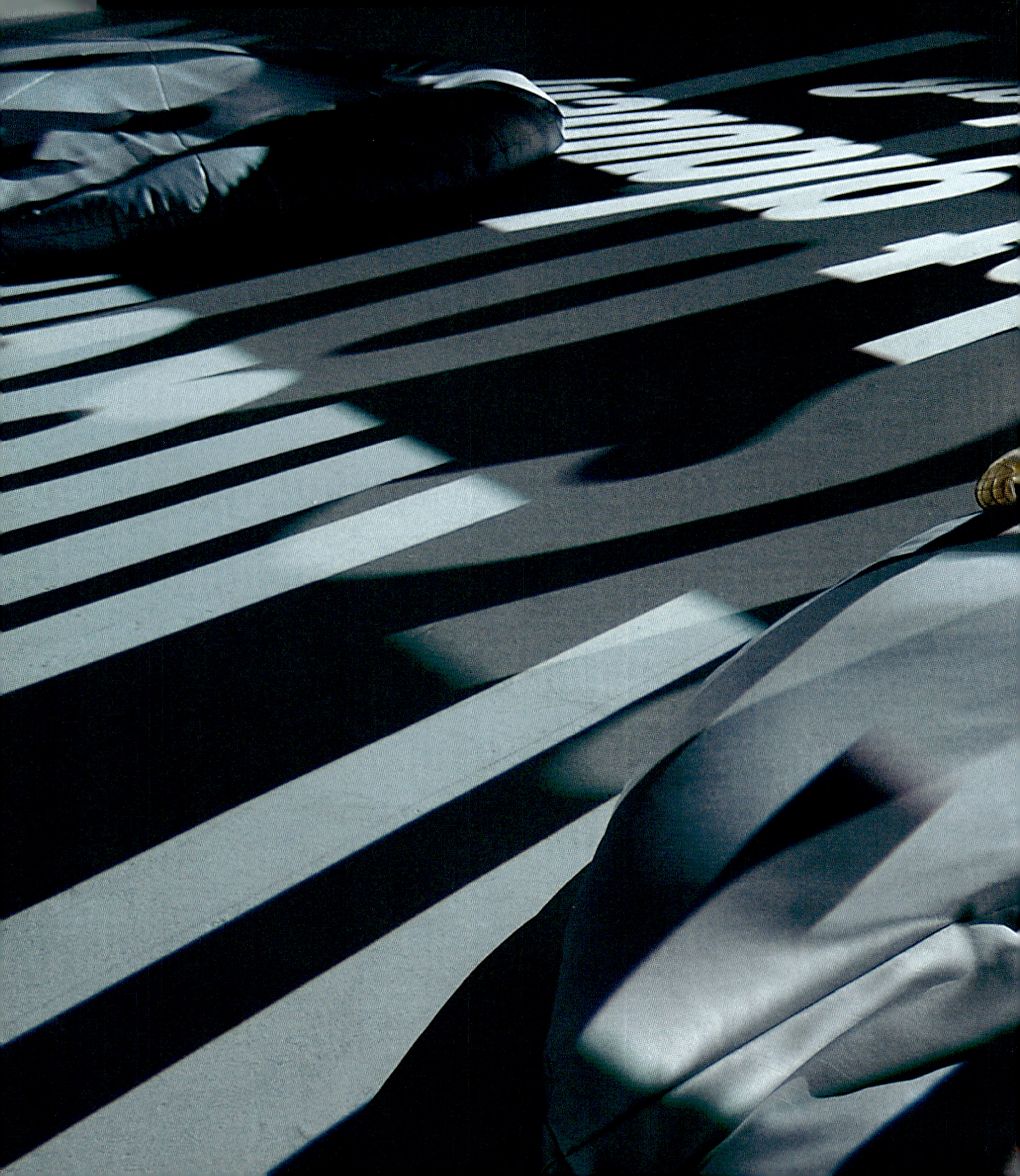

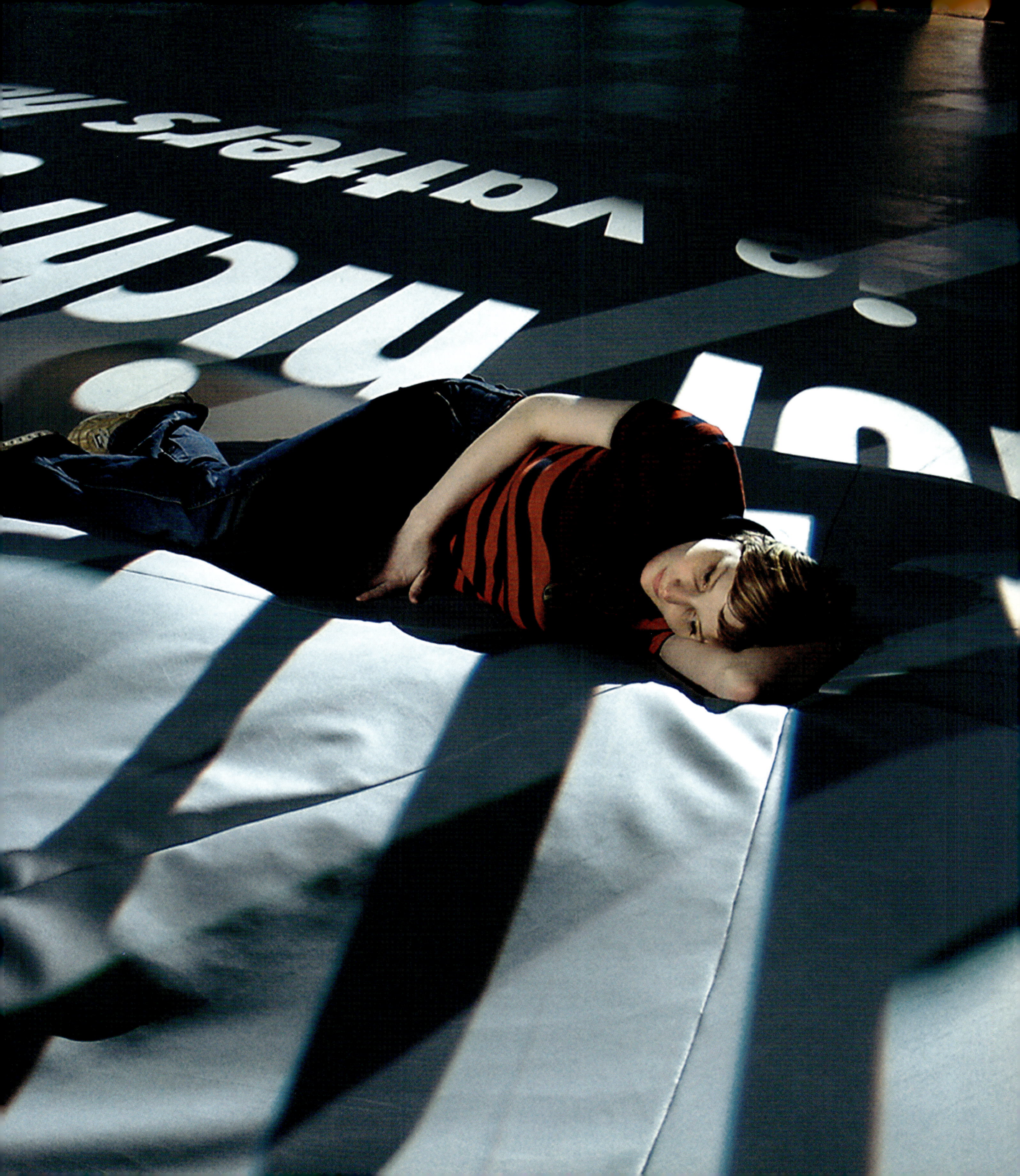

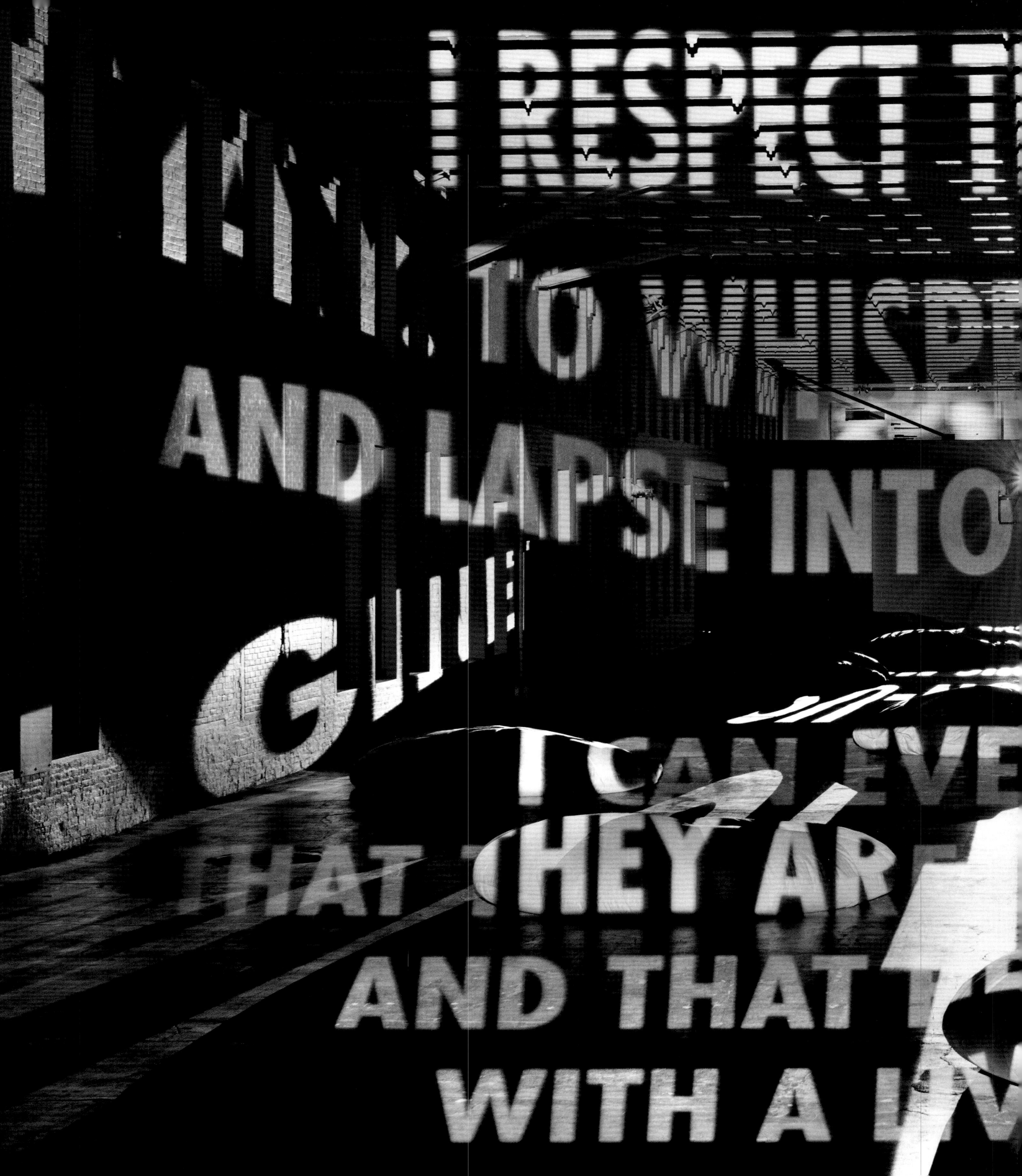
I RESPECT T
TO WHISP
AND LAPSE INTO
I CAN EVE
THAT THEY AR
AND THAT T
WITH A LIV

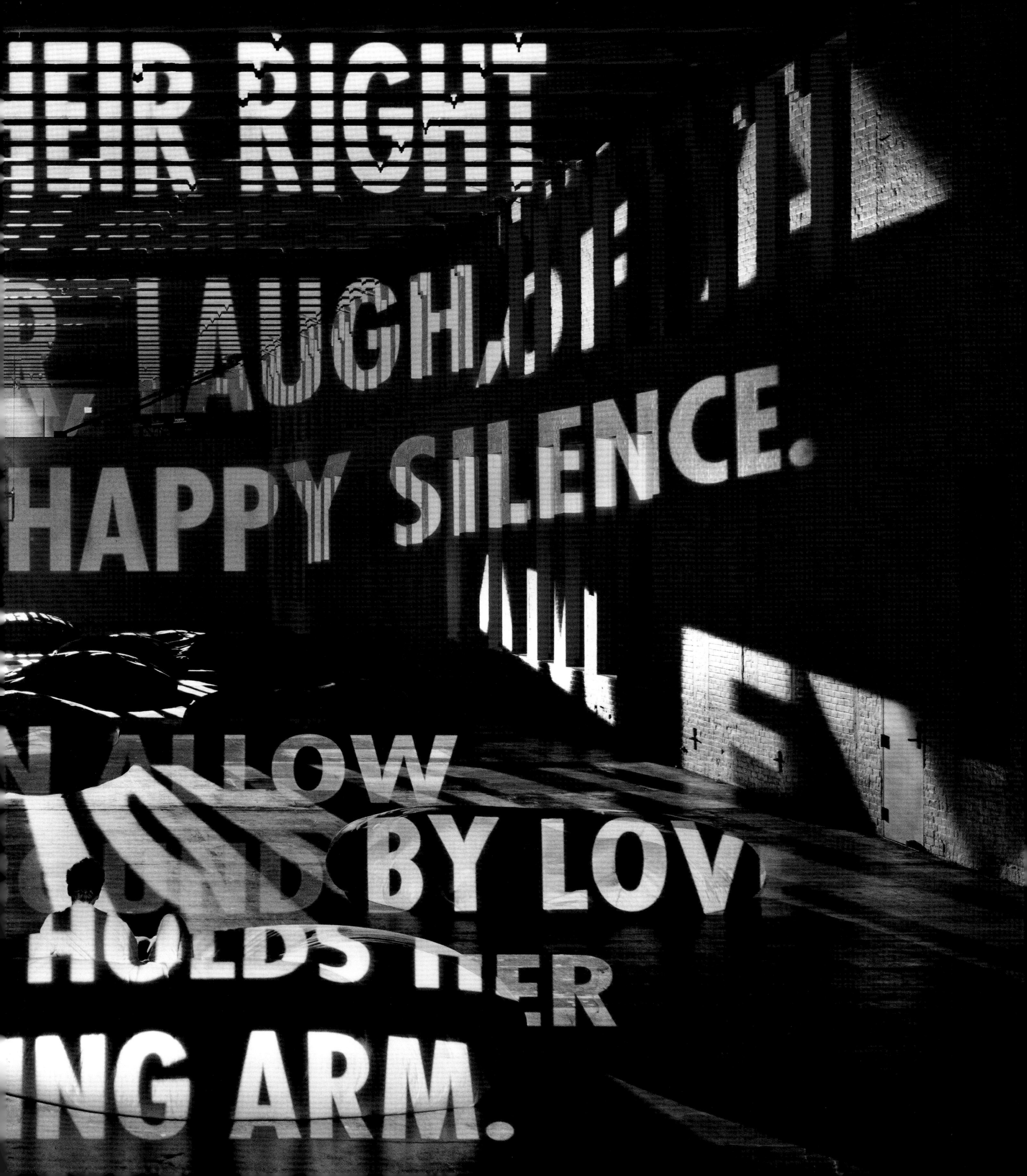

HEIR RIGHT
LAUGH
HAPPY SILENCE.
ALLOW
BY LOV
HOLDS HER
ING ARM.

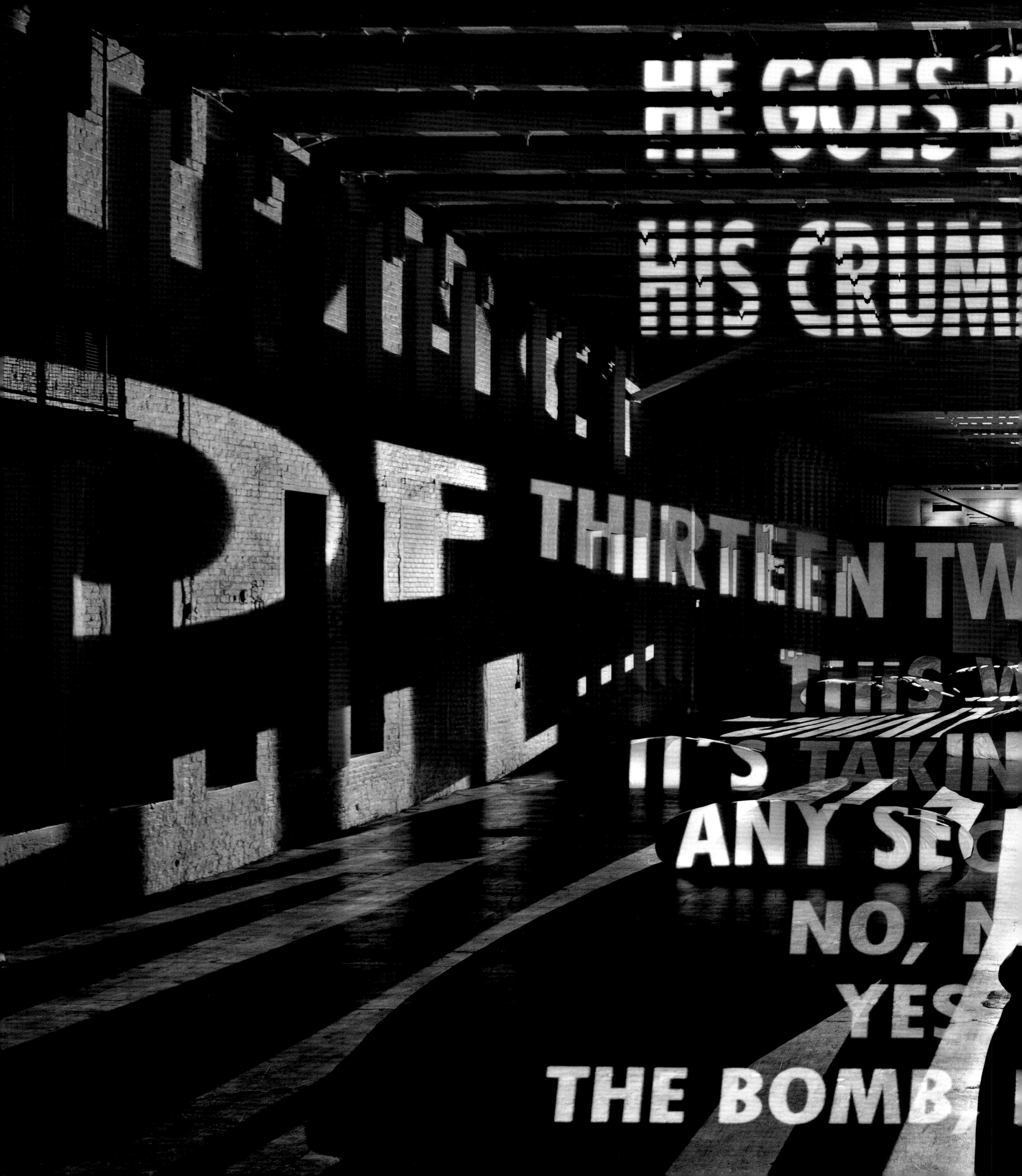

HE GOES B

HE GOES B

HIS CRUM

THIRTEEN TW

THIS W

IT'S TAKIN

ANY SEC

NO, N

YES

THE BOMB, I

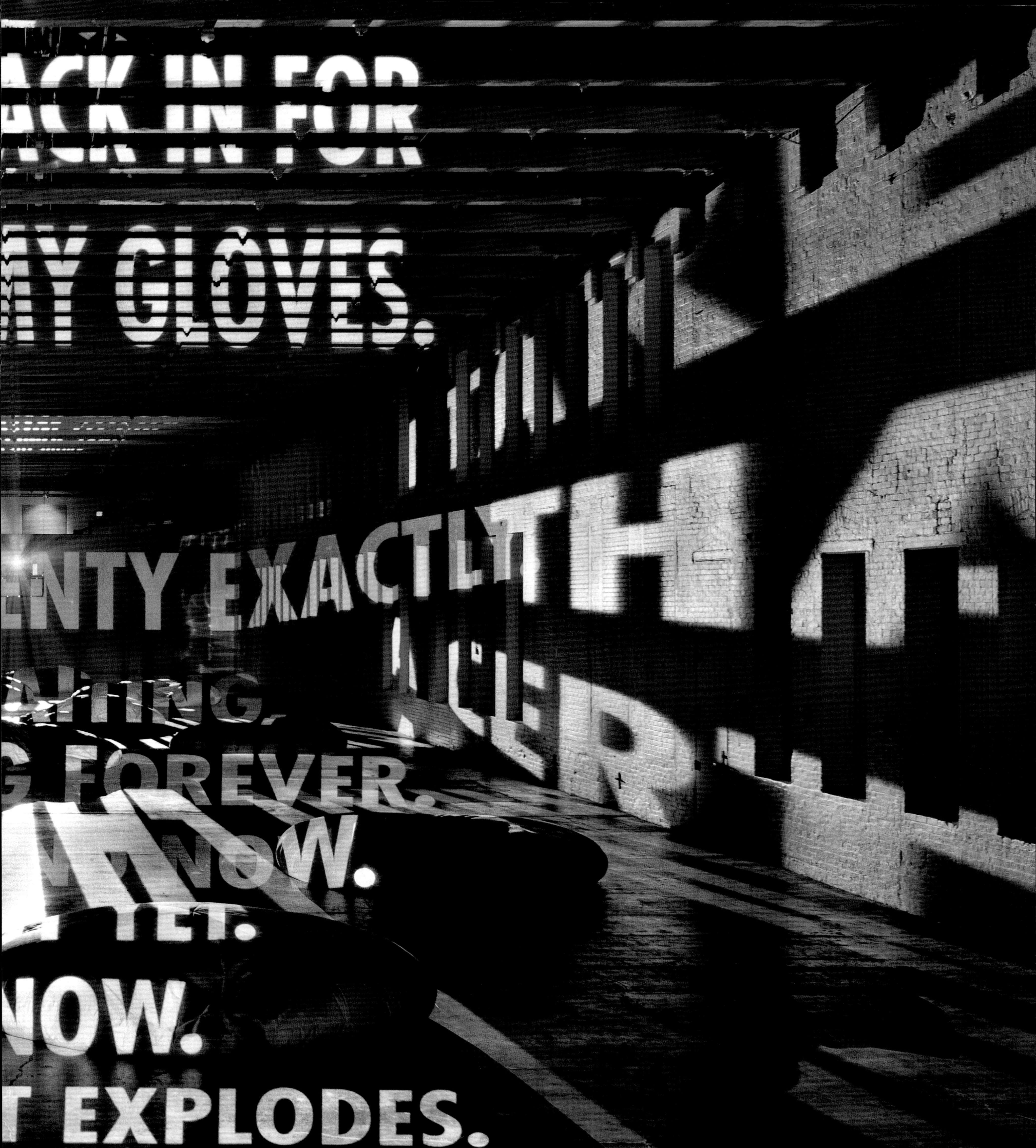

ACK IN FOR
MY GLOVES.
ENTY EXACTLY.
G FOREVER.
NOW.
YET.
NOW.
T EXPLODES.

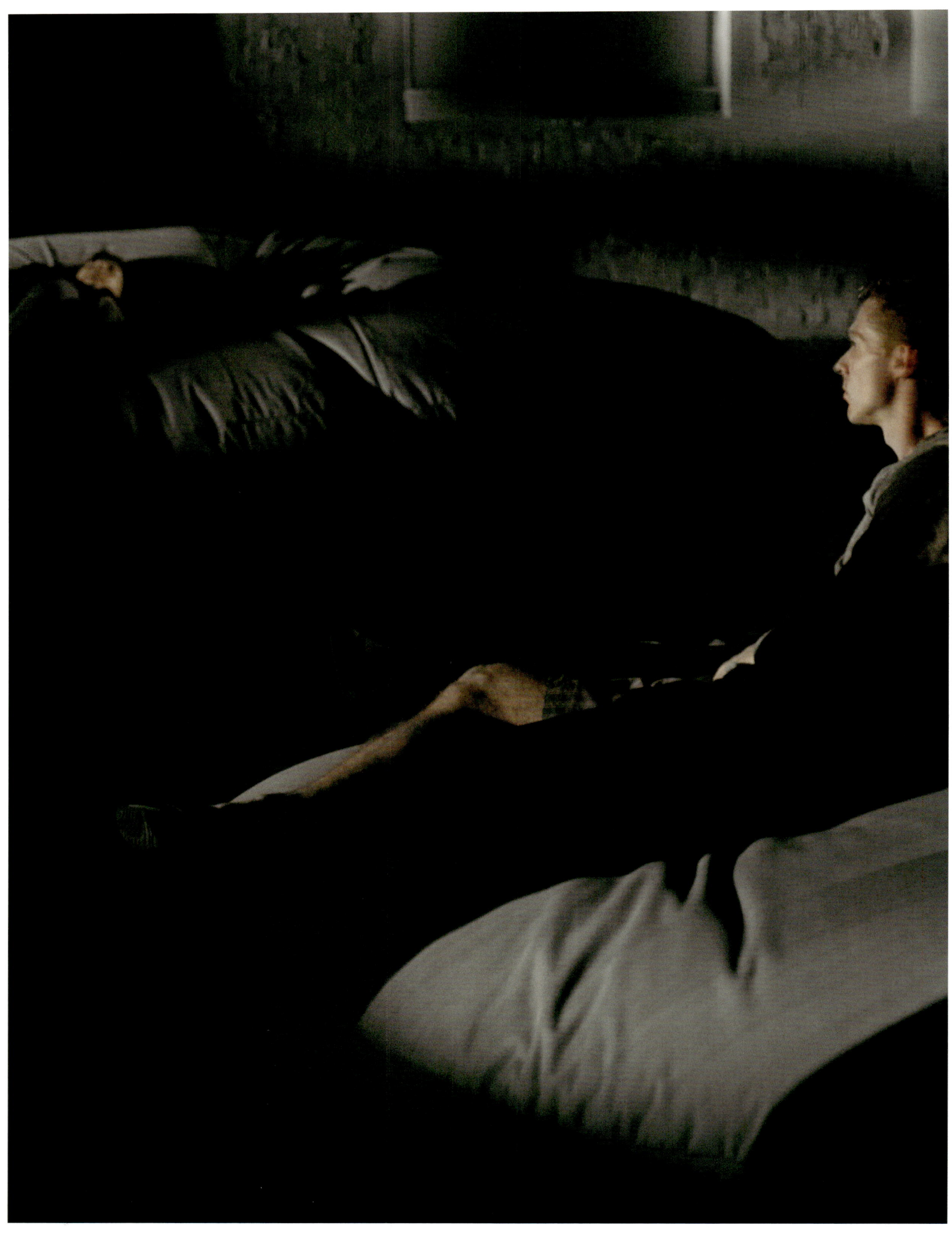

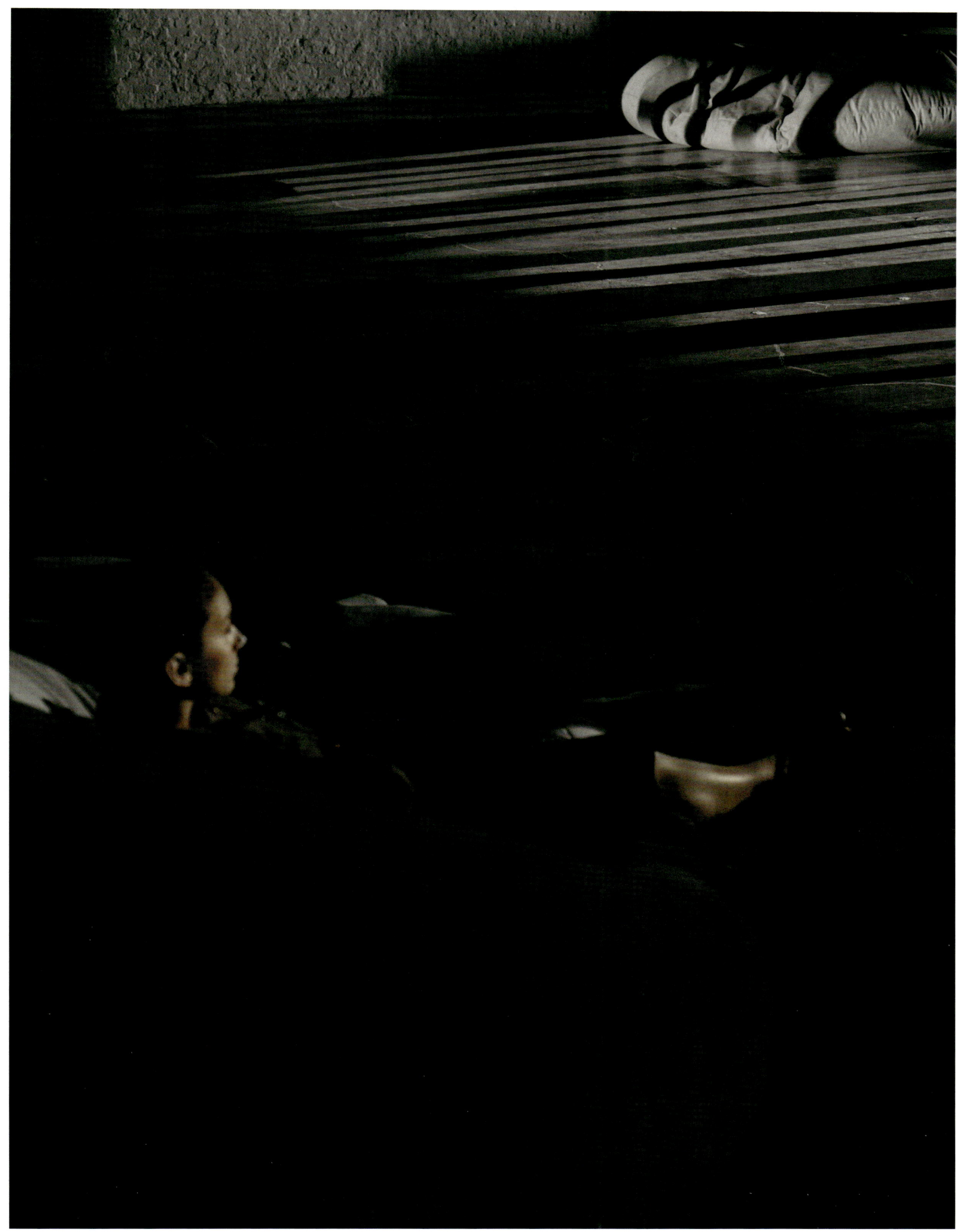

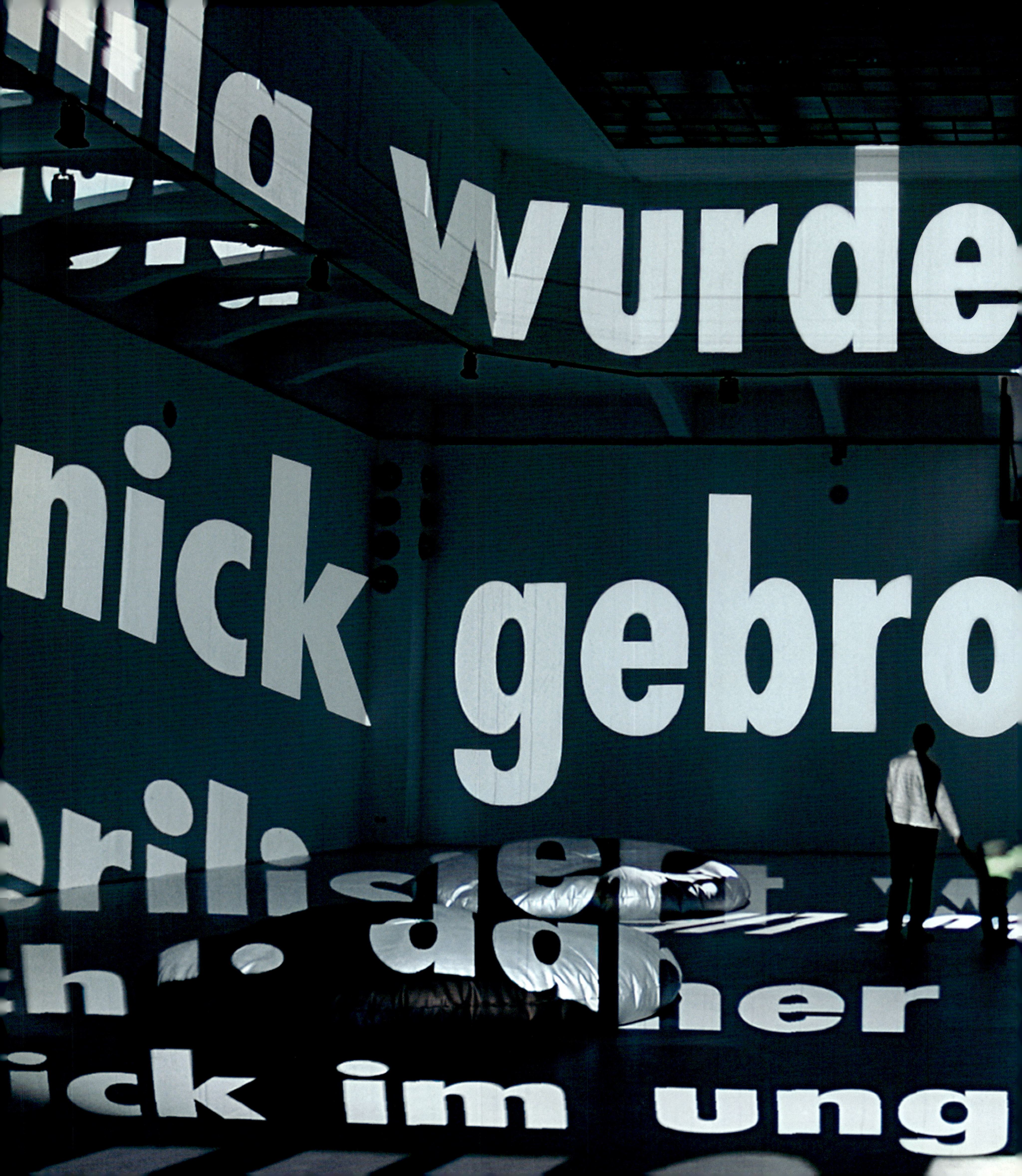

wurde

nick gebro

her

ick im ung

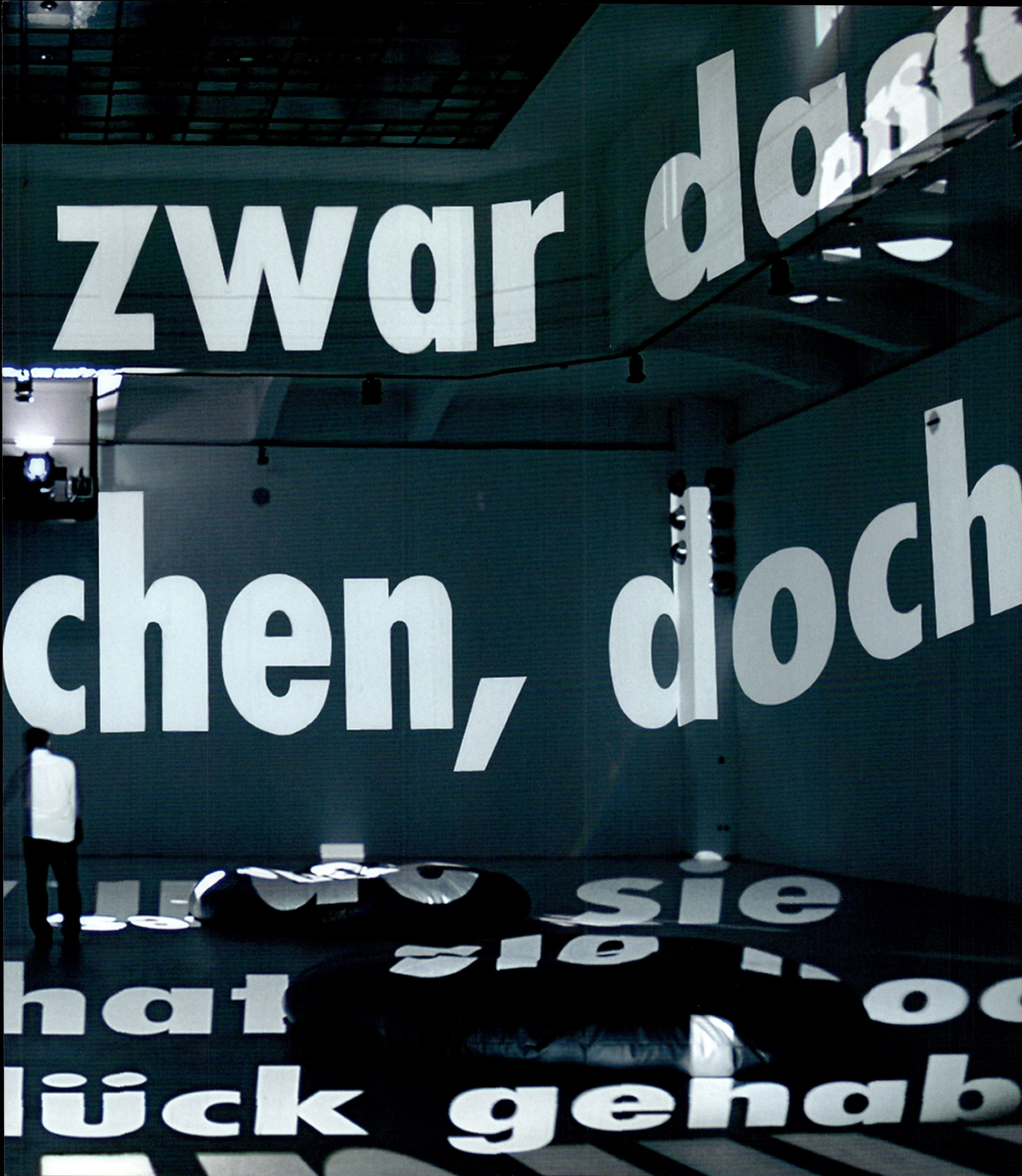

zwar
chen, doch
sie
hat
lück gehab

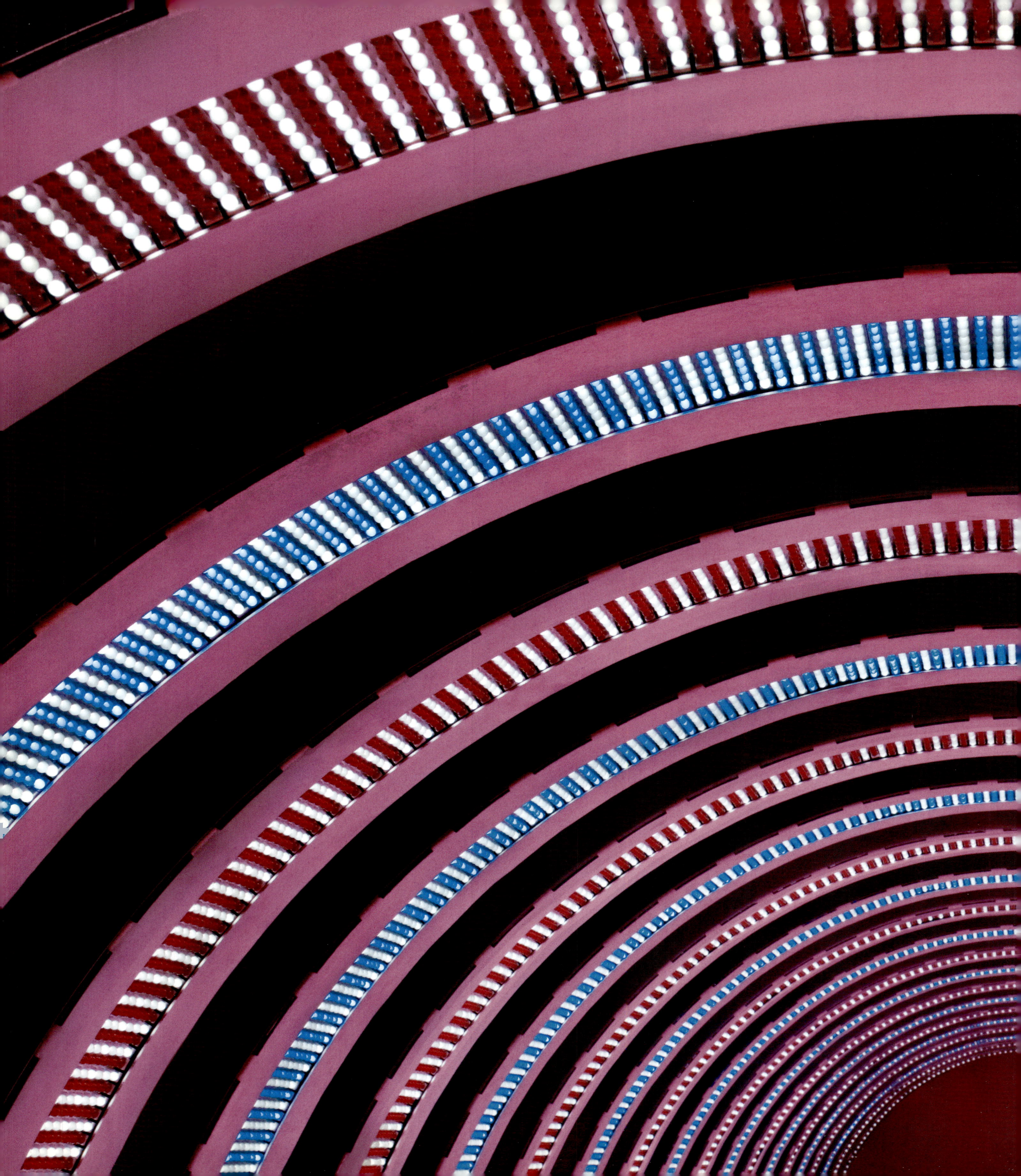

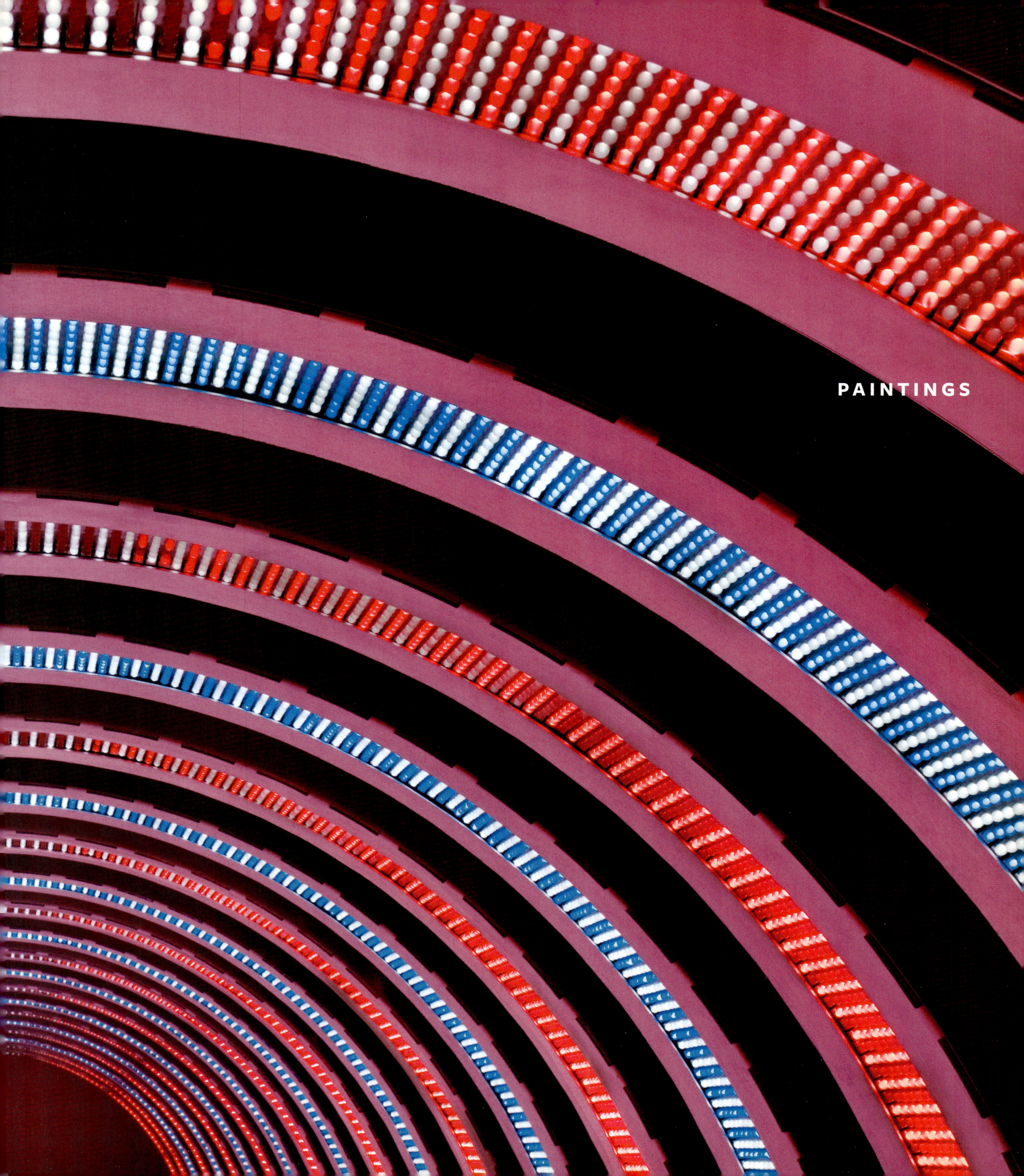

PAINTINGS

MAJOR CASE PRINTS

NAME: (Last, First, MI) ████	
SSN: ████	CASE: 0116-04-CID477
SIGNATURE: ████ b(7)(C)-2	TAKEN BY: SA ████ b(7)(C)-1
	DATE: 22 Nov 03

PALM, FINGERS & FINGERTIPS (LEFT HAND)

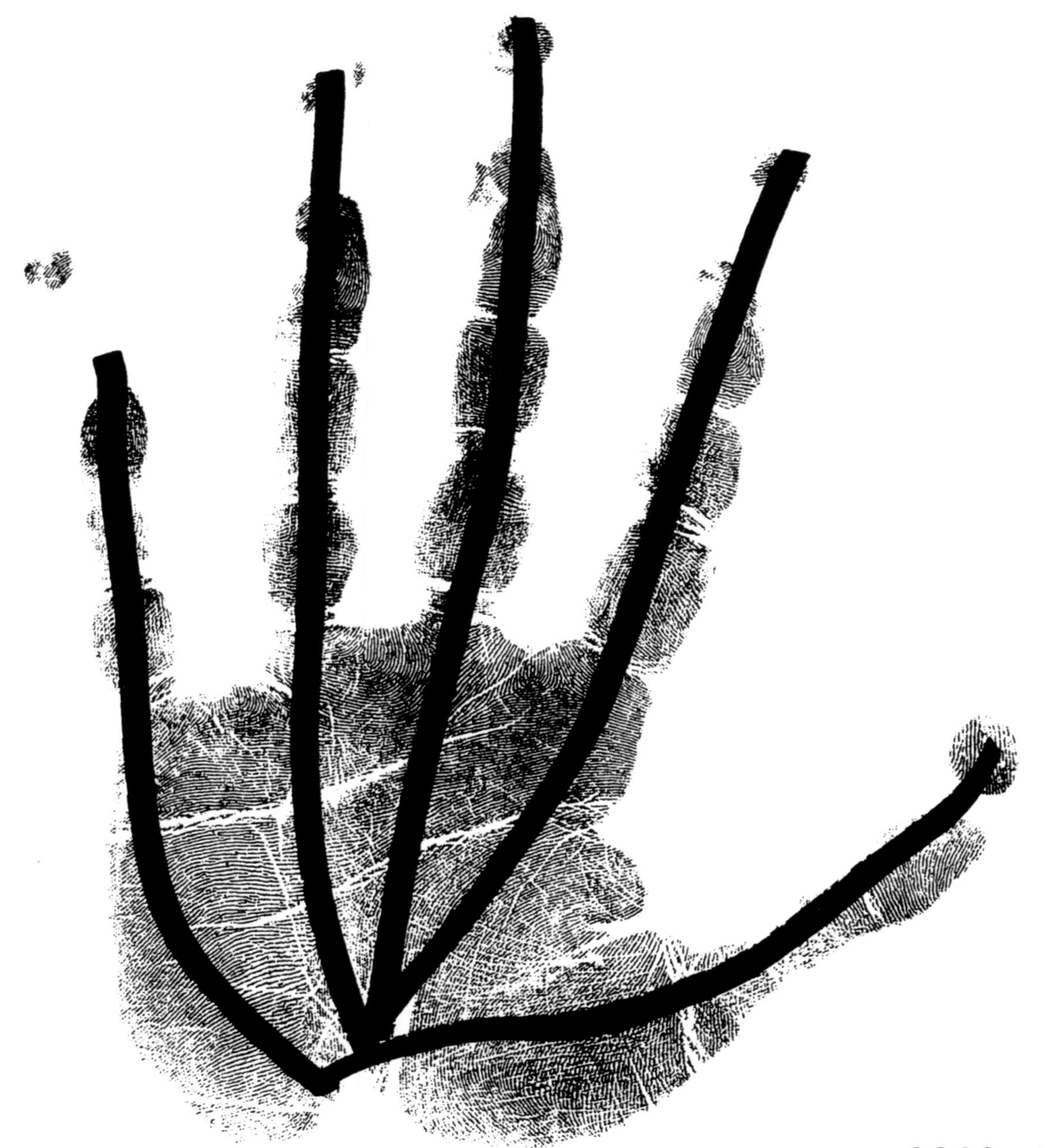

022974

FOR OFFICIAL USE ONLY

FOR OFFICIAL USE ONLY

Law Enforcement Sensitive

(EXHIBIT ______)

000406

DOD-044699

MAJOR CASE PRINTS

NAME: (Last, First, MI) [redacted]	CASE: 0116-04-CID477
SSN: [redacted]	TAKEN BY: SA [redacted] b(7)(c)-1
SIGNATURE: [redacted] b(7)(c)-2	DATE: 22 Nov 03

PALM, FINGERS & FINGERTIPS (RIGHT HAND)

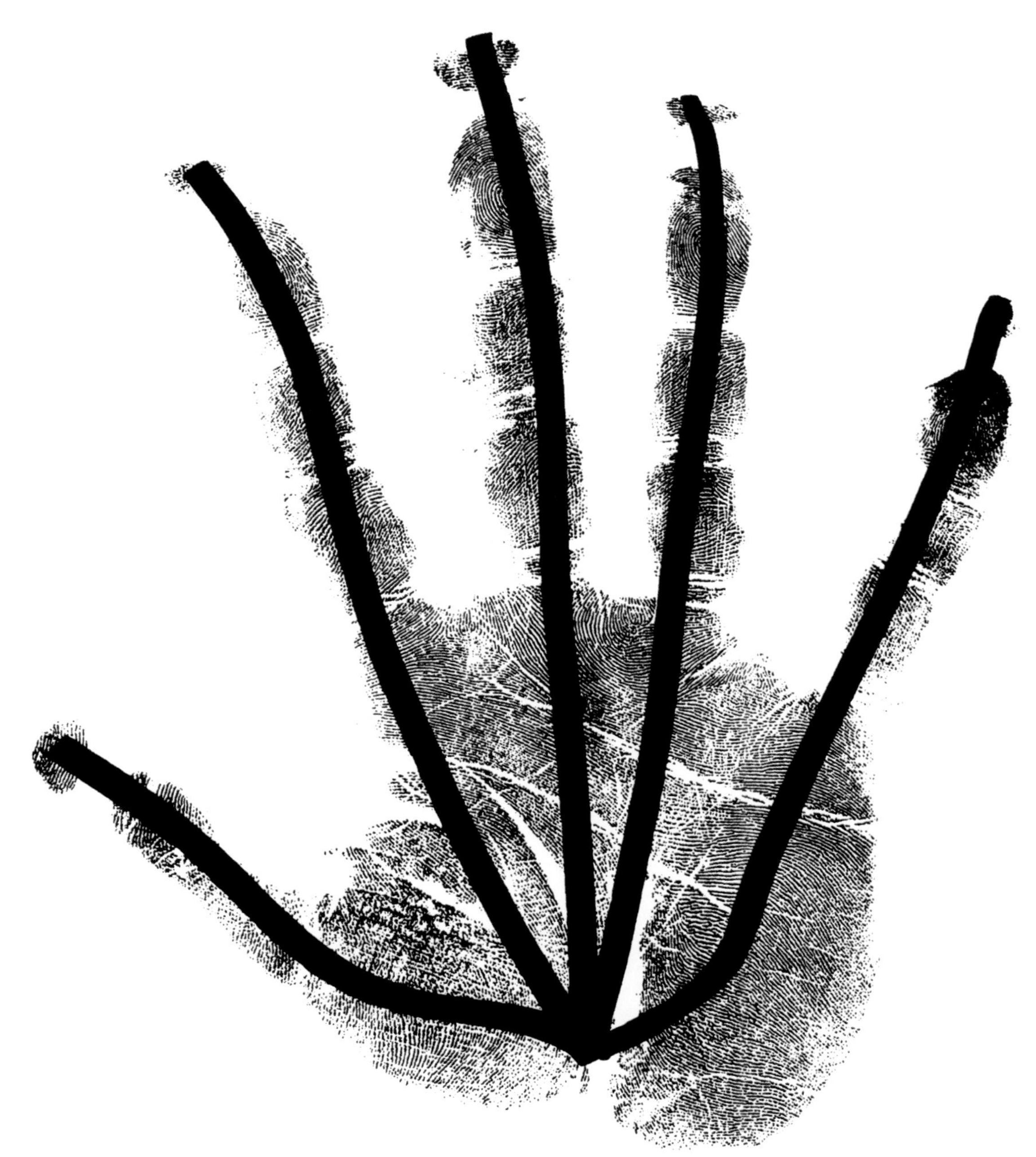

022975

FOR OFFICIAL USE ONLY

FOR OFFICIAL USE ONLY

Law Enforcement Sensitive

(EXHIBIT________)

000407

DOD-044700

0406-04-CID025-

Left Hand
(Palm Rolled)

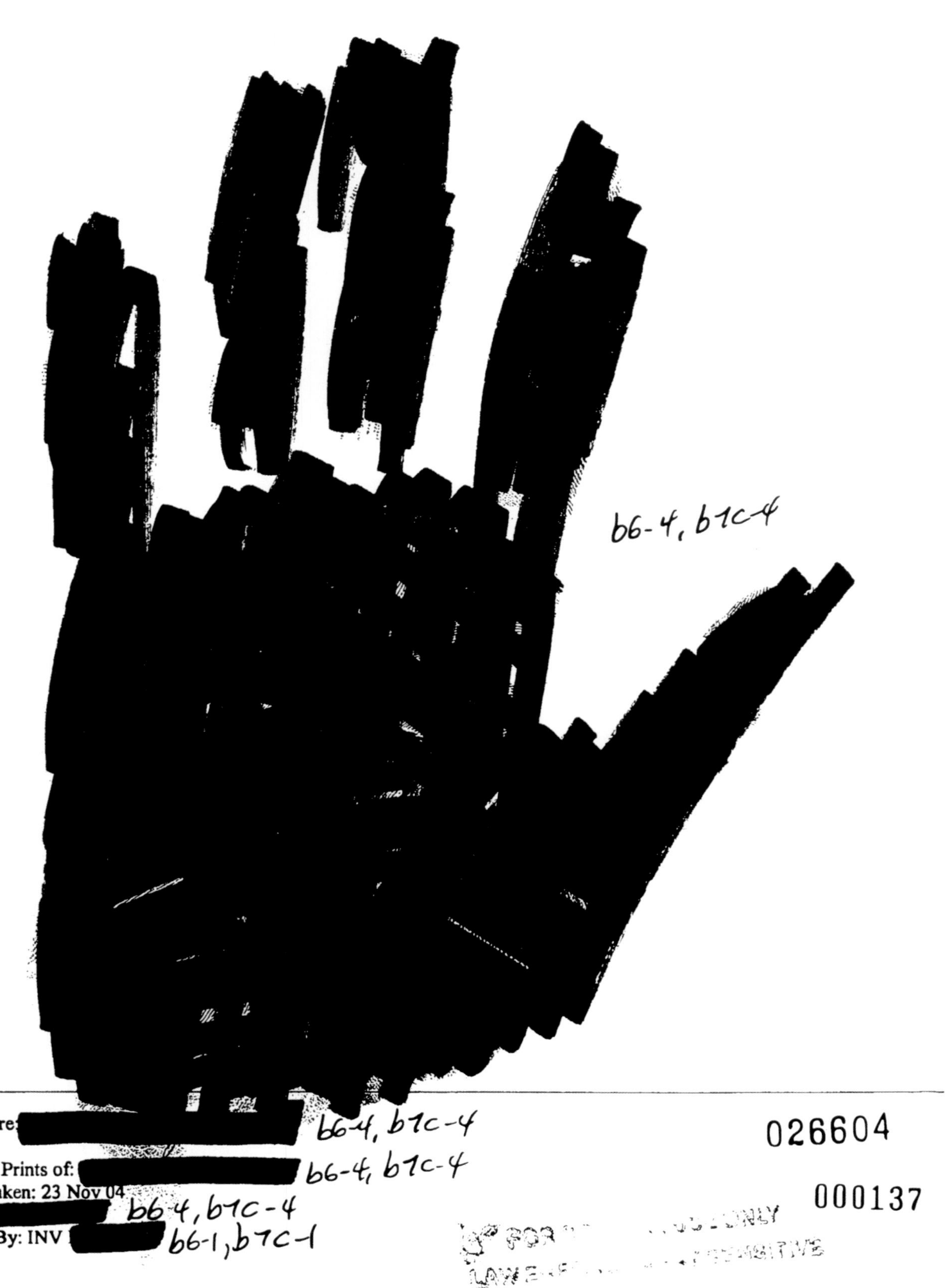

Signature: b6-4, b7c-4

026604

Record Prints of: b6-4, b7c-4

Date Taken: 23 Nov 04

SSN: b6-4, b7c-4

Taken By: INV b6-1, b7c-1

000137

DOD-052103

Right Hand
(Palm Rolled)

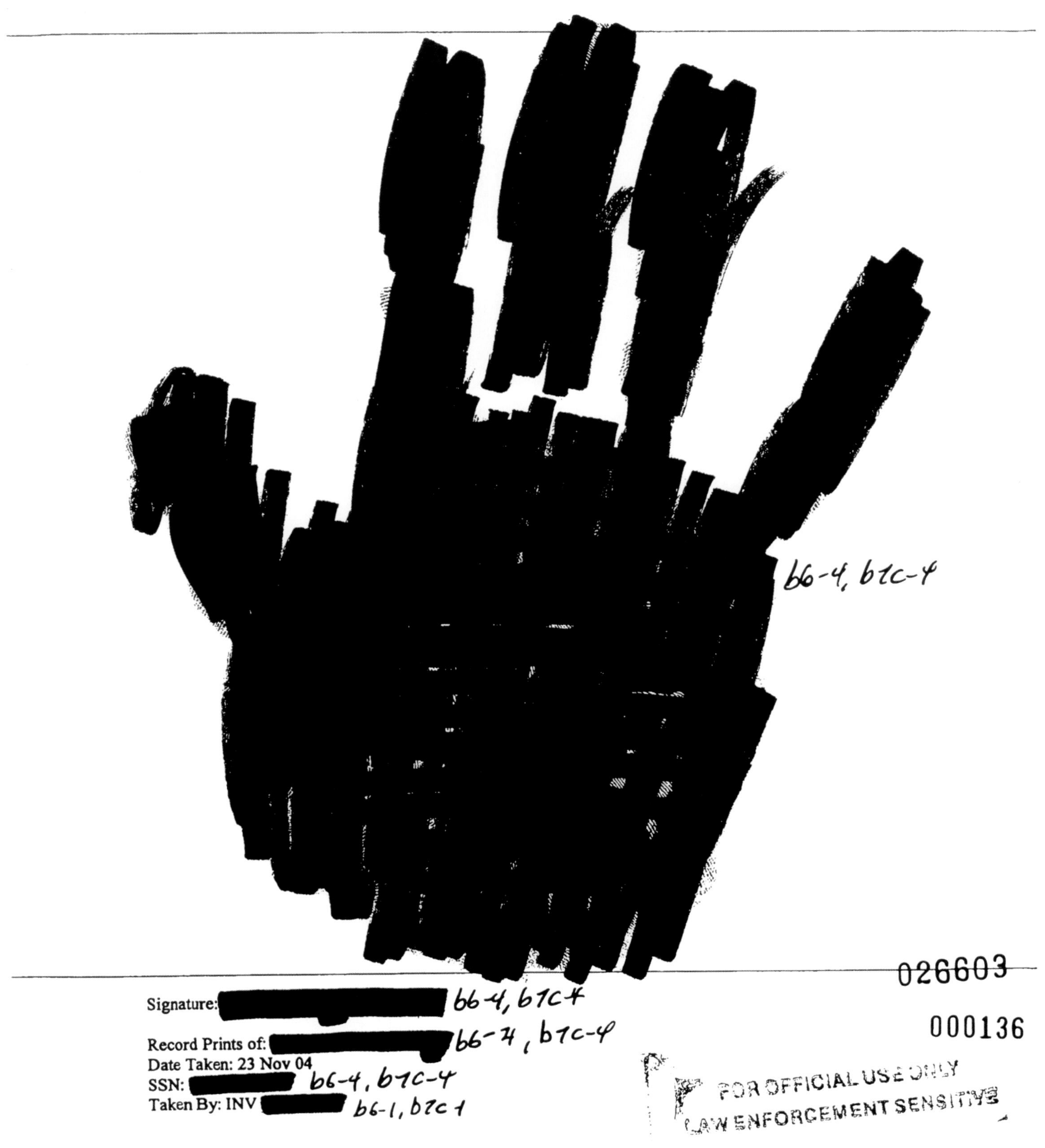

b6-4, b7c-4

026603

000136

Signature: [redacted] b6-4, b7c4

Record Prints of: [redacted] b6-4, b7c-4

Date Taken: 23 Nov 04

SSN: [redacted] b6-4, b7c-4

Taken By: INV [redacted] b6-1, b7c1

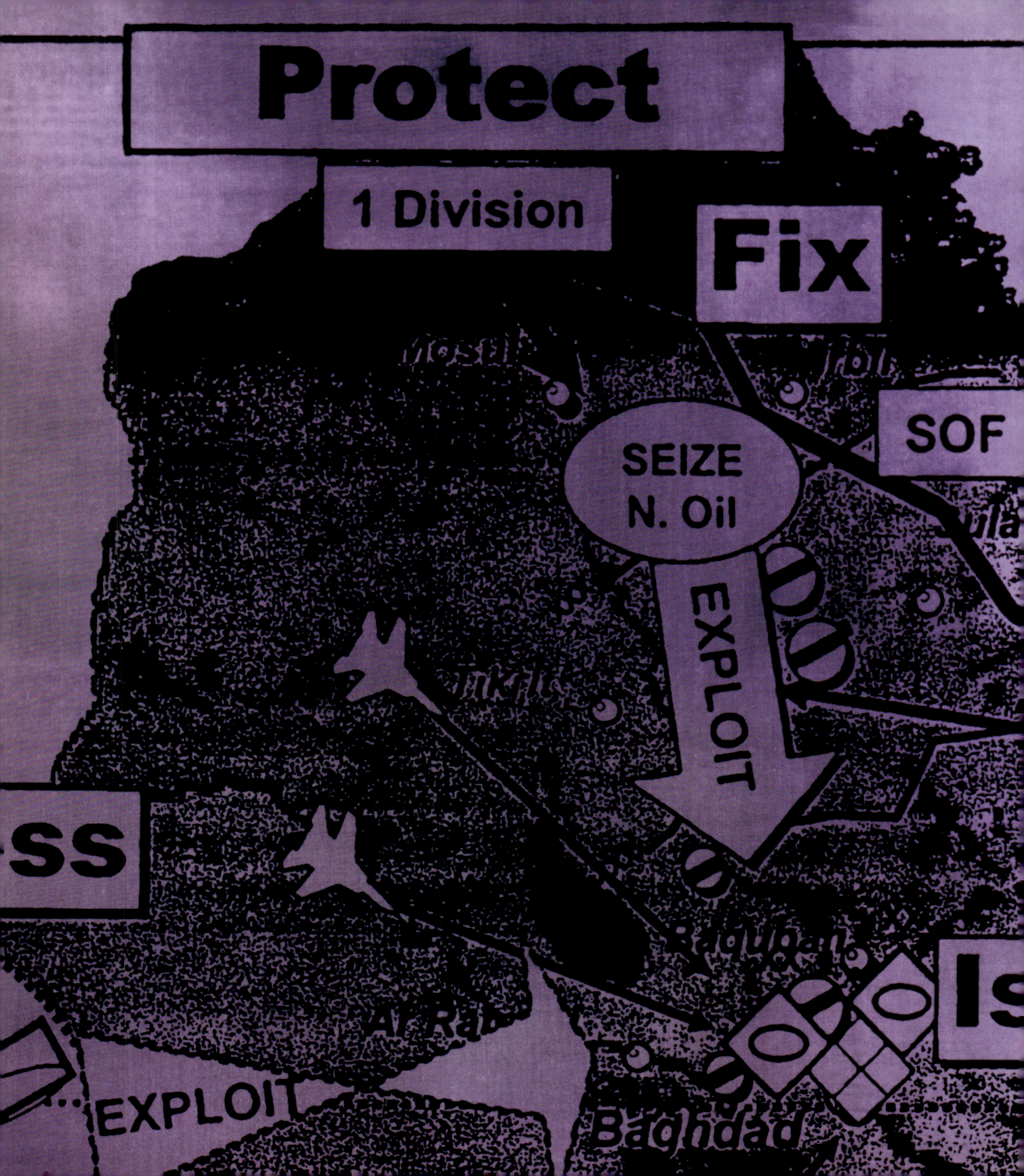

Protect

1 Division

Fix

SOF

SEIZE
N. Oil

EXPLOIT

SS

EXPLOIT

Baghdad

Is

SECRET//ORCON,REL TO USA,CMFI

DECLASSIFIED BY: RADM R.T. Moeller
DECLASSIFY ON: 16 June 2005
ACTION OFFICER: Mr. M.D. Fitzgerald, Civ

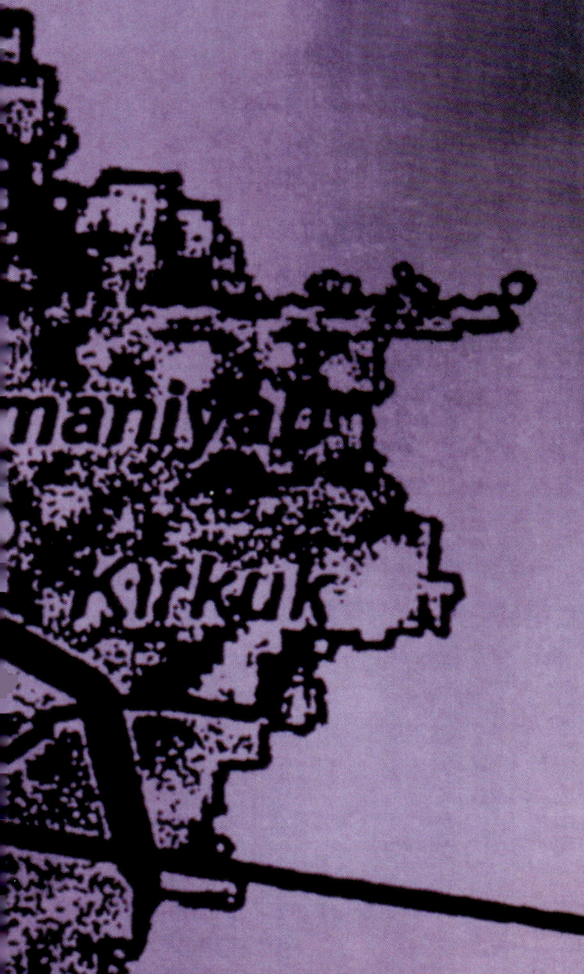

Simultaneous Security and Stability ops

olate

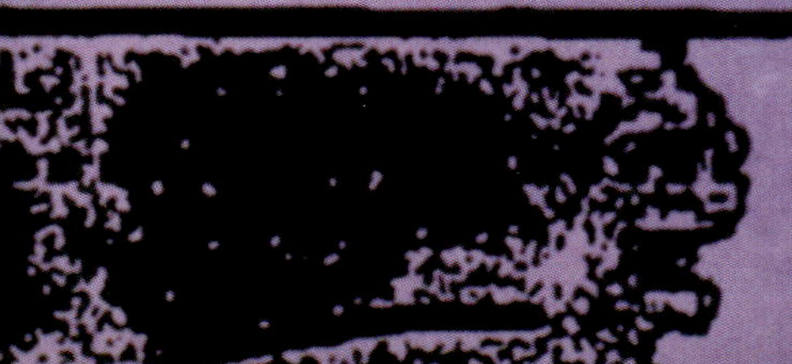

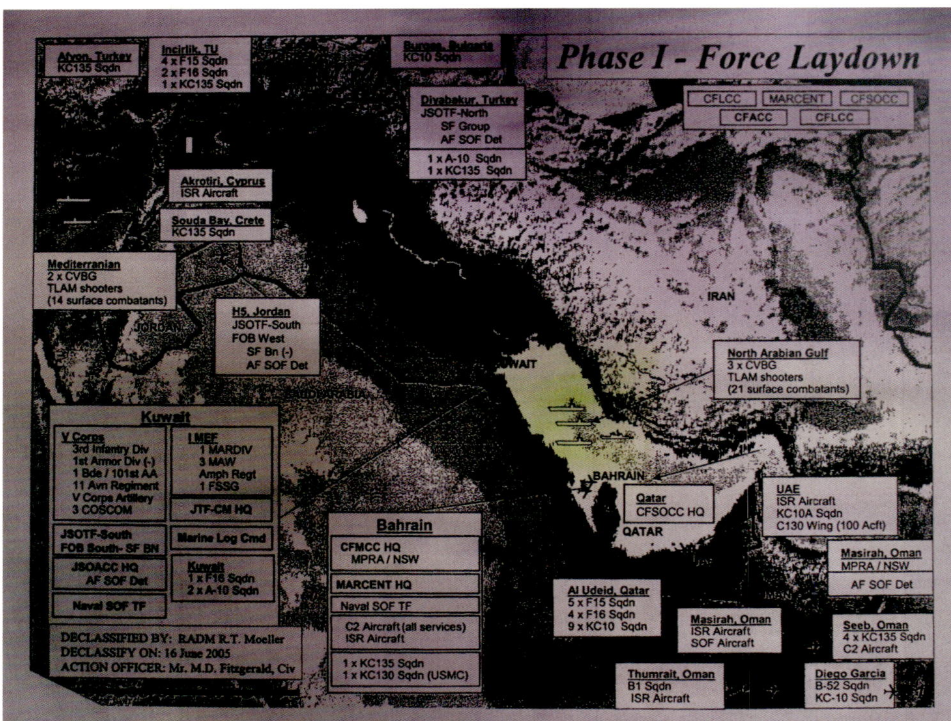
Phase I - Force Laydown
CFLCC MARCENT CFSOCC
CFACC CFLCC
Incirlik, TU
4 x F15 Sqdn
2 x F16 Sqdn
1 x KC135 Sqdn
Diyabakur, Turkey
JSOTF-North
SF Group
AF SOF Det
1 x A-10 Sqdn
1 x KC135 Sqdn
Akrotiri, Cyprus
ISR Aircraft
Souda Bay, Crete
KC135 Sqdn
Mediterranian
2 x CVBG
TLAM shooters
(14 surface combatants)
H5, Jordan
JSOTF-South
FOB West
SF Bn (-)
AF SOF Det
IRAN
KUWAIT
North Arabian Gulf
3 x CVBG
TLAM shooters
(21 surface combatants)
Kuwait
V Corps
3rd Infantry Div
1st Armor Div (-)
1 Bde / 101st AA
11 Avn Regiment
V Corps Artillery
3 COSCOM
I MEF
1 MARDIV
3 MAW
Amph Regt
1 FSSG
JTF-CM HQ
Marine Log Cmd
JSOTF-South
FOB South- SF BN
JSOACC HQ
AF SOF Det
Kuwait
1 x F16 Sqdn
2 x A-10 Sqdn
Naval SOF TF
BAHRAIN
Qatar
CFSOCC HQ
QATAR
UAE
ISR Aircraft
KC10A Sqdn
C130 Wing (100 Acft)
Bahrain
CFMCC HQ
MPRA / NSW
MARCENT HQ
Naval SOF TF
C2 Aircraft (all services)
ISR Aircraft
1 x KC135 Sqdn
1 x KC130 Sqdn (USMC)
Al Udeid, Qatar
5 x F15 Sqdn
4 x F16 Sqdn
9 x KC10 Sqdn
Masirah, Oman
ISR Aircraft
SOF Aircraft
Masirah, Oman
MPRA / NSW
AF SOF Det
Seeb, Oman
4 x KC135 Sqdn
C2 Aircraft
Thumrait, Oman
B1 Sqdn
ISR Aircraft
Diego Garcia
B-52 Sqdn
KC-10 Sqdn
DECLASSIFIED BY: RADM R.T. Moeller
DECLASSIFY ON: 16 June 2005
ACTION OFFICER: Mr. M.D. Fitzgerald, Civ

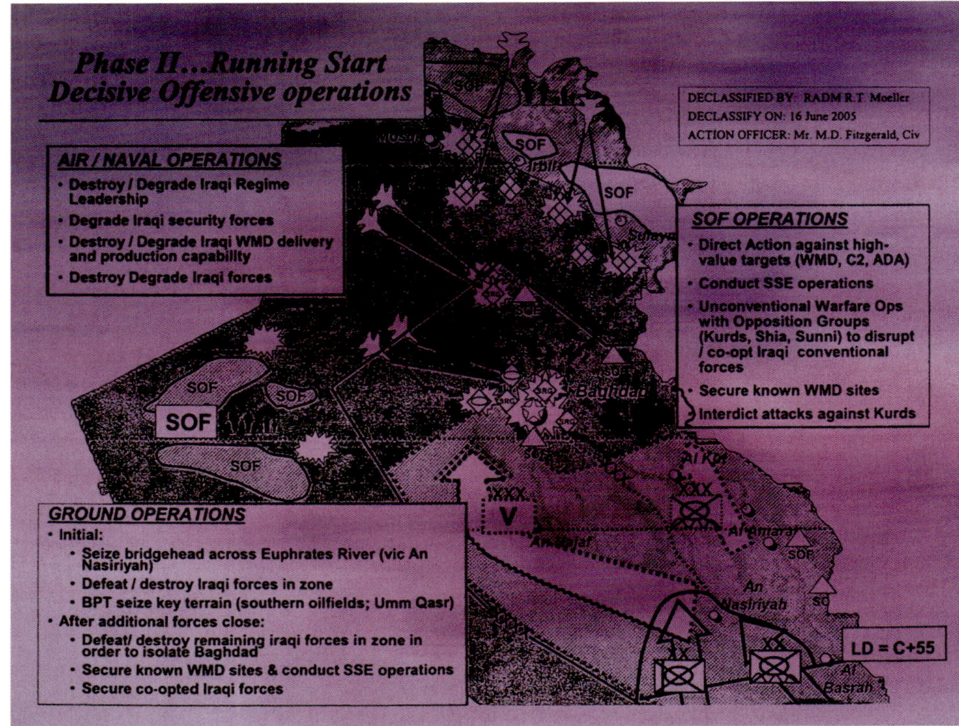
Phase II…Running Start
Decisive Offensive operations
DECLASSIFIED BY: RADM R.T. Moeller
DECLASSIFY ON: 16 June 2005
ACTION OFFICER: Mr. M.D. Fitzgerald, Civ
AIR / NAVAL OPERATIONS
• Destroy / Degrade Iraqi Regime Leadership
• Degrade Iraqi security forces
• Destroy / Degrade Iraqi WMD delivery and production capability
• Destroy Degrade Iraqi forces
SOF OPERATIONS
• Direct Action against high-value targets (WMD, C2, ADA)
• Conduct SSE operations
• Unconventional Warfare Ops with Opposition Groups (Kurds, Shia, Sunni) to disrupt / co-opt Iraqi conventional forces
• Secure known WMD sites
• Interdict attacks against Kurds
SOF
GROUND OPERATIONS
• Initial:
• Seize bridgehead across Euphrates River (vic An Nasiriyah)
• Defeat / destroy Iraqi forces in zone
• BPT seize key terrain (southern oilfields; Umm Qasr)
• After additional forces close:
• Defeat/ destroy remaining Iraqi forces in zone in order to isolate Baghdad
• Secure known WMD sites & conduct SSE operations
• Secure co-opted Iraqi forces
Baghdad
Al Kut
An Nasiriyah
V
LD = C+55
Al Basrah

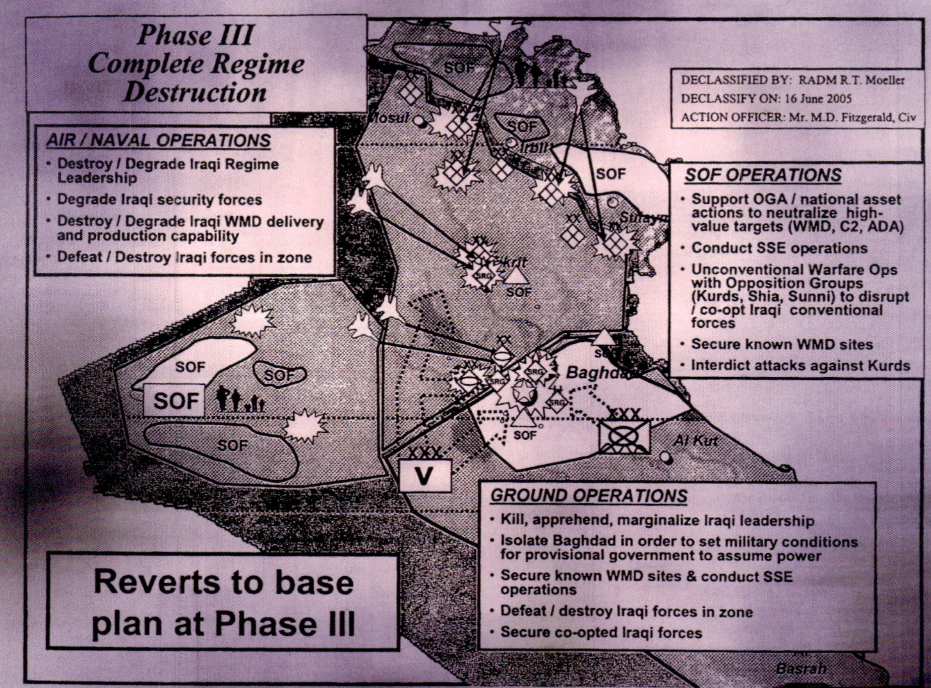
Phase III
Complete Regime
Destruction
DECLASSIFIED BY: RADM R.T. Moeller
DECLASSIFY ON: 16 June 2005
ACTION OFFICER: Mr. M.D. Fitzgerald, Civ
AIR / NAVAL OPERATIONS
• Destroy / Degrade Iraqi Regime Leadership
• Degrade Iraqi security forces
• Destroy / Degrade Iraqi WMD delivery and production capability
• Defeat / Destroy Iraqi forces in zone
SOF OPERATIONS
• Support OGA / national asset actions to neutralize high-value targets (WMD, C2, ADA)
• Conduct SSE operations
• Unconventional Warfare Ops with Opposition Groups (Kurds, Shia, Sunni) to disrupt / co-opt Iraqi conventional forces
• Secure known WMD sites
• Interdict attacks against Kurds
SOF
Baghdad
Al Kut
V
GROUND OPERATIONS
• Kill, apprehend, marginalize Iraqi leadership
• Isolate Baghdad in order to set military conditions for provisional government to assume power
• Secure known WMD sites & conduct SSE operations
• Defeat / destroy Iraqi forces in zone
• Secure co-opted Iraqi forces
Reverts to base plan at Phase III
Basrah

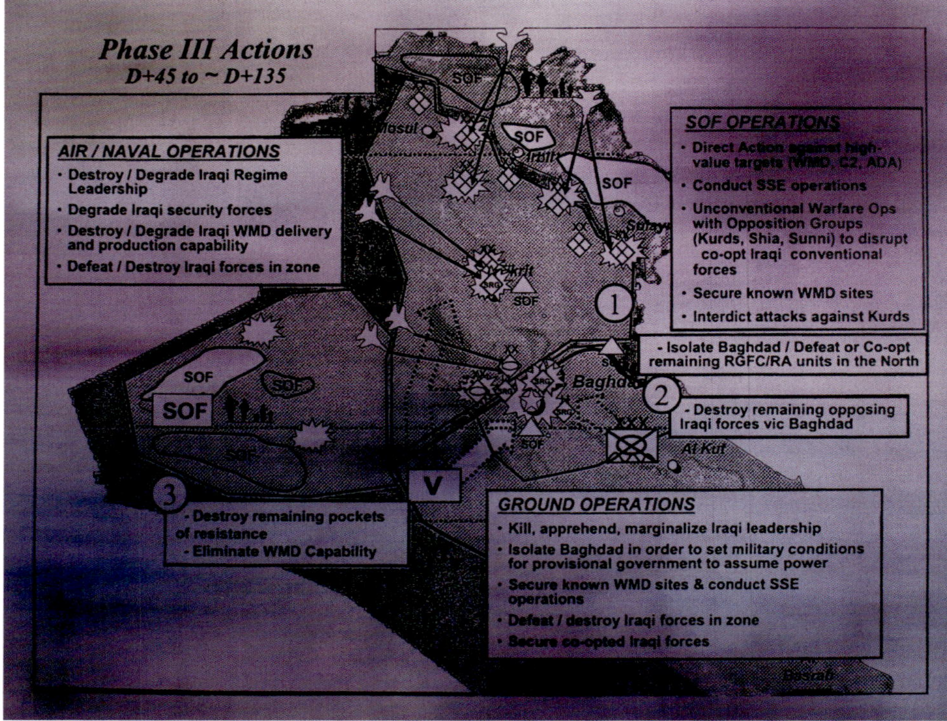
Phase III Actions
D+45 to ~ D+135
AIR / NAVAL OPERATIONS
• Destroy / Degrade Iraqi Regime Leadership
• Degrade Iraqi security forces
• Destroy / Degrade Iraqi WMD delivery and production capability
• Defeat / Destroy Iraqi forces in zone
SOF OPERATIONS
• Direct Action against high-value targets (WMD, C2, ADA)
• Conduct SSE operations
• Unconventional Warfare Ops with Opposition Groups (Kurds, Shia, Sunni) to disrupt co-opt Iraqi conventional forces
• Secure known WMD sites
• Interdict attacks against Kurds
1
- Isolate Baghdad / Defeat or Co-opt remaining RGFC/RA units in the North
2
- Destroy remaining opposing Iraqi forces vic Baghdad
3
- Destroy remaining pockets of resistance
- Eliminate WMD Capability
SOF
V
GROUND OPERATIONS
• Kill, apprehend, marginalize Iraqi leadership
• Isolate Baghdad in order to set military conditions for provisional government to assume power
• Secure known WMD sites & conduct SSE operations
• Defeat / destroy Iraqi forces in zone
• Secure co-opted Iraqi forces
Basrah

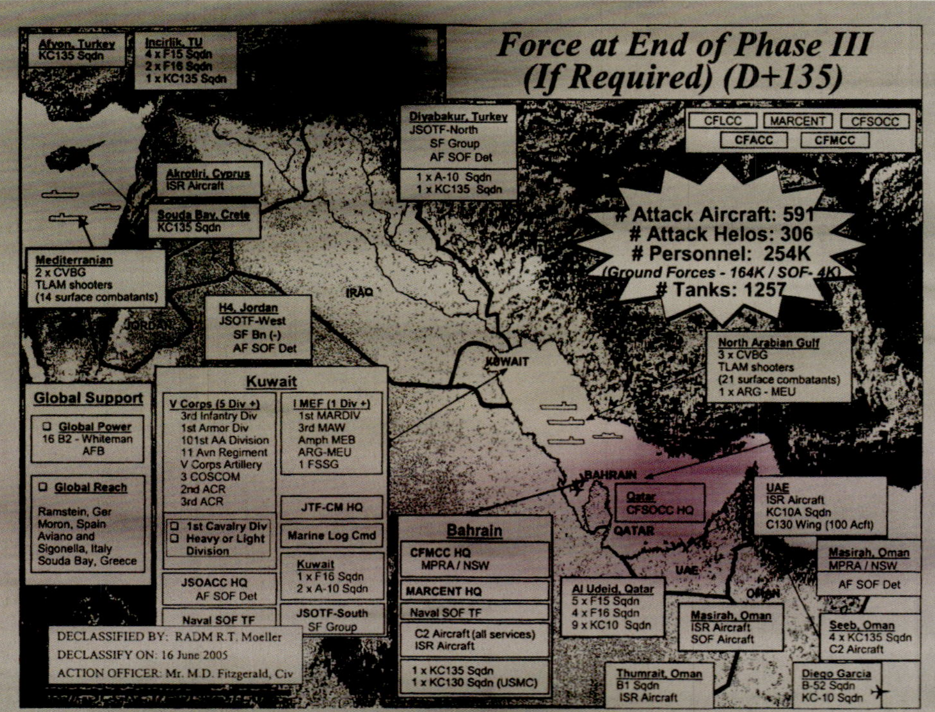
Force at End of Phase III
(If Required) (D+135)
Incirlik, TU
4 x F15 Sqdn
2 x F16 Sqdn
1 x KC135 Sqdn
Diyabakur, Turkey
JSOTF-North
SF Group
AF SOF Det
1 x A-10 Sqdn
1 x KC135 Sqdn
CFLCC MARCENT CFSOCC
CFACC CFMCC
Akrotiri, Cyprus
ISR Aircraft
Souda Bay, Crete
KC135 Sqdn
Attack Aircraft: 591
Attack Helos: 306
Personnel: 254K
(Ground Forces - 164K / SOF- 4K)
Tanks: 1257
Mediterranian
2 x CVBG
TLAM shooters
(14 surface combatants)
H4, Jordan
JSOTF-West
SF Bn (-)
AF SOF Det
IRAQ
KUWAIT
North Arabian Gulf
3 x CVBG
TLAM shooters
(21 surface combatants)
1 x ARG - MEU
Global Support
Global Power
16 B2 - Whiteman AFB
Global Reach
Ramstein, Ger
Moron, Spain
Aviano and Sigonella, Italy
Souda Bay, Greece
Kuwait
V Corps (5 Div +)
3rd Infantry Div
1st Armor Div
101st AA Division
11 Avn Regiment
V Corps Artillery
3 COSCOM
2nd ACR
3rd ACR
I MEF (1 Div +)
1st MARDIV
3rd MAW
Amph MEB
ARG-MEU
1 FSSG
JTF-CM HQ
1st Cavalry Div
Heavy or Light Division
Marine Log Cmd
JSOACC HQ
AF SOF Det
Kuwait
1 x F16 Sqdn
2 x A-10 Sqdn
JSOTF-South
SF Group
Naval SOF TF
BAHRAIN
Qatar
CFSOCC HQ
QATAR
UAE
ISR Aircraft
KC10A Sqdn
C130 Wing (100 Acft)
Bahrain
CFMCC HQ
MPRA / NSW
MARCENT HQ
Naval SOF TF
C2 Aircraft (all services)
ISR Aircraft
1 x KC135 Sqdn
1 x KC130 Sqdn (USMC)
Al Udeid, Qatar
5 x F15 Sqdn
4 x F16 Sqdn
9 x KC10 Sqdn
Masirah, Oman
ISR Aircraft
SOF Aircraft
Masirah, Oman
MPRA / NSW
AF SOF Det
Seeb, Oman
4 x KC135 Sqdn
C2 Aircraft
Thumrait, Oman
B1 Sqdn
ISR Aircraft
Diego Garcia
B-52 Sqdn
KC-10 Sqdn
DECLASSIFIED BY: RADM R.T. Moeller
DECLASSIFY ON: 16 June 2005
ACTION OFFICER: Mr. M.D. Fitzgerald, Civ

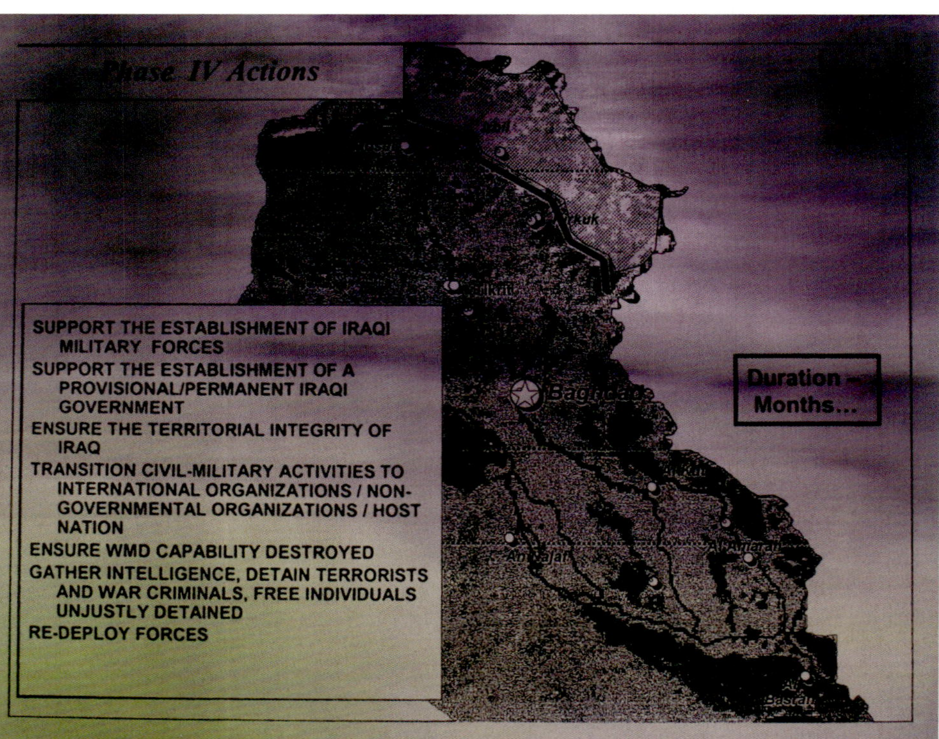
Phase IV Actions
SUPPORT THE ESTABLISHMENT OF IRAQI MILITARY FORCES
SUPPORT THE ESTABLISHMENT OF A PROVISIONAL/PERMANENT IRAQI GOVERNMENT
ENSURE THE TERRITORIAL INTEGRITY OF IRAQ
TRANSITION CIVIL-MILITARY ACTIVITIES TO INTERNATIONAL ORGANIZATIONS / NON-GOVERNMENTAL ORGANIZATIONS / HOST NATION
ENSURE WMD CAPABILITY DESTROYED
GATHER INTELLIGENCE, DETAIN TERRORISTS AND WAR CRIMINALS, FREE INDIVIDUALS UNJUSTLY DETAINED
RE-DEPLOY FORCES
Duration – Months…
Baghdad
Basrah

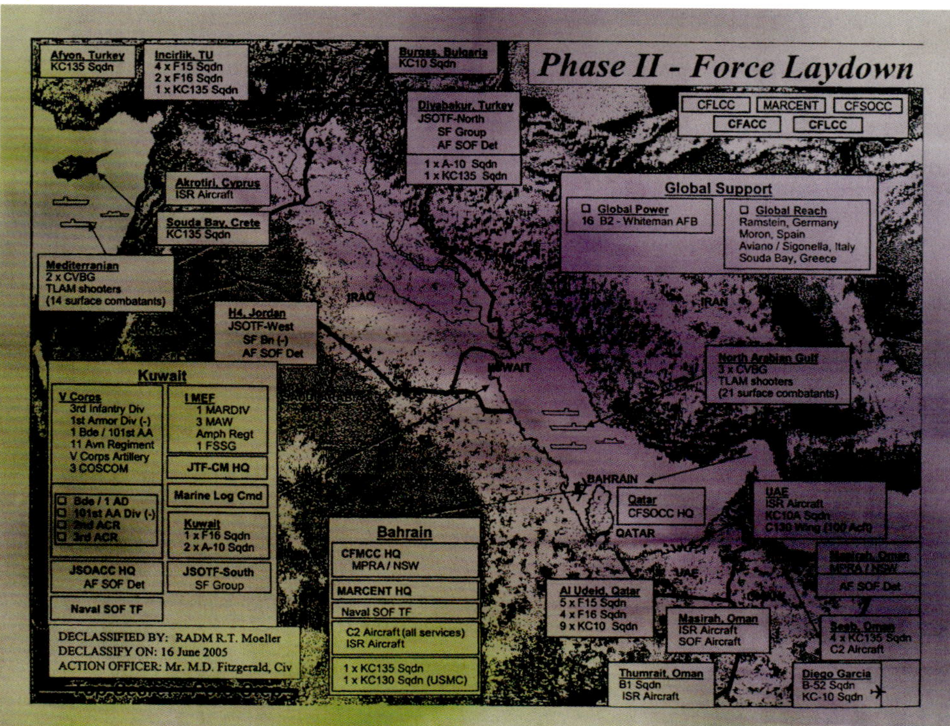
Phase II - Force Laydown
Afyon, Turkey
KC135 Sqdn
Incirlik, TU
4 x F15 Sqdn
2 x F16 Sqdn
1 x KC135 Sqdn
Burgas, Bulgaria
KC10 Sqdn
Diyabakur, Turkey
JSOTF-North
SF Group
AF SOF Det
1 x A-10 Sqdn
1 x KC135 Sqdn
CFLCC
MARCENT
CFSOCC
CFACC
CFLCC
Akrotiri, Cyprus
ISR Aircraft
Souda Bay, Crete
KC135 Sqdn
Global Support
Global Power
16 B2 - Whiteman AFB
Global Reach
Ramstein, Germany
Moron, Spain
Aviano / Sigonella, Italy
Souda Bay, Greece
Mediterranian
2 x CVBG
TLAM shooters
(14 surface combatants)
IRAQ
IRAN
H4, Jordan
JSOTF-West
SF Bn (-)
AF SOF Det
KUWAIT
North Arabian Gulf
3 x CVBG
TLAM shooters
(21 surface combatants)
Kuwait
V Corps
3rd Infantry Div
1st Armor Div (-)
1 Bde / 101st AA
11 Avn Regiment
V Corps Artillery
3 COSCOM
I MEF
1 MARDIV
3 MAW
Amph Regt
1 FSSG
JTF-CM HQ
Marine Log Cmd
Bde / 1 AD
101st AA Div (-)
2nd ACR
3rd ACR
Kuwait
1 x F16 Sqdn
2 x A-10 Sqdn
JSOACC HQ
AF SOF Det
JSOTF-South
SF Group
Naval SOF TF
Bahrain
CFMCC HQ
MPRA / NSW
MARCENT HQ
Naval SOF TF
C2 Aircraft (all services)
ISR Aircraft
1 x KC135 Sqdn
1 x KC130 Sqdn (USMC)
BAHRAIN
Qatar
CFSOCC HQ
QATAR
UAE
ISR Aircraft
KC10A Sqdn
C130 Wing (100 Acft)
Masirah, Oman
MPRA / NSW
AF SOF Det
Al Udeid, Qatar
5 x F15 Sqdn
4 x F16 Sqdn
9 x KC10 Sqdn
Masirah, Oman
ISR Aircraft
SOF Aircraft
Seeb, Oman
4 x KC135 Sqdn
C2 Aircraft
Thumrait, Oman
B1 Sqdn
ISR Aircraft
Diego Garcia
B-52 Sqdn
KC-10 Sqdn
DECLASSIFIED BY: RADM R.T. Moeller
DECLASSIFY ON: 16 June 2005
ACTION OFFICER: Mr. M.D. Fitzgerald, Civ

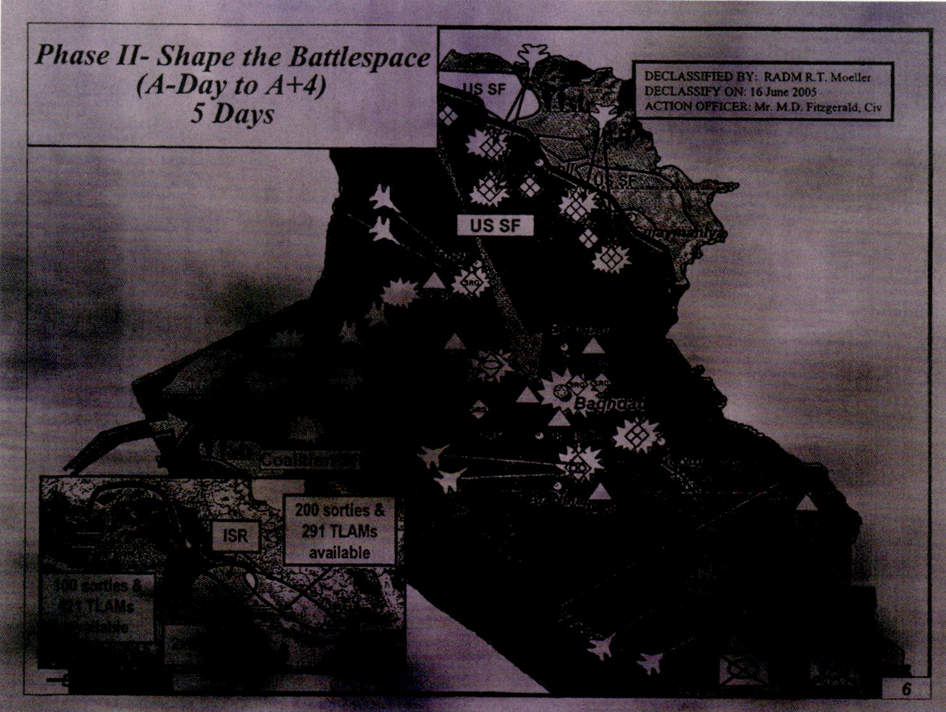
Phase II- Shape the Battlespace
(A-Day to A+4)
5 Days
DECLASSIFIED BY: RADM R.T. Moeller
DECLASSIFY ON: 16 June 2005
ACTION OFFICER: Mr. M.D. Fitzgerald, Civ
US SF
US SF
Baghdad
ISR
200 sorties &
291 TLAMs
available
6

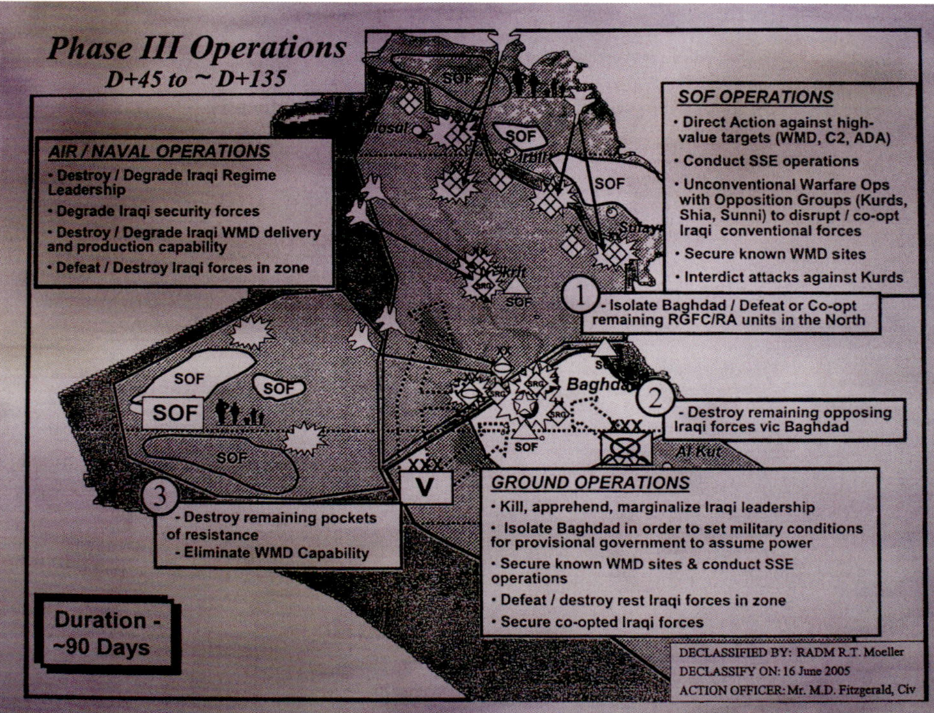
Phase III Operations
D+45 to ~ D+135
AIR / NAVAL OPERATIONS
• Destroy / Degrade Iraqi Regime Leadership
• Degrade Iraqi security forces
• Destroy / Degrade Iraqi WMD delivery and production capability
• Defeat / Destroy Iraqi forces in zone
SOF OPERATIONS
• Direct Action against high-value targets (WMD, C2, ADA)
• Conduct SSE operations
• Unconventional Warfare Ops with Opposition Groups (Kurds, Shia, Sunni) to disrupt / co-opt Iraqi conventional forces
• Secure known WMD sites
• Interdict attacks against Kurds
1
- Isolate Baghdad / Defeat or Co-opt remaining RGFC/RA units in the North
2
- Destroy remaining opposing Iraqi forces vic Baghdad
3
- Destroy remaining pockets of resistance
- Eliminate WMD Capability
SOF
Baghdad
Al Kut
V
GROUND OPERATIONS
• Kill, apprehend, marginalize Iraqi leadership
• Isolate Baghdad in order to set military conditions for provisional government to assume power
• Secure known WMD sites & conduct SSE operations
• Defeat / destroy rest Iraqi forces in zone
• Secure co-opted Iraqi forces
Duration -
~90 Days
DECLASSIFIED BY: RADM R.T. Moeller
DECLASSIFY ON: 16 June 2005
ACTION OFFICER: Mr. M.D. Fitzgerald, Civ

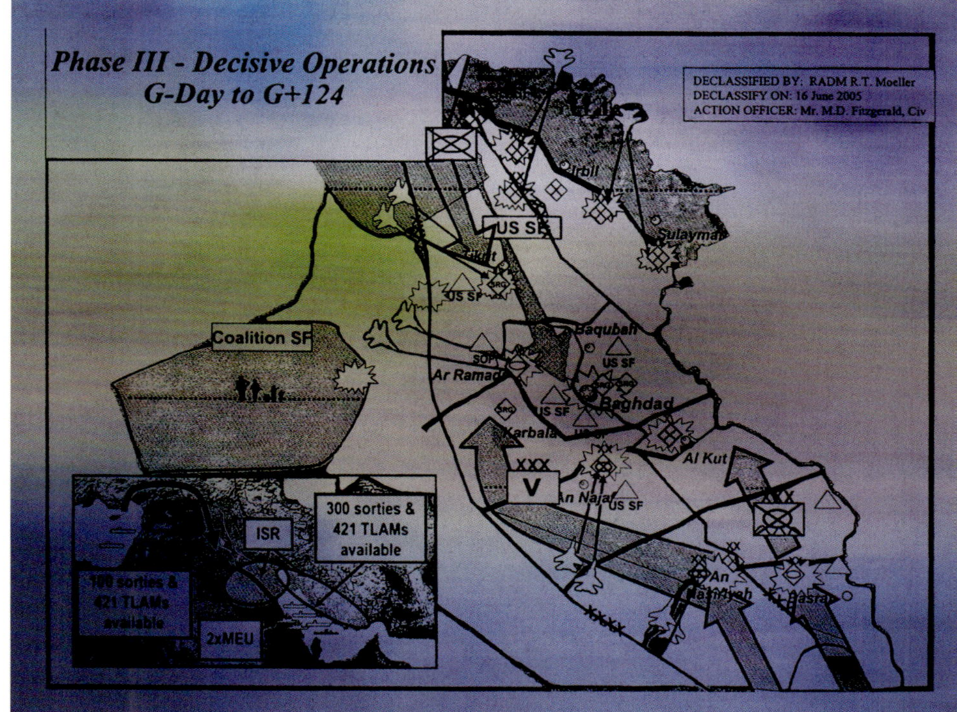
Phase III - Decisive Operations
G-Day to G+124
DECLASSIFIED BY: RADM R.T. Moeller
DECLASSIFY ON: 16 June 2005
ACTION OFFICER: Mr. M.D. Fitzgerald, Civ
US SF
Coalition SF
Baqubah
Ar Ramadi
Baghdad
Al Kut
An Najaf
V
ISR
300 sorties &
421 TLAMs
available
2xMEU

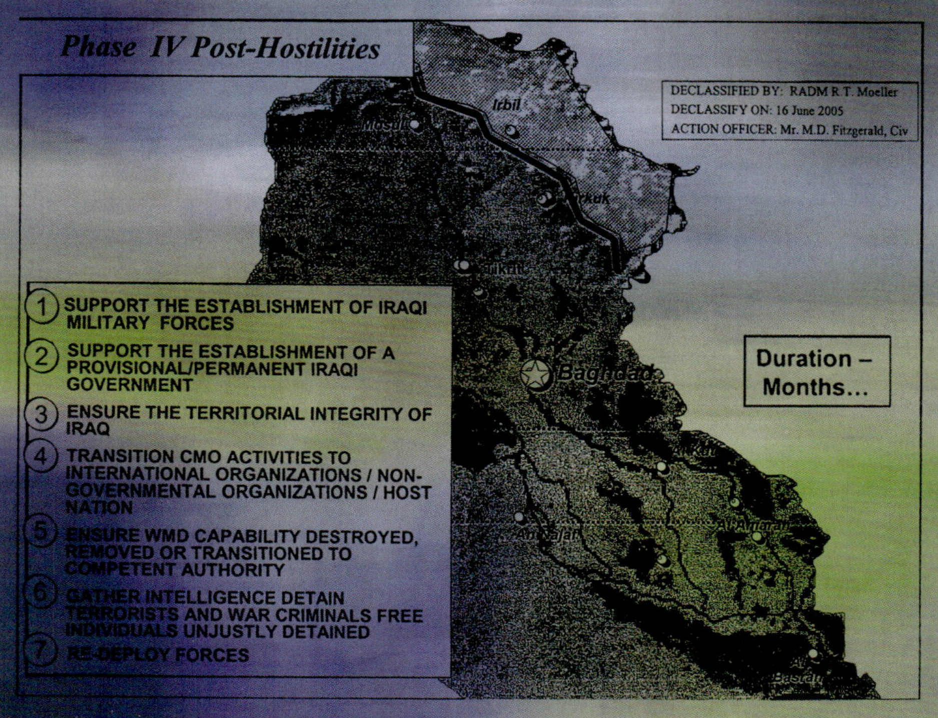
Phase IV Post-Hostilities
DECLASSIFIED BY: RADM R.T. Moeller
DECLASSIFY ON: 16 June 2005
ACTION OFFICER: Mr. M.D. Fitzgerald, Civ
Irbil
Mosul
Baghdad
1 SUPPORT THE ESTABLISHMENT OF IRAQI MILITARY FORCES
2 SUPPORT THE ESTABLISHMENT OF A PROVISIONAL/PERMANENT IRAQI GOVERNMENT
3 ENSURE THE TERRITORIAL INTEGRITY OF IRAQ
4 TRANSITION CMO ACTIVITIES TO INTERNATIONAL ORGANIZATIONS / NON-GOVERNMENTAL ORGANIZATIONS / HOST NATION
5 ENSURE WMD CAPABILITY DESTROYED, REMOVED OR TRANSITIONED TO COMPETENT AUTHORITY
6 GATHER INTELLIGENCE DETAIN TERRORISTS AND WAR CRIMINALS FREE INDIVIDUALS UNJUSTLY DETAINED
7 RE-DEPLOY FORCES
Duration –
Months...

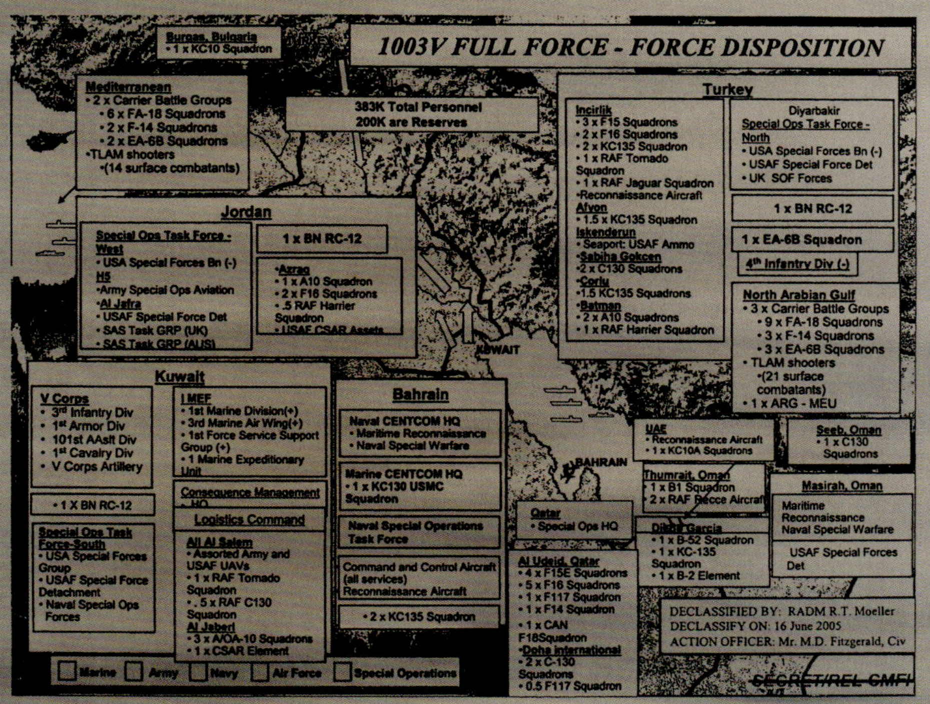
1003V FULL FORCE - FORCE DISPOSITION
Burgas, Bulgaria
• 1 x KC10 Squadron
Mediterranean
• 2 x Carrier Battle Groups
• 6 x FA-18 Squadrons
• 2 x F-14 Squadrons
• 2 x EA-6B Squadrons
•TLAM shooters
•(14 surface combatants)
383K Total Personnel
200K are Reserves
Turkey
Incirlik
• 3 x F15 Squadrons
• 2 x F16 Squadrons
• 2 x KC135 Squadron
• 1 x RAF Tornado Squadron
• 1 x RAF Jaguar Squadron
•Reconnaissance Aircraft
Afyon
• 1.5 x KC135 Squadron
Iskenderun
• Seaport: USAF Ammo
•Sabiha Gokcen
•2 x C130 Squadrons
•Corlu
•1.5 KC135 Squadrons
•Batman
• 2 x A10 Squadrons
• 1 x RAF Harrier Squadron
Diyarbakir
Special Ops Task Force - North
• USA Special Forces Bn (-)
• USAF Special Force Det
• UK SOF Forces
1 x BN RC-12
1 x EA-6B Squadron
4th Infantry Div (-)
Jordan
Special Ops Task Force - West
• USA Special Forces Bn (-)
H5
•Army Special Ops Aviation
•Al Jafra
• USAF Special Force Det
• SAS Task GRP (UK)
• SAS Task GRP (AUS)
1 x BN RC-12
•Azraq
• 1 x A10 Squadron
• 2 x F16 Squadrons
• .5 RAF Harrier Squadron
• USAF CSAR Assets
North Arabian Gulf
• 3 x Carrier Battle Groups
• 9 x FA-18 Squadrons
• 3 x F-14 Squadrons
• 3 x EA-6B Squadrons
• TLAM shooters
•(21 surface combatants)
• 1 x ARG - MEU
Kuwait
V Corps
• 3rd Infantry Div
• 1st Armor Div
• 101st AAslt Div
• 1st Cavalry Div
• V Corps Artillery
• 1 X BN RC-12
Special Ops Task Force-South
• USA Special Forces Group
• USAF Special Force Detachment
• Naval Special Ops Forces
I MEF
• 1st Marine Division(+)
• 3rd Marine Air Wing(+)
• 1st Force Service Support Group (+)
• 1 Marine Expeditionary Unit
Consequence Management HQ
Logistics Command
Ali Al Salem
• Assorted Army and USAF UAVs
• 1 x RAF Tornado Squadron
• .5 x RAF C130 Squadron
Al Jaberi
• 3 x A/OA-10 Squadrons
• 1 x CSAR Element
Bahrain
Naval CENTCOM HQ
• Maritime Reconnaissance
• Naval Special Warfare
Marine CENTCOM HQ
• 1 x KC130 USMC Squadron
Naval Special Operations Task Force
Command and Control Aircraft (all services)
Reconnaissance Aircraft
• 2 x KC135 Squadron
BAHRAIN
KUWAIT
Qatar
• Special Ops HQ
Al Udeid, Qatar
• 4 x F15E Squadrons
• 5 x F16 Squadrons
• 1 x F117 Squadron
• 1 x F14 Squadron
• 1 x CAN F18Squadron
•Doha International
• 2 x C-130 Squadrons
• 0.5 F117 Squadron
UAE
• Reconnaissance Aircraft
• 1 x KC10A Squadrons
Thumrait, Oman
• 1 x B1 Squadron
• 2 x RAF Recce Aircraft
Diego Garcia
• 1 x B-52 Squadron
• 1 x KC-135 Squadron
• 1 x B-2 Element
Seeb, Oman
• 1 x C130 Squadrons
Masirah, Oman
Maritime Reconnaissance
Naval Special Warfare
USAF Special Forces Det
Marine
Army
Navy
Air Force
Special Operations
DECLASSIFIED BY: RADM R.T. Moeller
DECLASSIFY ON: 16 June 2005
ACTION OFFICER: Mr. M.D. Fitzgerald, Civ
SECRET/REL CMFI

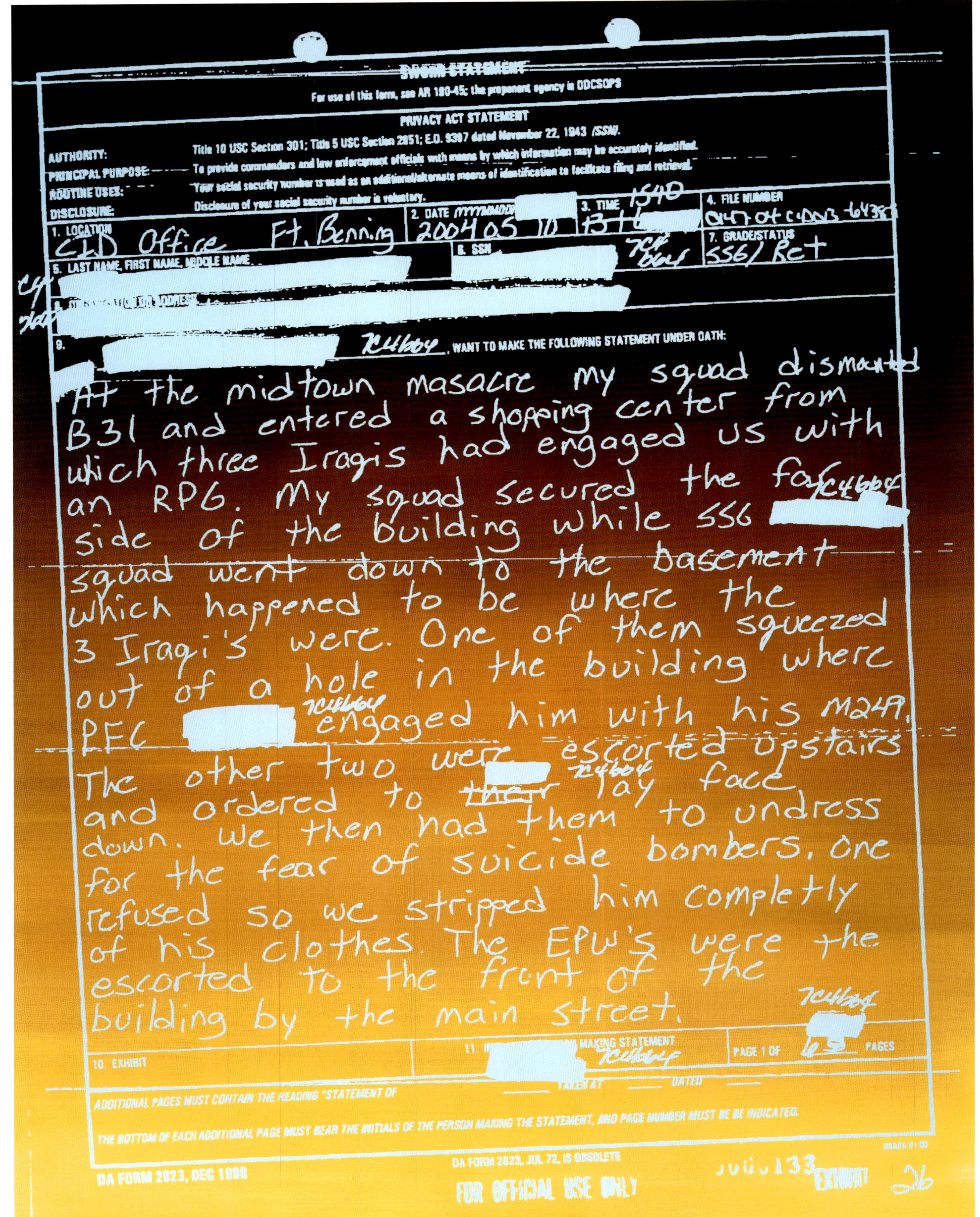

SWORN STATEMENT

For use of this form, see AR 190-45; the proponent agency is ODCSOPS

PRIVACY ACT STATEMENT

AUTHORITY: Title 10 USC Section 301; Title 5 USC Section 2951; E.O. 9397 dated November 22, 1943 (SSN).

PRINCIPAL PURPOSE: To provide commanders and law enforcement officials with means by which information may be accurately identified.

ROUTINE USES: Your social security number is used as an additional/alternate means of identification to facilitate filing and retrieval.

DISCLOSURE: Disclosure of your social security number is voluntary.

1. LOCATION	2. DATE (YYYYMMDD)	3. TIME	4. FILE NUMBER
CID Office Ft. Benning	20040510	1540	0047-04 CID03 -64383

5. LAST NAME, FIRST NAME, MIDDLE NAME	6. SSN	7. GRADE/STATUS
		SSG / Rct

8. ORGANIZATION OR ADDRESS

9. I, ______ 7C4b6 , WANT TO MAKE THE FOLLOWING STATEMENT UNDER OATH:

At the midtown masacre my squad dismanted B31 and entered a shopping center from which three Iraqis had engaged us with an RPG. My squad secured the far side of the building while SSG ______ squad went down to the basement which happened to be where the 3 Iraqi's were. One of them squeezed out of a hole in the building where PFC ______ engaged him with his M249. The other two were escorted upstairs and ordered to ~~their~~ lay face down. We then had them to undress for the fear of suicide bombers. One refused so we stripped him completly of his clothes. The EPW's were the escorted to the front of the building by the main street.

10. EXHIBIT	11. INITIALS OF PERSON MAKING STATEMENT	PAGE 1 OF 5 PAGES

ADDITIONAL PAGES MUST CONTAIN THE HEADING "STATEMENT OF ______ TAKEN AT ______ DATED ______"

THE BOTTOM OF EACH ADDITIONAL PAGE MUST BEAR THE INITIALS OF THE PERSON MAKING THE STATEMENT, AND PAGE NUMBER MUST BE INDICATED.

DA FORM 2823, DEC 1998 — DA FORM 2823, JUL 72, IS OBSOLETE — USAPA V1.00

FOR OFFICIAL USE ONLY

JULIU133 EXHIBIT 26

DODDOACID 008455

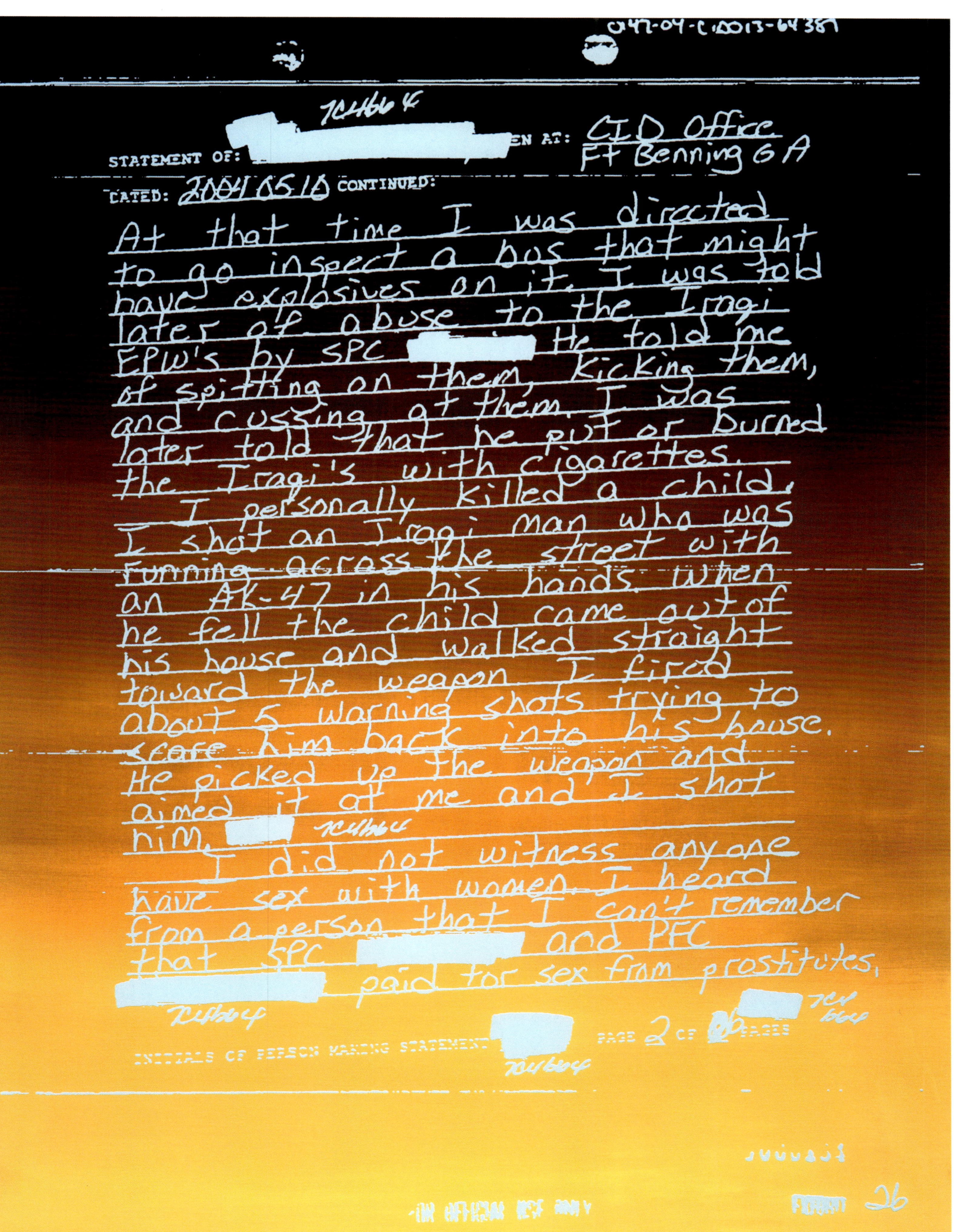

047-04-CID013-64389

STATEMENT OF: ... TAKEN AT: CID Office Ft Benning GA

DATED: 20040510 CONTINUED:

At that time I was directed to go inspect a bus that might have explosives on it. I was told later of abuse to the Iraqi EPW's by SPC [redacted]. He told me of spitting on them, kicking them, and cussing at them. I was later told that he put or burned the Iraqi's with cigarettes.

I personally killed a child. I shot an Iraqi man who was running across the street with an AK-47 in his hands. When he fell the child came out of his house and walked straight toward the weapon. I fired about 5 warning shots trying to scare him back into his house. He picked up the weapon and aimed it at me and I shot him.

I did not witness anyone have sex with women. I heard from a person that I can't remember that SPC [redacted] and PFC [redacted] paid for sex from prostitutes.

INITIALS OF PERSON MAKING STATEMENT [redacted] PAGE 2 OF 6 PAGES

FOR OFFICIAL USE ONLY

EXHIBIT 26

DODDOACID 008456

AUTOPSY REPORT ME04-14

(b)(6)-4

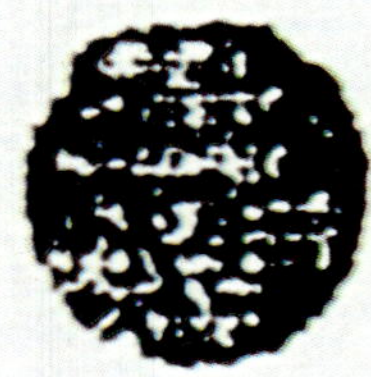

This 47-year-old White male, (b)(6)-4
The autopsy disclosed multiple blunt
chest wall, numerous displaced rib fra
mesentery of the small and large intes
revealed hemorrhage into the strap mu
hyoid bone. According to the investig
decedent was shackled to the top of a
lost consciousness and became pulsele

The severe blunt force injuries, the ha
cavity with a gag contributed to this in
homicide.

(b)(6)-2

(b)(6)-2

CDR, MC, USN, DMO/FS
Chief Deputy Medical Examiner

OPINION

] died of blunt force injuries and asphyxia.
rce injuries, including deep contusions of the
ures, lung contusions, and hemorrhage into the
ne. An examination of the neck structures
cles and fractures of the thyroid cartilage and
ive report provided by U.S. Army CID, the
orframe with a gag in his mouth at the time he
.

ing position, and the obstruction of the oral
vidual's death. The manner of death is

b.1
1.46

Alternative Interrogation Techniques (Wish List)
4Th Infantry Division, ICE

Open Hand Strikes (face and midsection) (no distance greater than 24 inches)

Fairly self-explanatory.

Pressure Point Manipulation

Manipulation of specific points on the human body can cause acute temporary pain but cause no long term effects or damage.

Close Quarter Confinement

Confinement of subject in extremely close quarters. Discomfort induces compliance and cooperation.

White Noise Exposure

Overexposure of subject to noise found to be meaningless and many times monotonous to subject. Often used in conjunction with Sleep Deprivation.

Sleep Deprivation

An initial period of total deprivation (usually 12 to 24 hours) followed by regular and irregular sleep patterns over several days.

Stimulus Deprivation

The human mind requires stimulation, however small, to maintain resistance to suggestion, mental and emotional manipulation and self will. Subject is deprived of this stimulation for 12 to 24 hours during initial stages. Effects on subject's resistance are monitored with short intense interrogations (15-60 minutes at most). Subject's resistance will usually rapidly decay after 36 to 48 hours. This technique requires no physical pressure to be applied. However, subject must be carefully monitored.

***There are a number of "coercive" techniques that may be employed that cause no permanent harm to the subject. These techniques, however, often call for medical personnel to be on call for unforeseen complications. They include but are not limited to the following:**

Phone Book Strikes
Low Voltage Electrocution
Closed-Fist Strikes
Muscle Fatigue Inducement

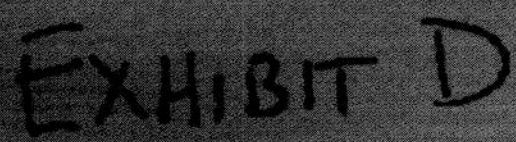

6627

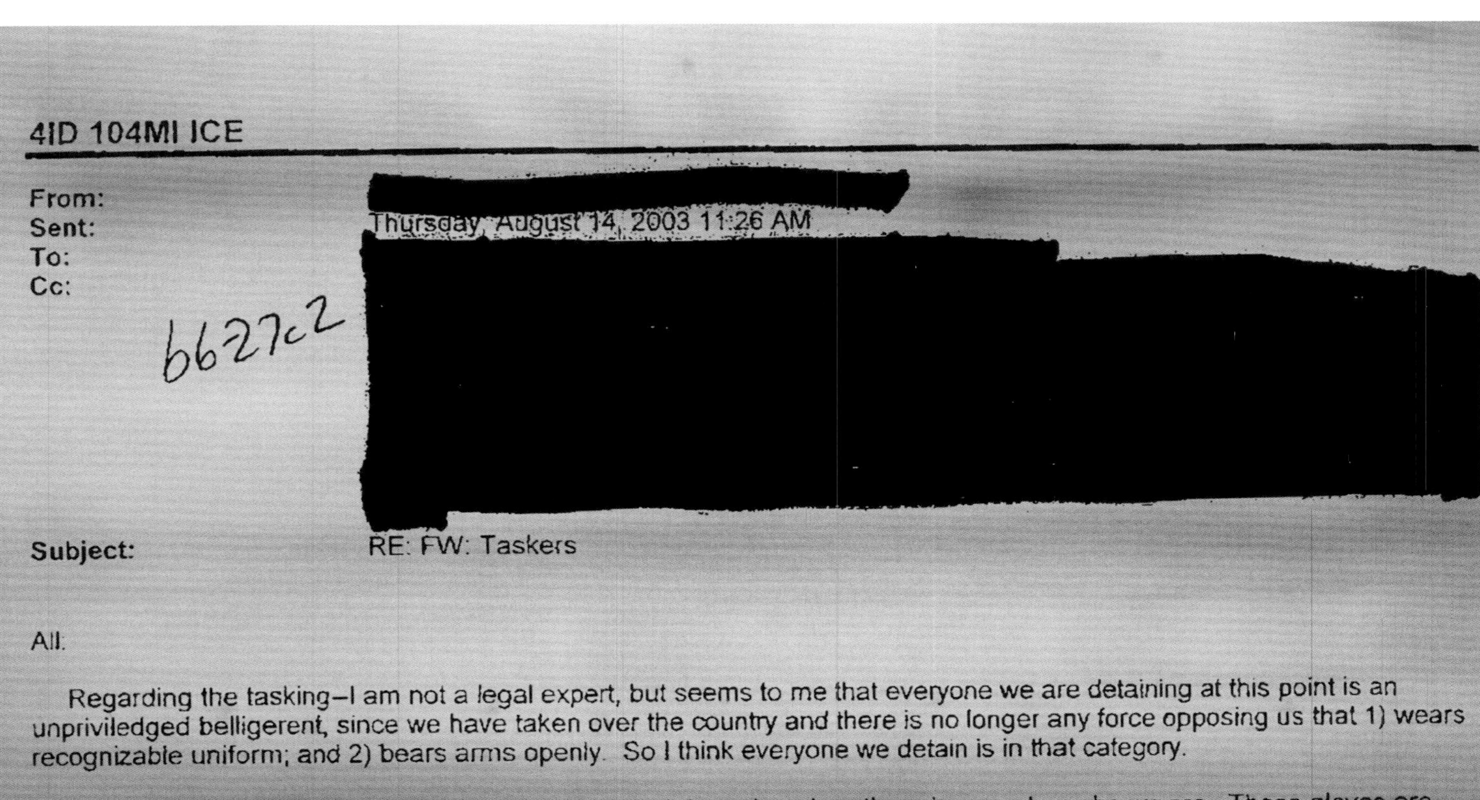

4ID 104MI ICE

From:
Sent: Thursday, August 14, 2003 11:26 AM
To:
Cc:

b6 2/7c2

Subject: RE: FW: Taskers

All:

Regarding the tasking--I am not a legal expert, but seems to me that everyone we are detaining at this point is an unpriviledged belligerent, since we have taken over the country and there is no longer any force opposing us that 1) wears recognizable uniform; and 2) bears arms openly. So I think everyone we detain is in that category.

As for "the gloves need to come off..." we need to take a deep breath and remember who we are. Those gloves are most definitely NOT based on Cold War or WWII enemies--they are based on clearly established standards of international law to which we are signatories and in part the originators. Those in turn derive from practices commonly accepted as morally correct, the so-called "usages of war." It comes down to standards of right and wrong--something we cannot just put aside when we find it inconvenient, any more than we can declare that we will "take no prisoners" and therefore shoot those who surrender to us simply because we find prisoners inconvenient.

"The casualties are mounting..." we have taken casualties in every war we have ever fought--that is part of the very nature of war. We also inflict casualties, generally many more than we take. **That in no way justifies letting go of our standards.** We have NEVER considered our enemies justified in doing such things to us. Casualties are part of war--if you cannot take casualties then you cannot engage in war. Period.

BOTTOM LINE. We are American soldiers, heirs of a long tradition of staying on the high ground. We need to stay there.

b6 2/7c2

Psalm 24: 3-8

-----Original Message-----
From:
[mailto:
Sent: Thursday, August 14, 2003 3:56 PM
To:
Cc:

b6 2/7c2

Subject: Re: FW: Taskers

I sent several months in Afghanistan interrogating the Taliban and al Qaeda. Restrictions on interrogation techniques had a negative impact

1

EXHIBIT A

6621

on our ability to gather intelligence. Our interrogation doctrine is based on former Cold War amd WWII enemies. Todays enemy particularly those in SWA, understand force, not psychological mind games or incentives. I would propose a baseline interrogation technique that at a minimum allows for physical contact resembling that used by SERE instructors. This allows open handed facial slaps from a distance of no more than about two feet and back handed blows to the midsection from a distance of about 18 inches. Again, this is open handed. I will not comment on the effectiveness of these techniques as both a control measure and an ability to send a clear message. I also believe that this should be a minimum baseline.

Other techniques would include close confinement quarters, sleep deprivation, white noise, and a litnany of harsher fear-up approaches...fear of dogs and snakes appear to work nicely. I firmly agree that the gloves need to come off.

V/R

b62/7c2

----- Original Message -----
From: " b62/7c2
Date: Thursday, August 14, 2003 2:51 pm
Subject: FW: Taskers

> Sounds crazy, but we're just passing this on.
>
> -----Original Message-----
> From: b62/7c2
> [mailto
> Sent: Thursday, August 14, 2003 1:51 AM
> To: b62 7c2
> Cc:
> Subject: Taskers
>
>
> ALCON
>
> Just wanted to make sure we are all clear on the taskers at hand
>
> 1- A list identifying individuals who we have in detention that
> fall under
> the category of "unlawful combatants" I've included a definition
> form the
> SJA folks:
>
> In order to properly address your request for a legal definition of
> the term "unlawful combatant," I must first provide you with a
> framework of definitions with which to work. According to the Law
> of Land Warfare,
> the term "combatant" is defined as anyone engaging in hostilities
> in an
> armed conflict on behalf of a party to the conflict. Combatants are
> lawful targets, unless out of combat. With that said, "lawful
> combatants" receive protections of the Geneva Conventions and
> gain combat
> immunity for their warlike acts, as well as become prisoners of
> war if
> captured. In comparison, "unprivileged belligerents," commonly
> referred to as "unlawful combatants," may be treated as criminals
> under the
> domestic law of the captor. Unprivileged belligerents may
> include spies,

6622

September 26, 2003

To Whom It May Concern:

(b)(6)

I am writing this letter for my wife and myself. The purpose of this letter is to appeal to you, as a parent, for relief for my son (1st Lt. [redacted] b6-5) in his current situation. I understand that the U.S. Army wants to court martial him and send him to prison. Without getting into the specifics of the charges against him I simply want to appeal to you, as a father, to allow him to resign with an honorable discharge. My son is not the type of person that deserves to be placed in prison. He has never been in any trouble what so ever until these charges.

I know you don't know me, or my son, so if you don't mind please read this letter because it is important to me that you know who I am, and more importantly, who my son is before you make a recommendation about how to treat him.

First, so that you know a little about me and my perspective on young men I have written a little about my background. I have been in secondary education for 30 years. I have been a [redacted] b6-2 for 10 years. This June, Florida Governor Jeb Bush appointed me as [redacted] b6-2 b6-2 [redacted] Our school system has 40,000 students and 5,200 employees. My headquarters are located in b6-2 [redacted], a small city that is the home to Congressman Cliff Stearns and former Florida governor Buddy McKay. So you understand that I evaluate the quality and nature of my employees and interact with my community's leaders on a weekly basis. I am also heavily involved in activities with our Veteran's groups.

My family is very important to me and all of us are totally involved in our community. My wife recently retired after spending 17 years as the business manager of our 1,000-member church. My two daughters and their husbands are teachers. One daughter recently became our church's full time youth director. We are committed to our city, our county, and our country.

My son, b6-5 [redacted] has always been a leader academically and athletically, and has excelled at everything he has attempted. He has been chosen by adults throughout his life to be a leader in boy scouts, chosen as a camp counselor on several occasions, and represented our local VFW and our high school at Boys' State. This will be his first failure.

Quite frankly I find it hard to believe that he is not wanted and needed in our Army. He used to want to be a career officer. He had a great attitude and, I believe, the right morals to make the tough decisions every time. It breaks my heart to know that he no longer feels wanted by a country that he so wants to serve. Here are a couple of examples of what [redacted] has written to us in his letters from Iraq:

b6-2

(b)(6)

April 12, 2003—"...You both can't possibly imagine how appreciative I am of you. Not just thankful, but proud. Proud to be raised by you both. Proud to be in such a strong family with such strong morals...you never asked why I joined but today I know why more than ever. I am here to embrace those values, those memories that you gave me. Only by sharing, and in this case leading others, do I feel I can possibly repay the debt that I owe you and the society that would allow for such a life to exist...I couldn't think of a happier time in my life. I am doing exactly what it is I have always wanted to do. Without this experience I would feel incomplete for the rest of my life, debts unpaid and talents unrealized."

July 12, 2003—At the start of the investigation by the Army he writes: "Needless to say the Army has made a decision, or helped me make a decision, that I will only serve for 4 years. I still love my country and have faith in her virtues, though she has none in mine. If this goes to court martial it will be broadcast over the news and my name, and yours, will be tarnished forever. You didn't sign up for that, but I did. If this happens I apologize in advance. All I ever wanted to do was to serve and protect those who loved me, and spread freedom to others less fortunate...I have brought hundreds of criminals to prison, captured countless weapons, saved lives of coalition and civilian personnel, have my life threatened on a daily basis from insurgents and criminals alike. Yet all I ever wanted was to be left alone with my platoon so I could continue doing what I love the most..."

As you can tell my son loves his country and I assure you he is not a criminal. Please allow him to keep his dignity and pride. If he must be released from the Army, then please allow him to resign his commission and receive an honorable discharge. I often hear that Generals are treated as gods from my friends who have served. Please act like a compassionate god, and a reasonable man, and allow my son to be released from all charges with dignity. I beg of you, as a father, for my son's life.

Sincerely,

b6-2

008163

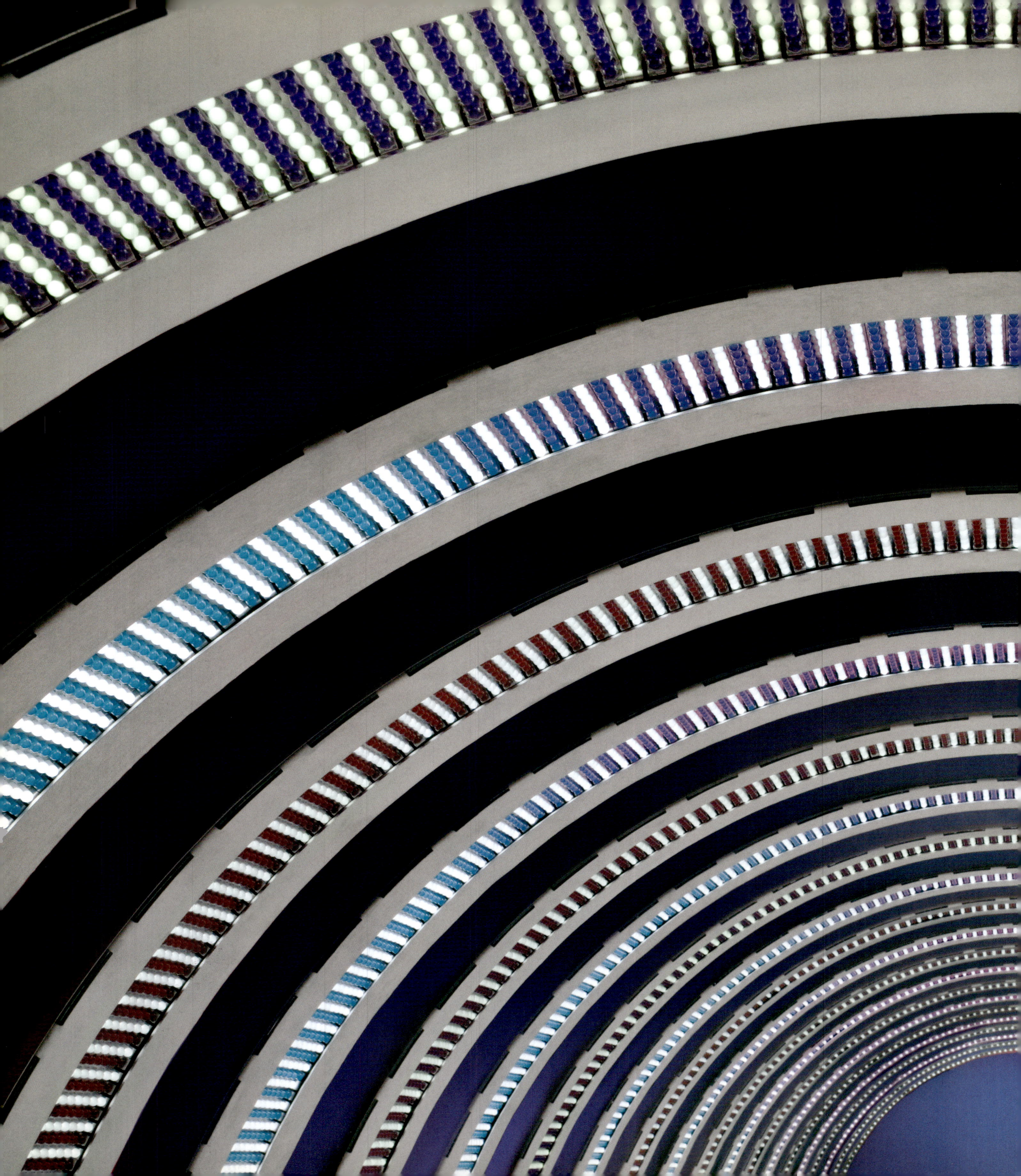

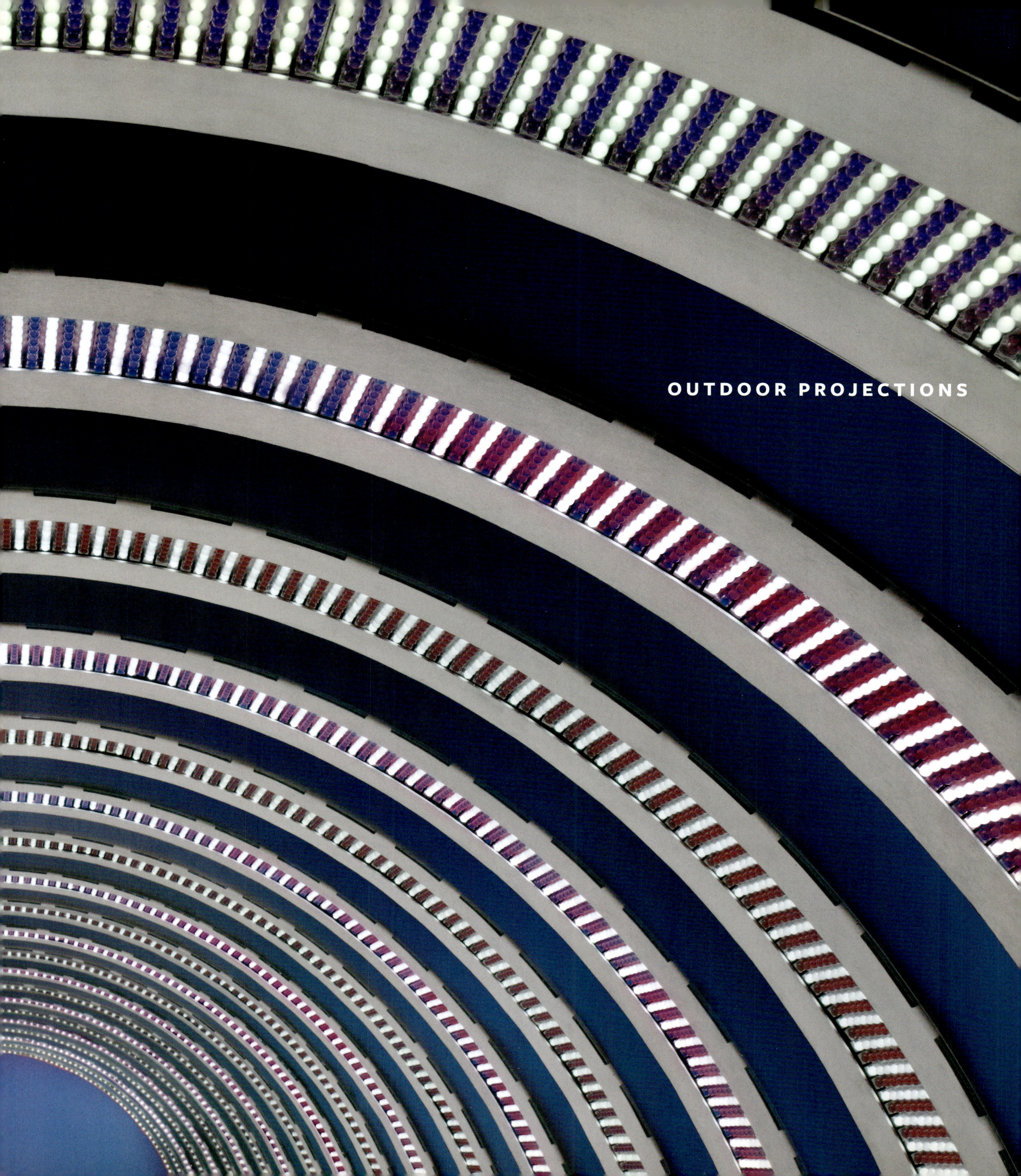

OUTDOOR PROJECTIONS

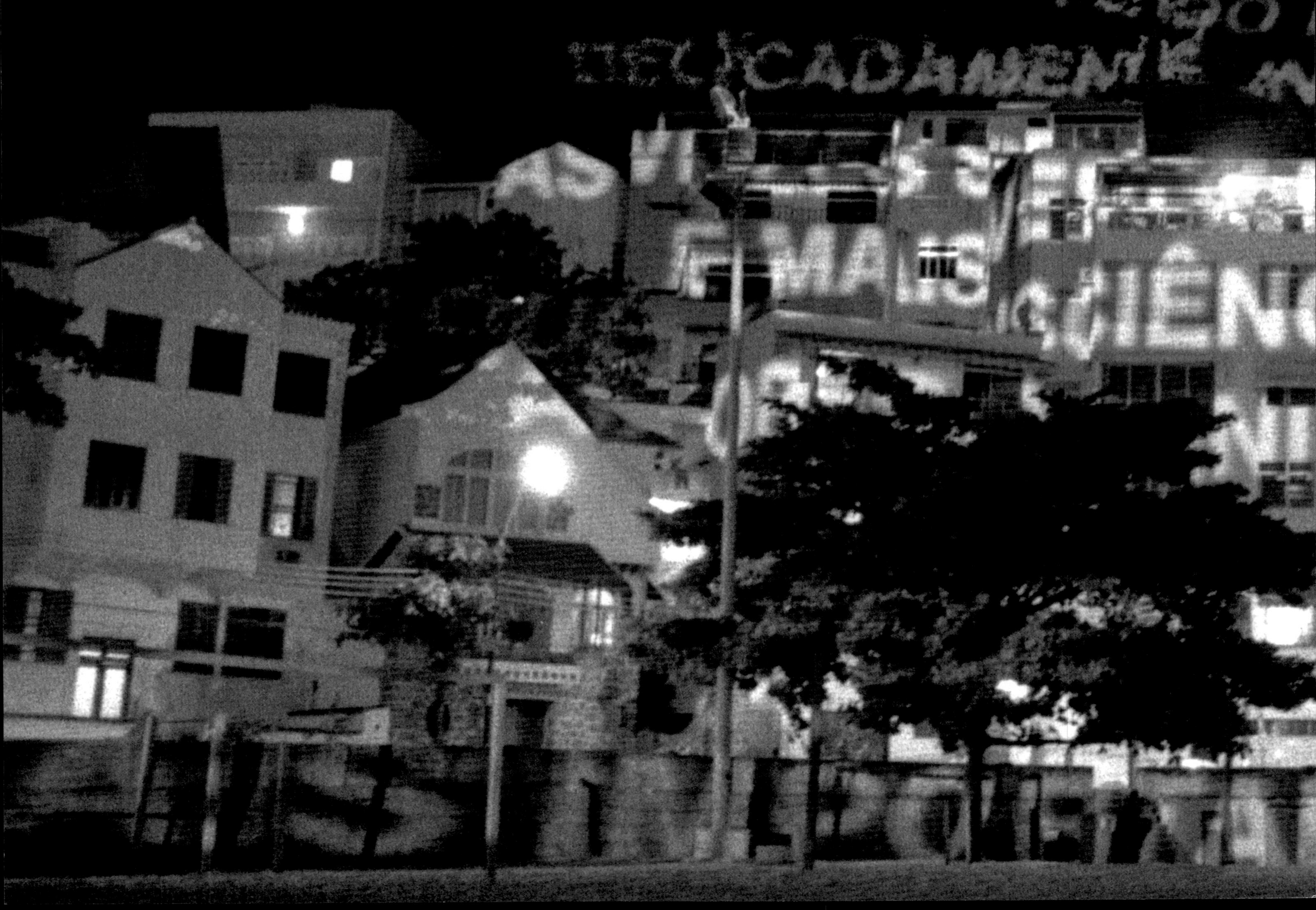
MAIS

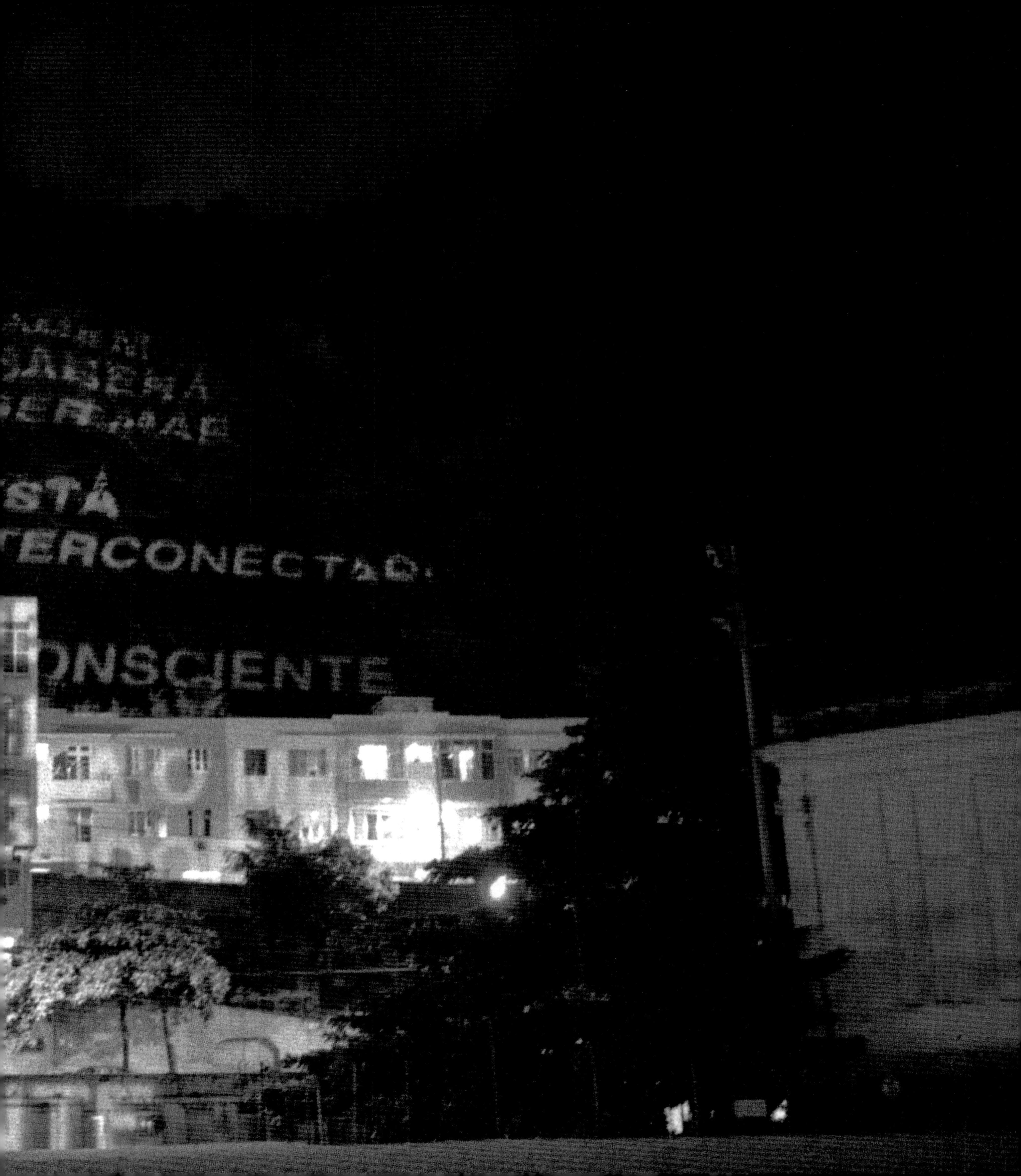

STÁ
ERCONECTAD
ONSCIENTE

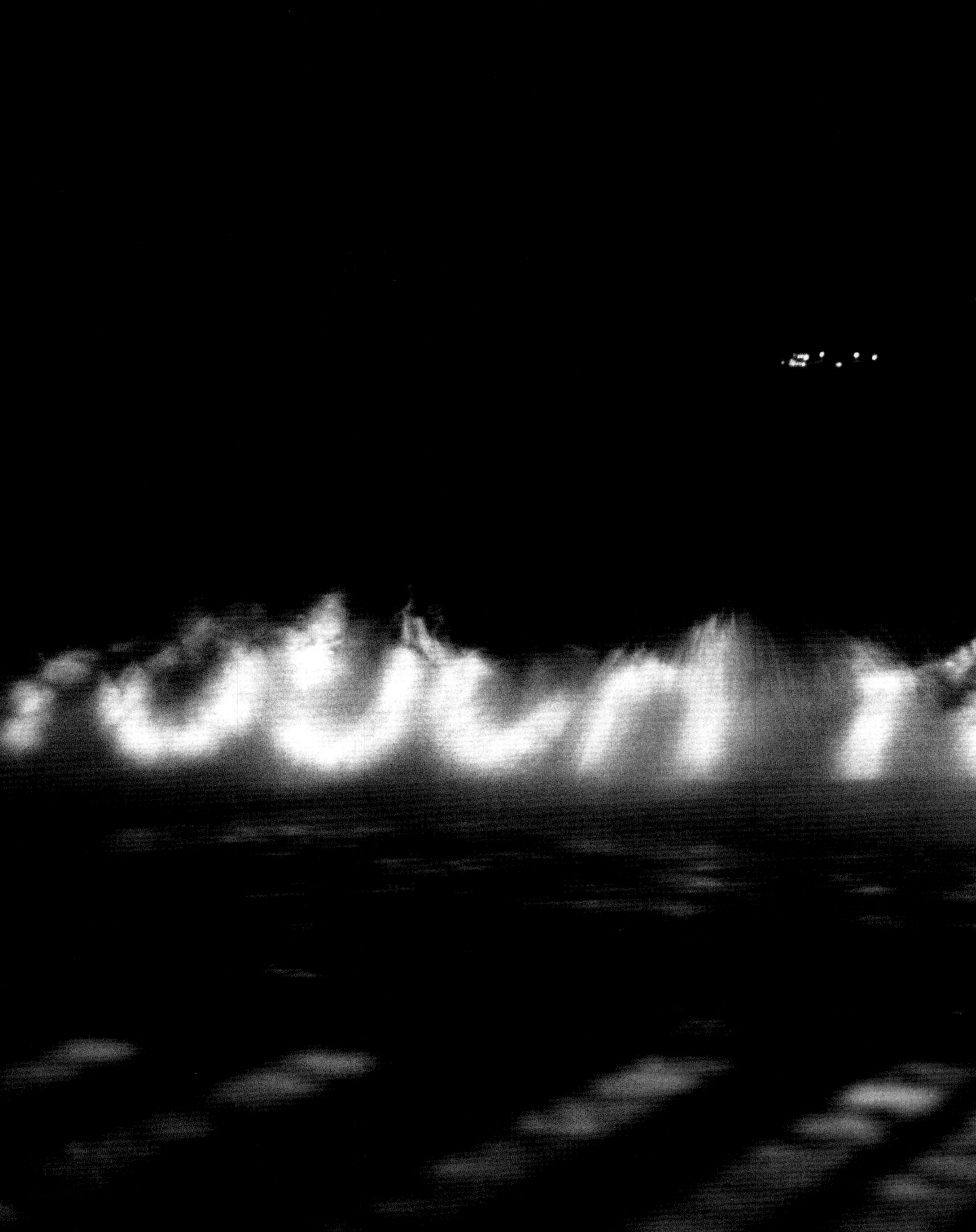

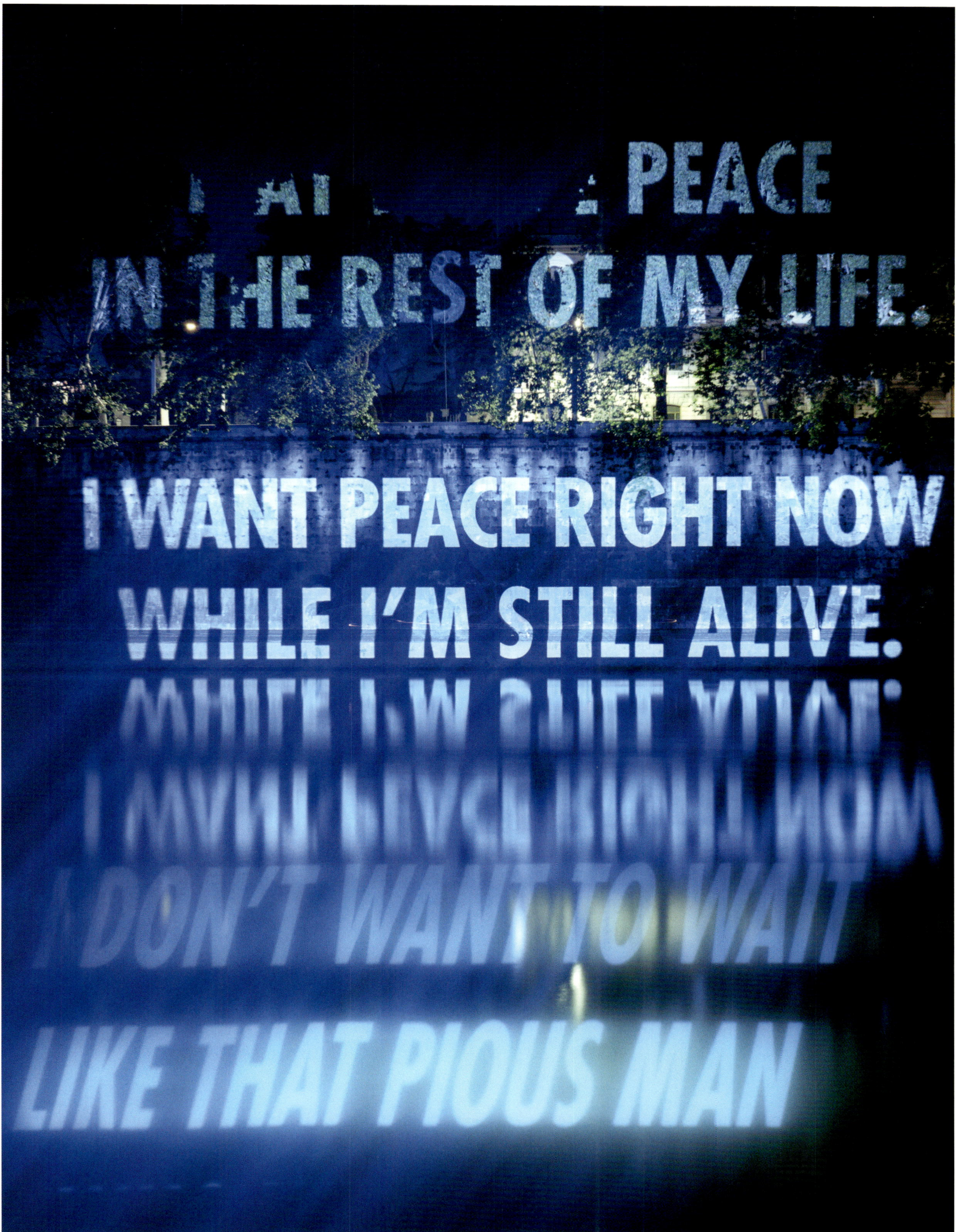
PEACE
IN THE REST OF MY LIFE.
I WANT PEACE RIGHT NOW
WHILE I'M STILL ALIVE.
DON'T WANT TO WAIT
LIKE THAT PIOUS MAN

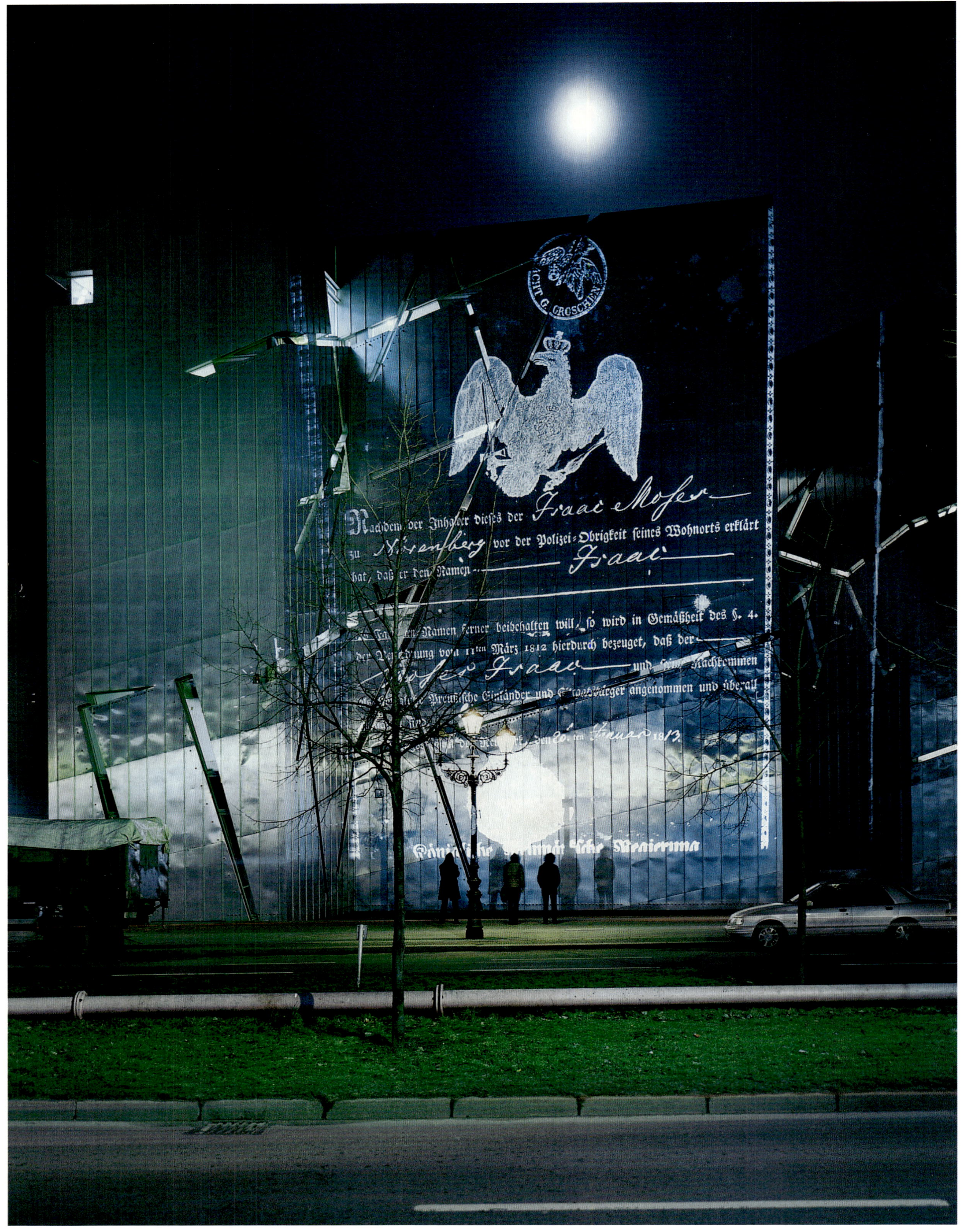
der Inhaber dieses der Isaac Moser
vor der Polizei-Obrigkeit seines Wohnorts erklärt
hat, daß er den Namen Isaac
Namen ferner beibehalten will, so wird in Gemäßheit des §. 4.
März 1812 hierdurch bezeuget, daß der
angenommen und überall

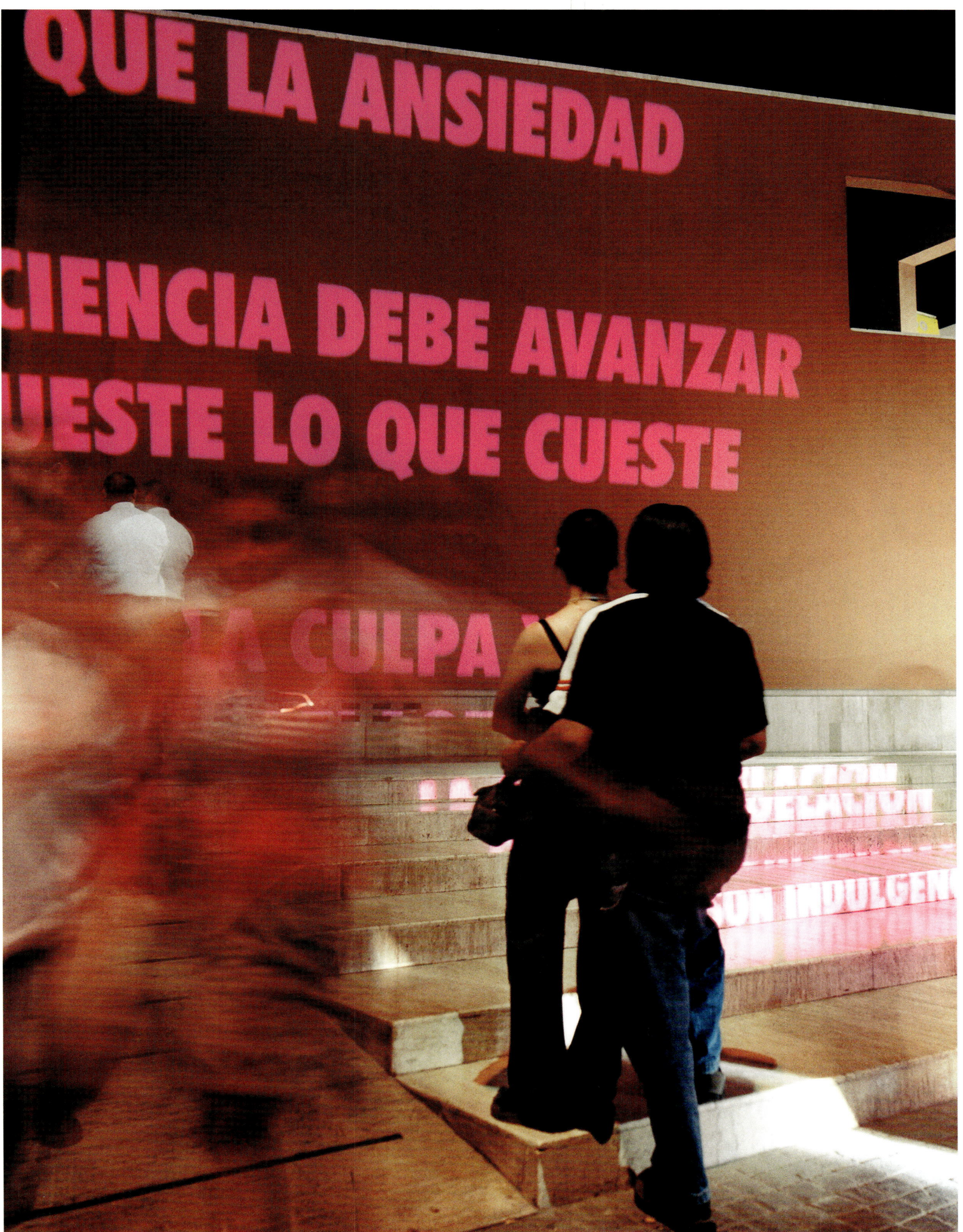
QUE LA ANSIEDAD
CIENCIA DEBE AVANZAR
UESTE LO QUE CUESTE
CULPA

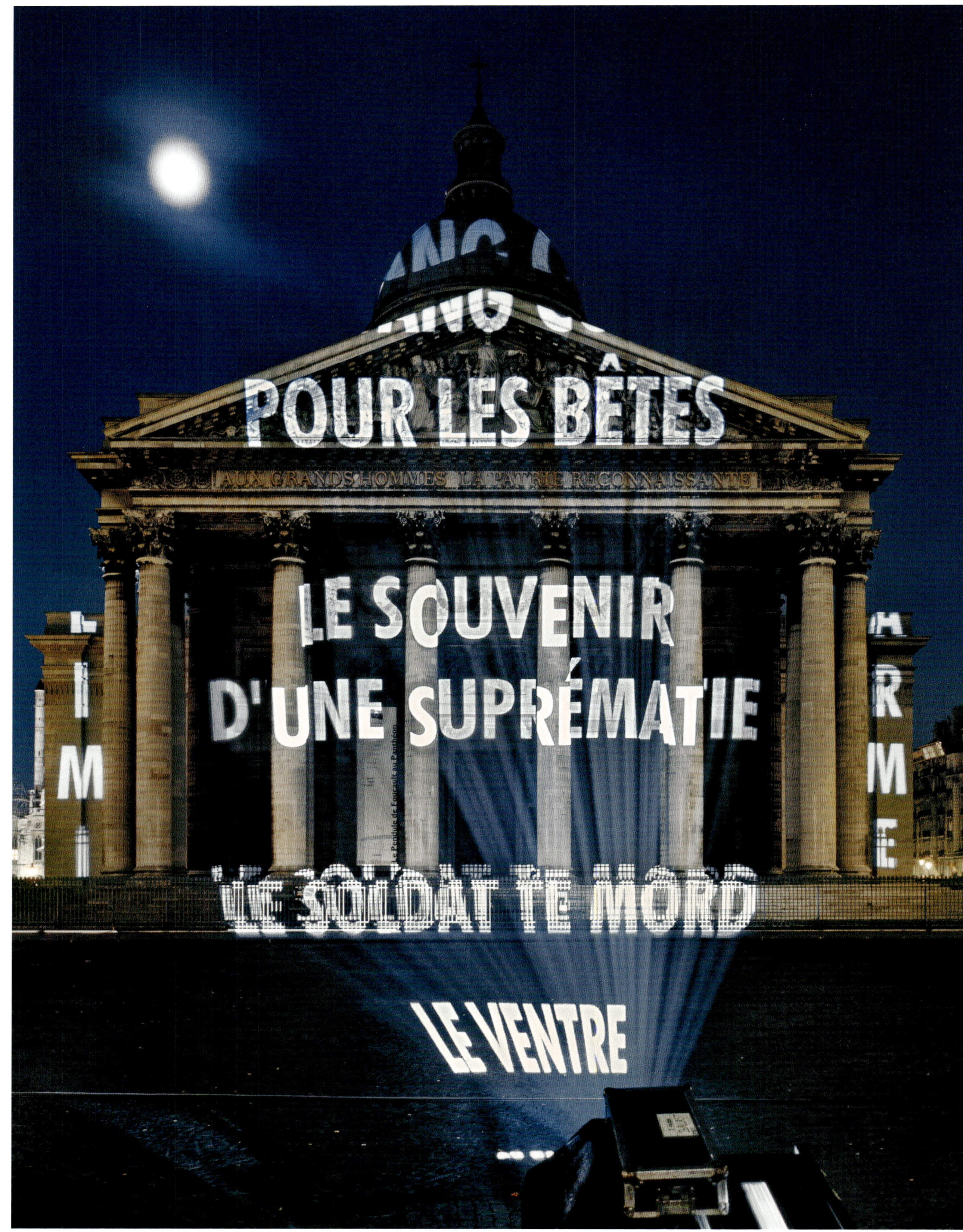
POUR LES BÊTES
AUX GRANDS HOMMES LA PATRIE RECONNAISSANTE
LE SOUVENIR
D'UNE SUPRÉMATIE
LE SOLDAT TE MORD
LE VENTRE

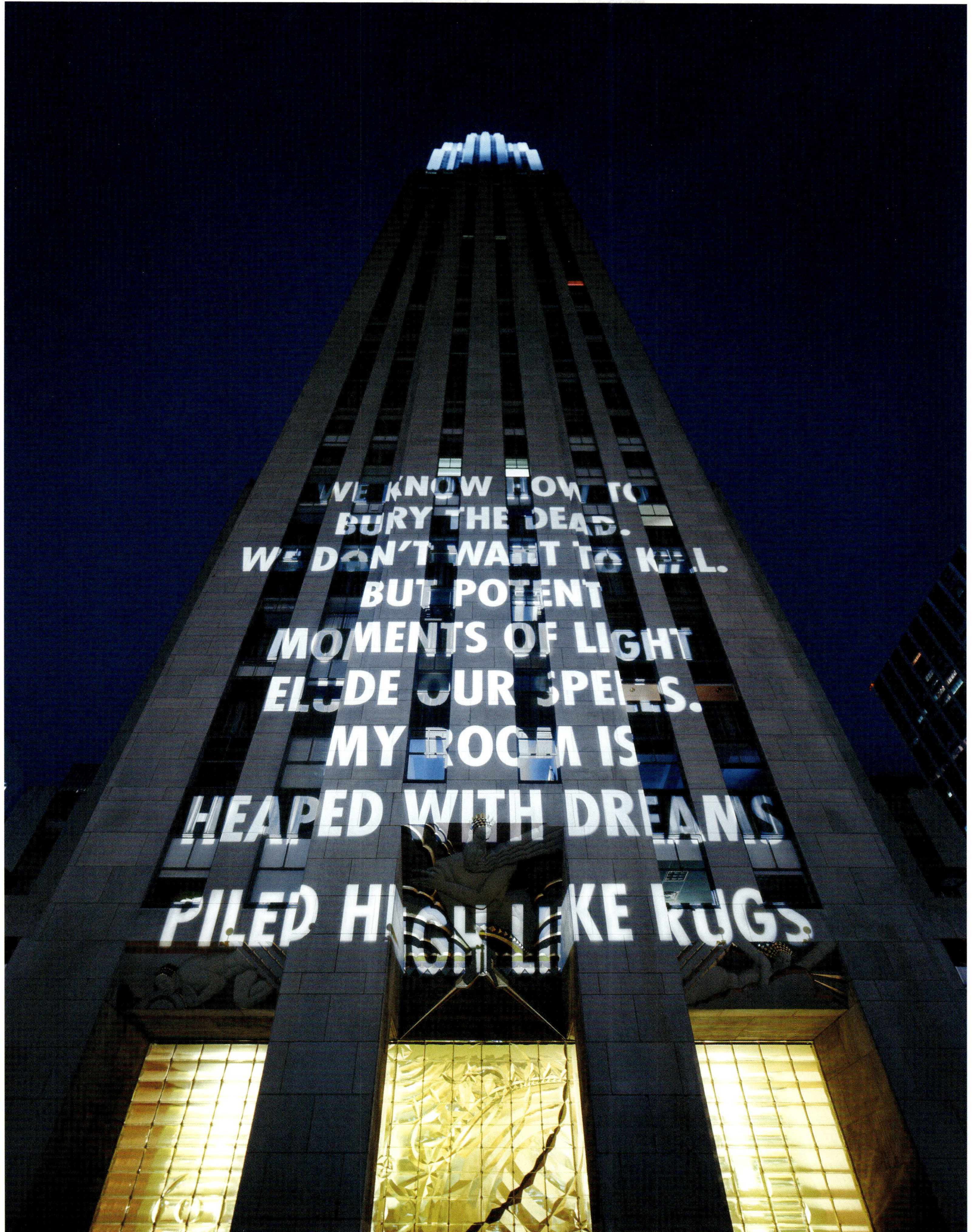
WE KNOW HOW TO
BURY THE DEAD.
WE DON'T WANT TO KILL.
BUT POTENT
MOMENTS OF LIGHT
ELUDE OUR SPELLS.
MY ROOM IS
HEAPED WITH DREAMS
PILED HIGH LIKE RUGS

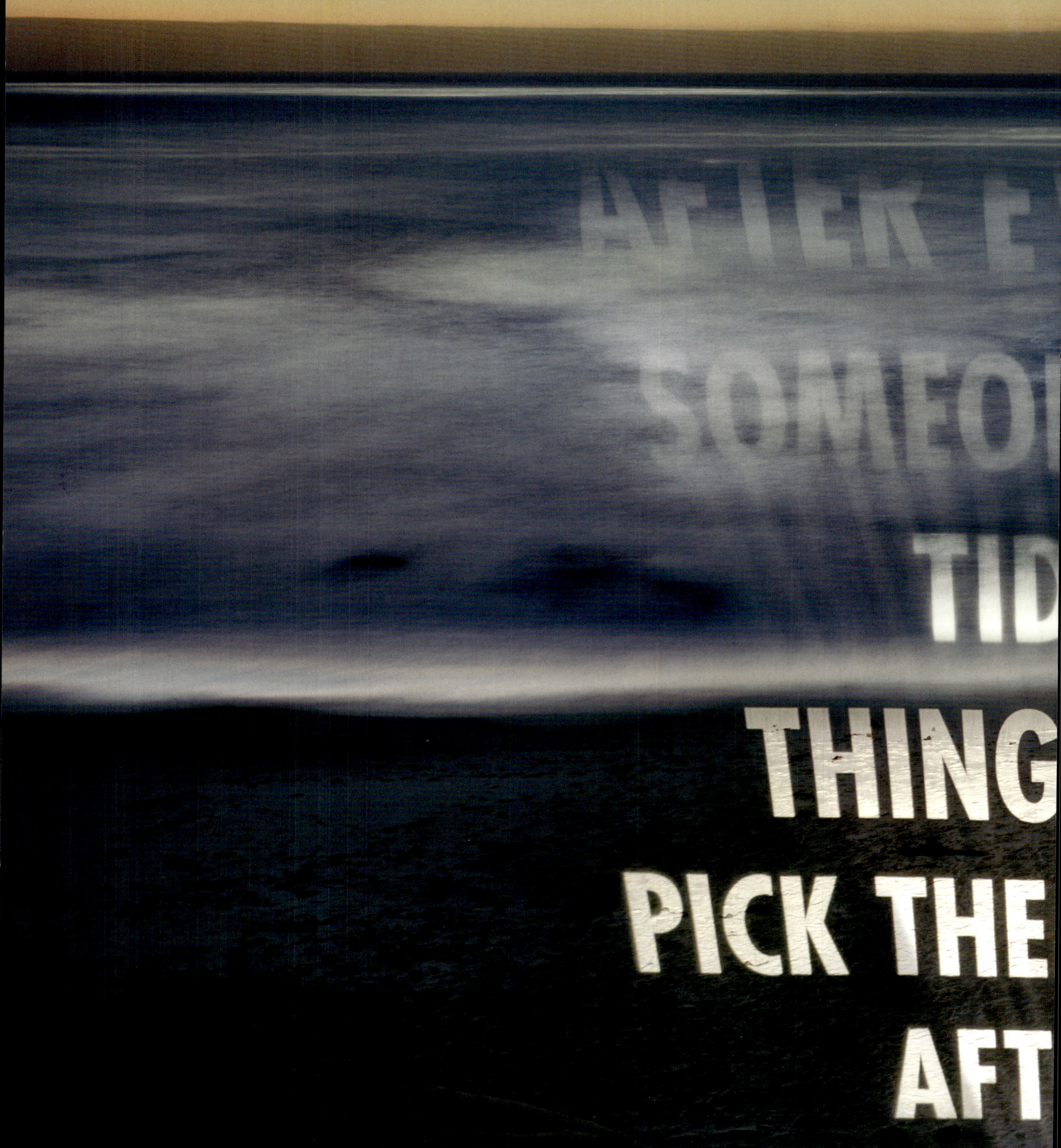
AFTER E
SOMEO
TID
THING
PICK THE
AFT

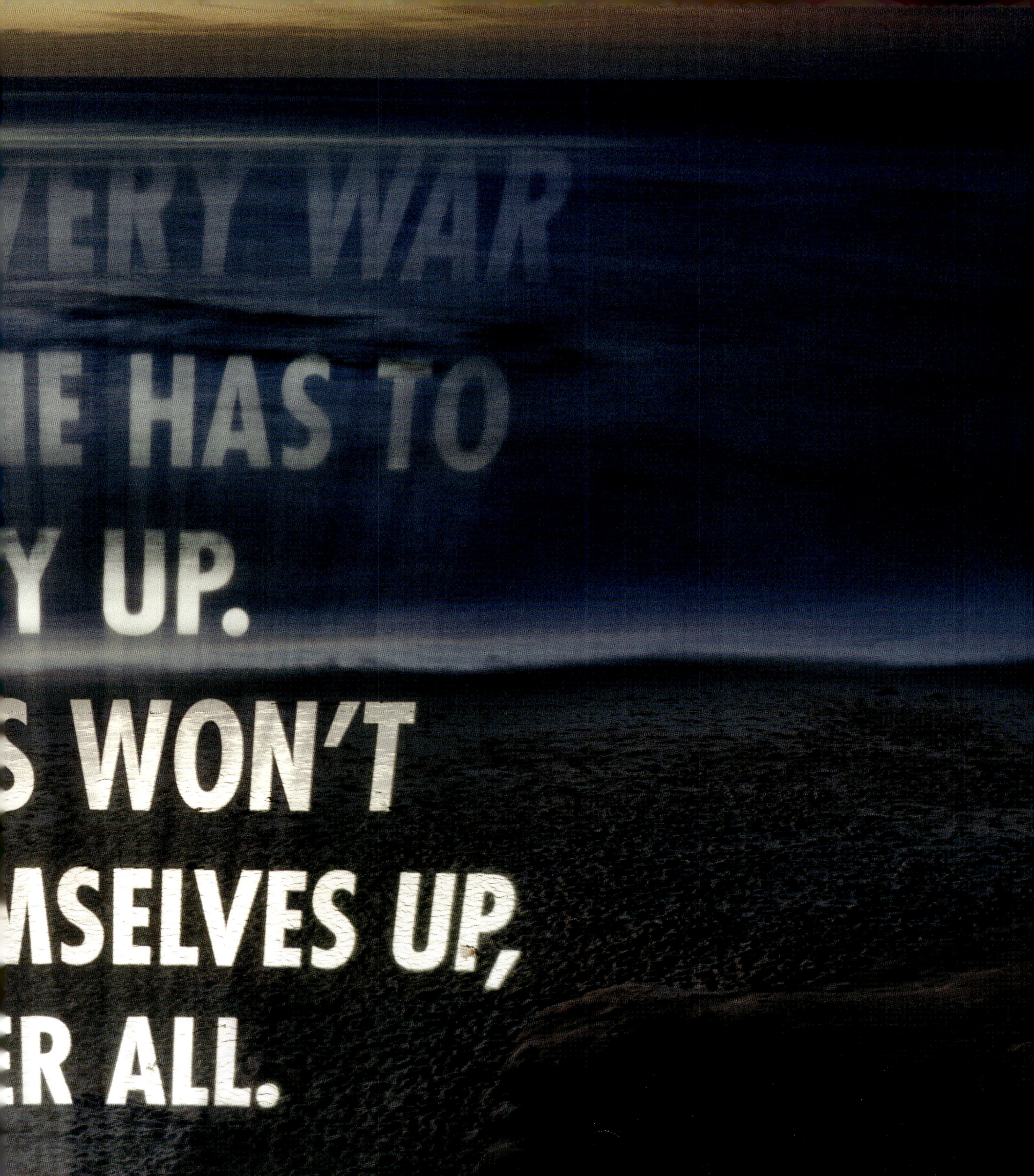
VERY WAR
HE HAS TO
Y UP.
S WON'T
MSELVES UP,
ER ALL.

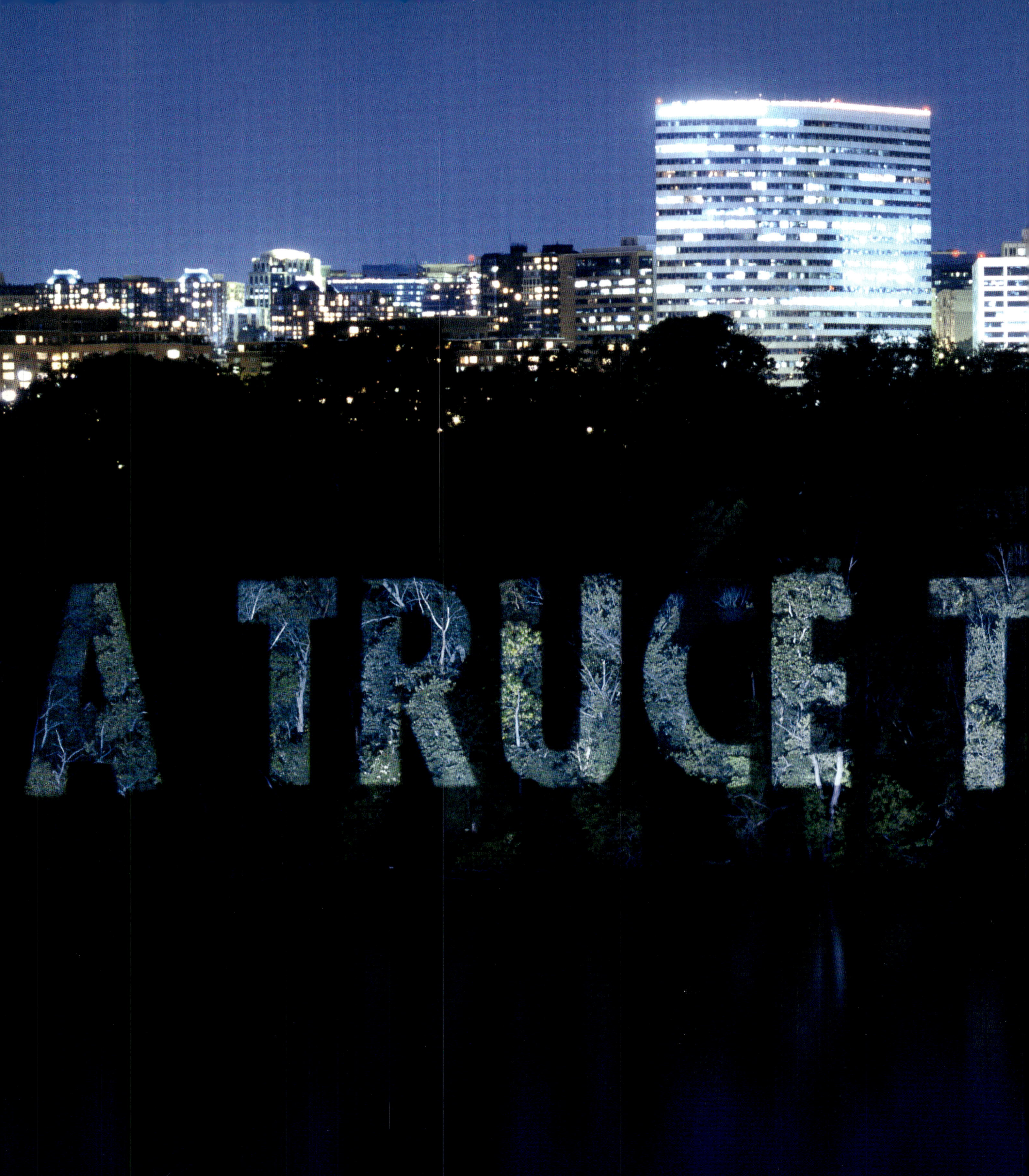
A TRUCE T

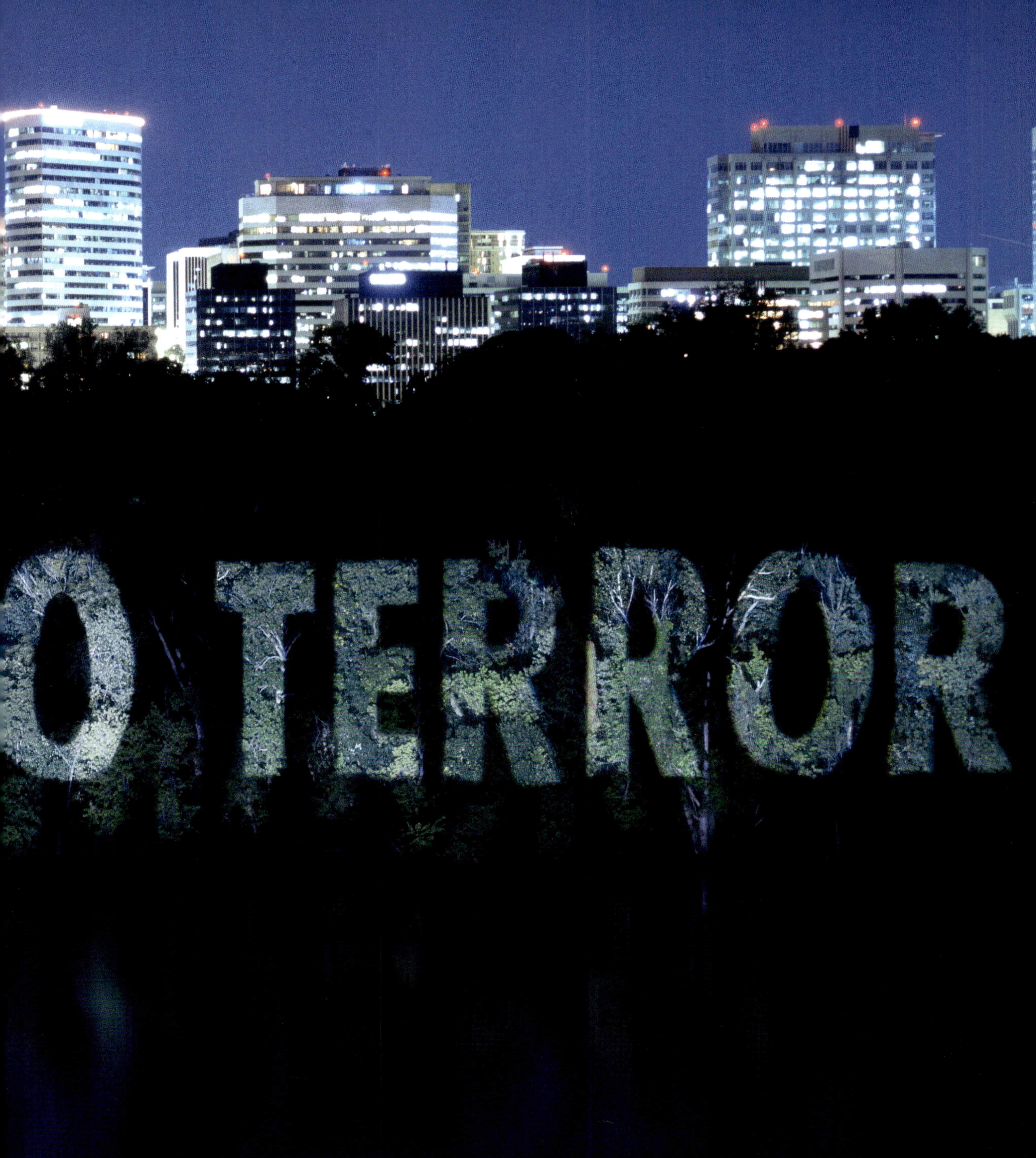

OTERROR

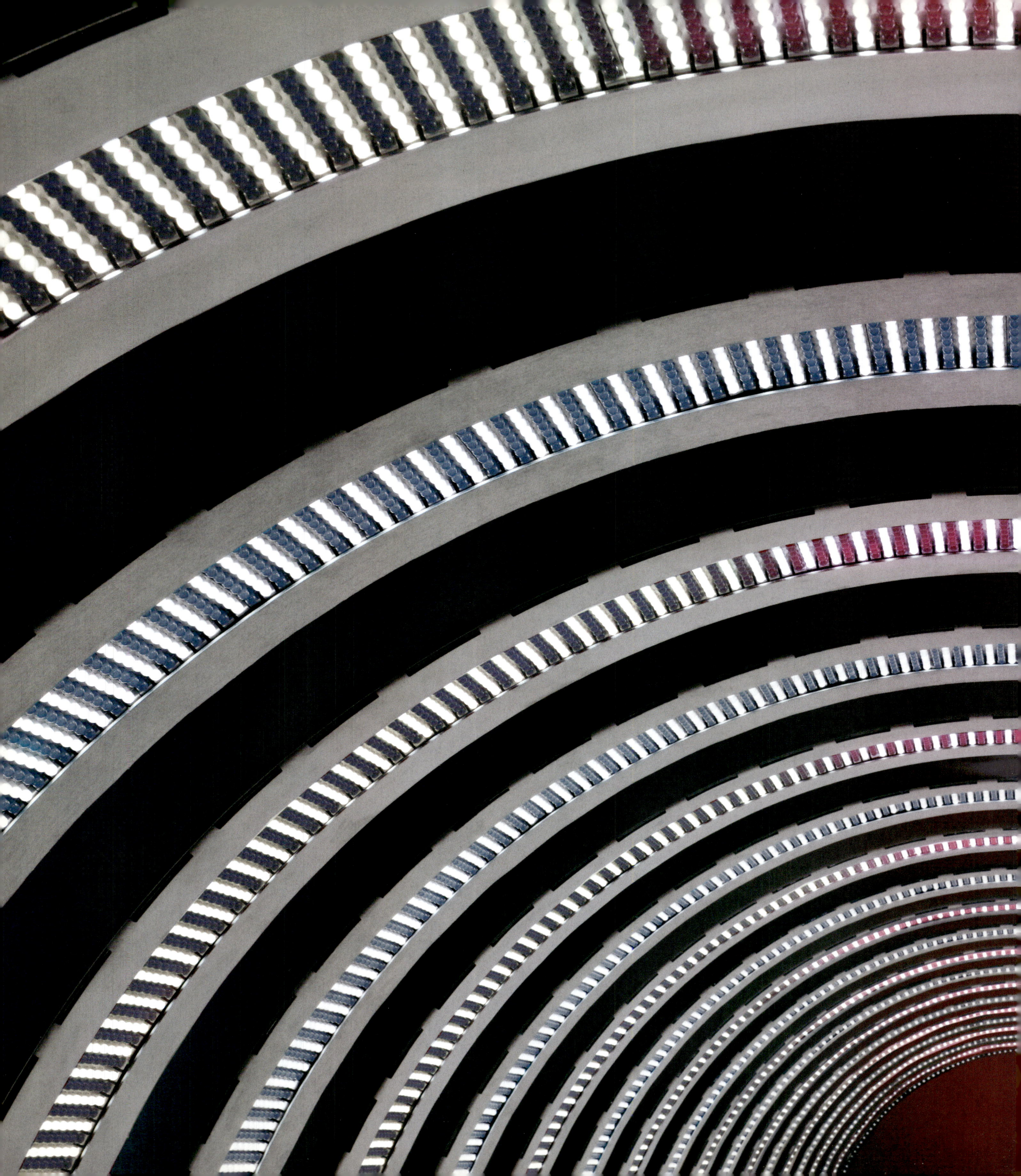

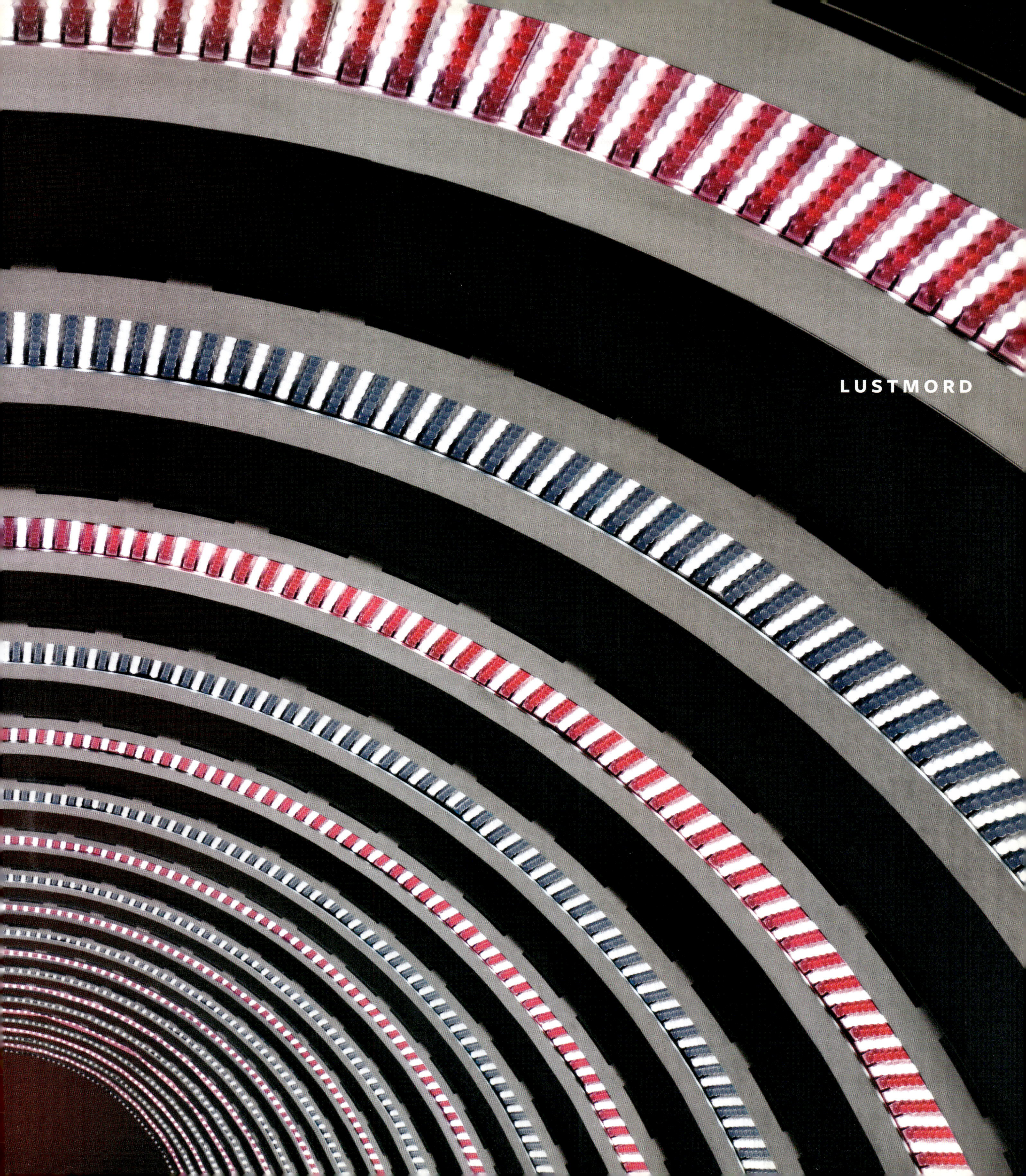
LUSTMORD

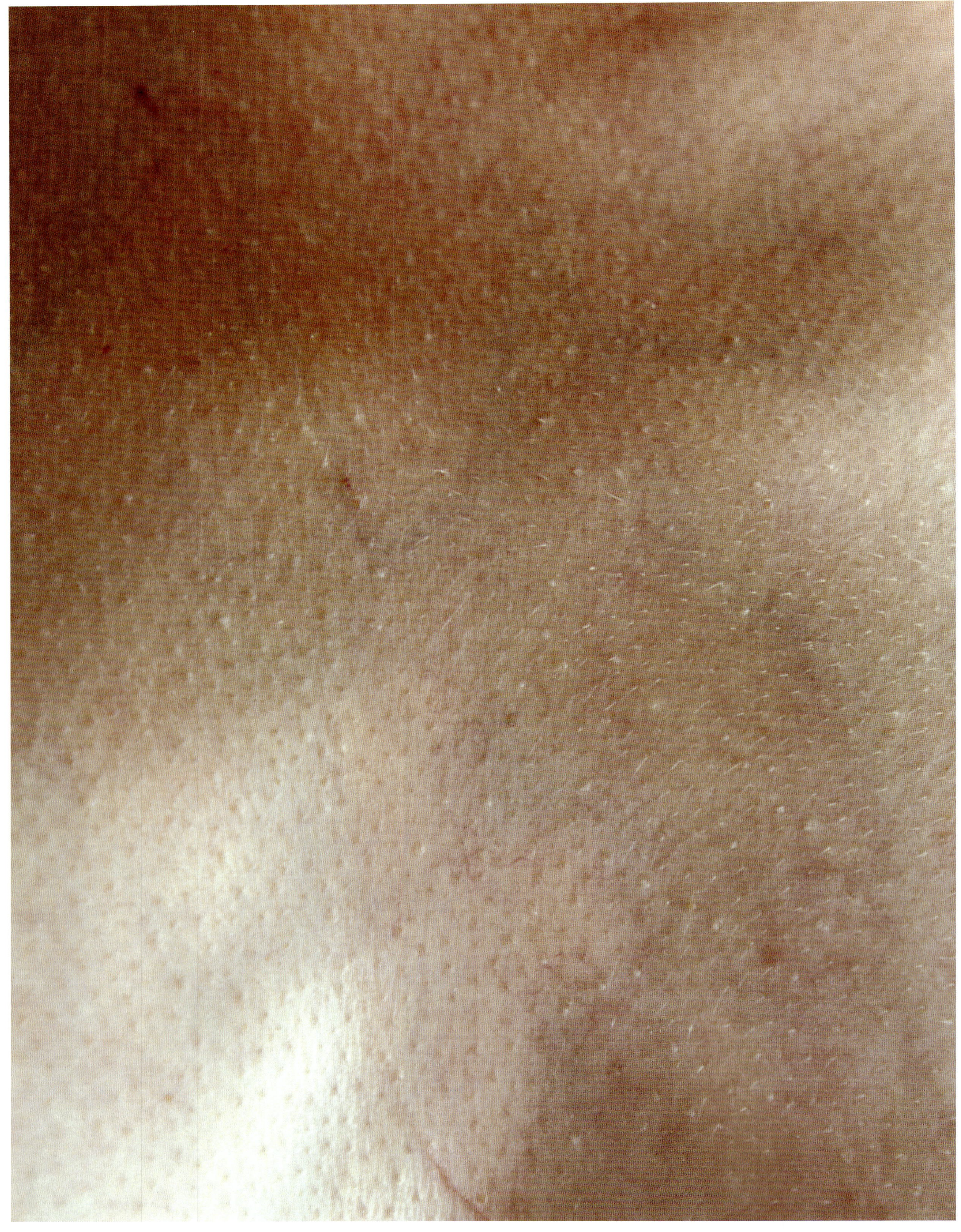

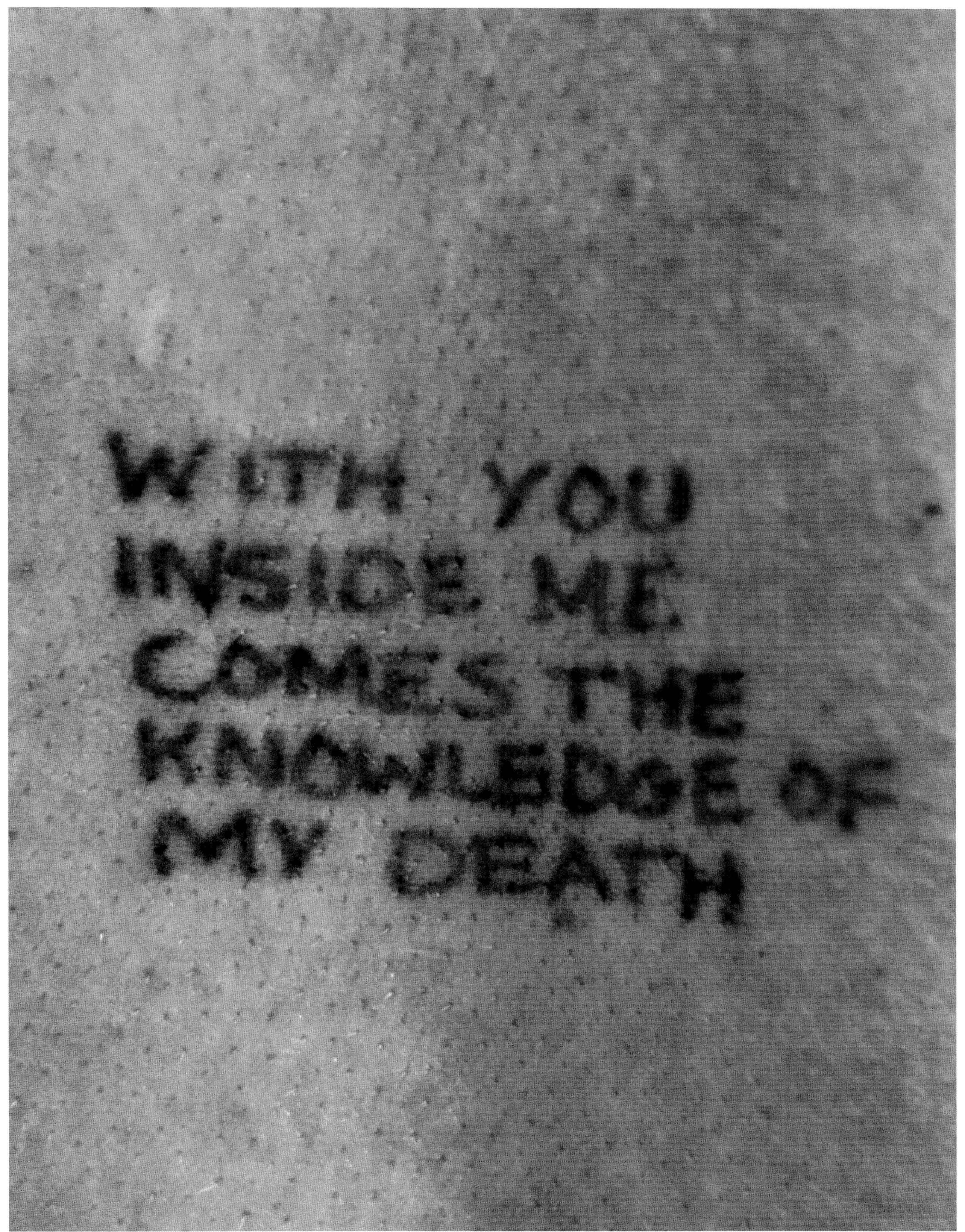
WITH YOU
INSIDE ME
COMES THE
KNOWLEDGE OF
MY DEATH

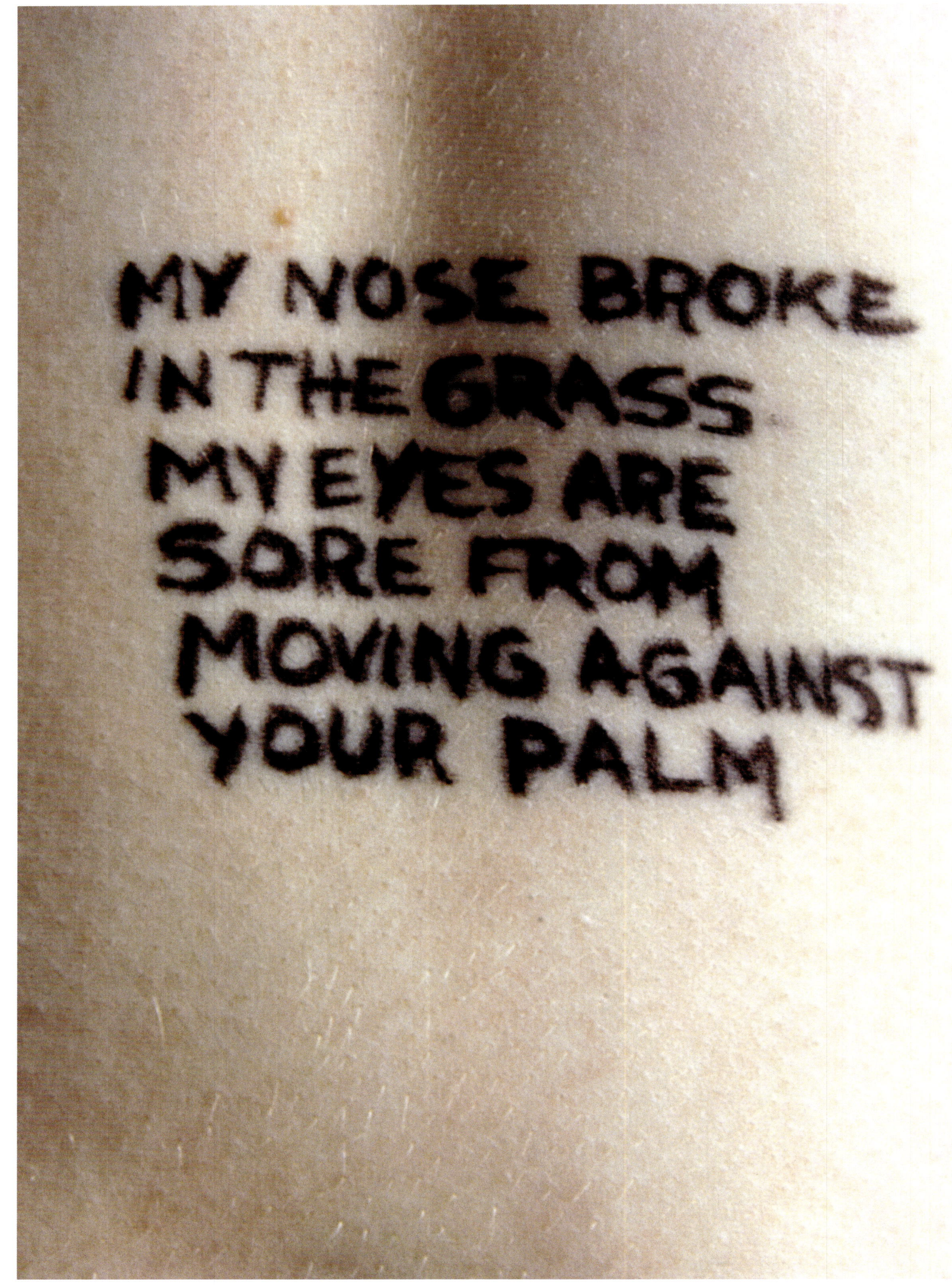
MY NOSE BROKE
IN THE GRASS
MY EYES ARE
SORE FROM
MOVING AGAINST
YOUR PALM

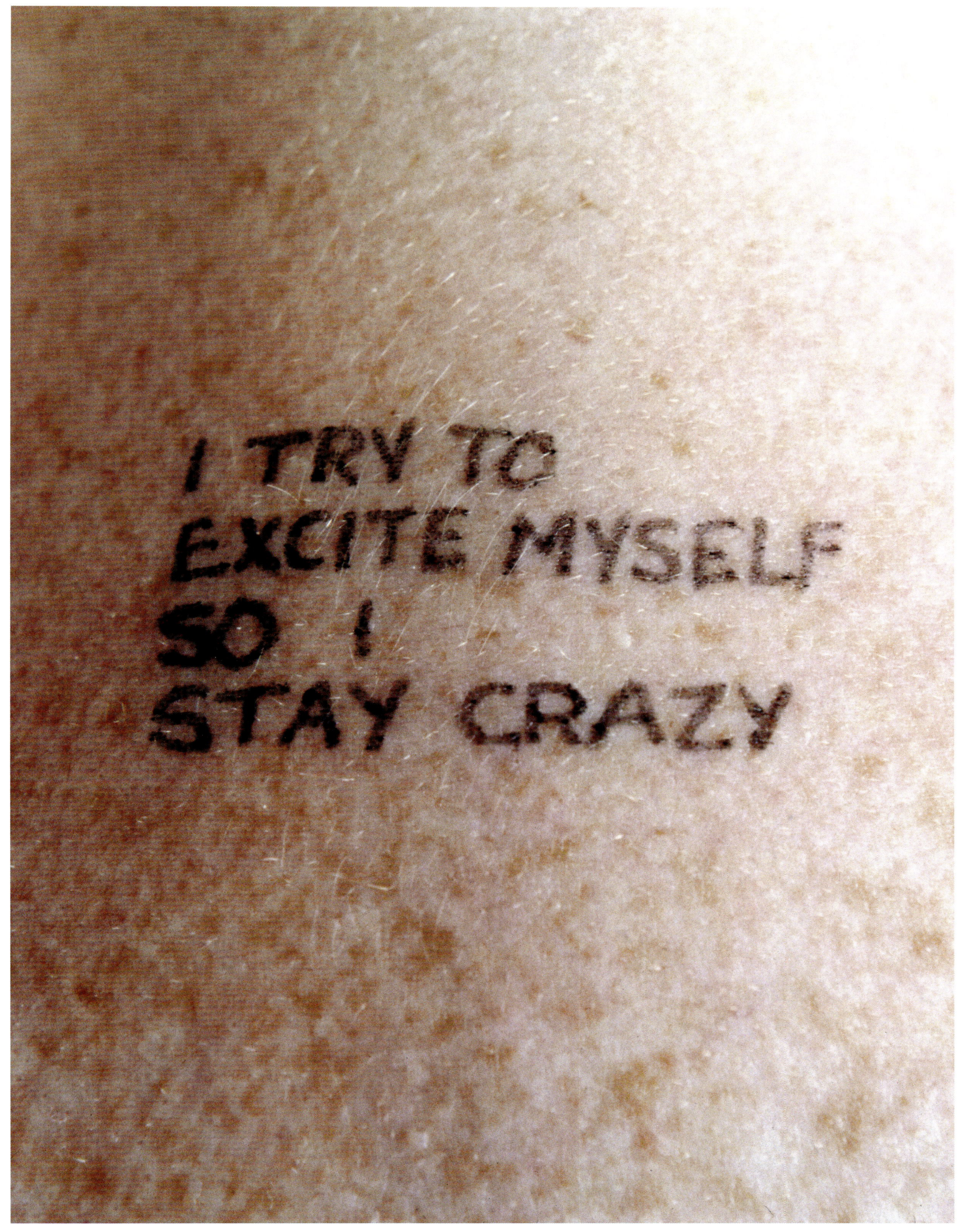
I TRY TO
EXCITE MYSELF
SO I
STAY CRAZY

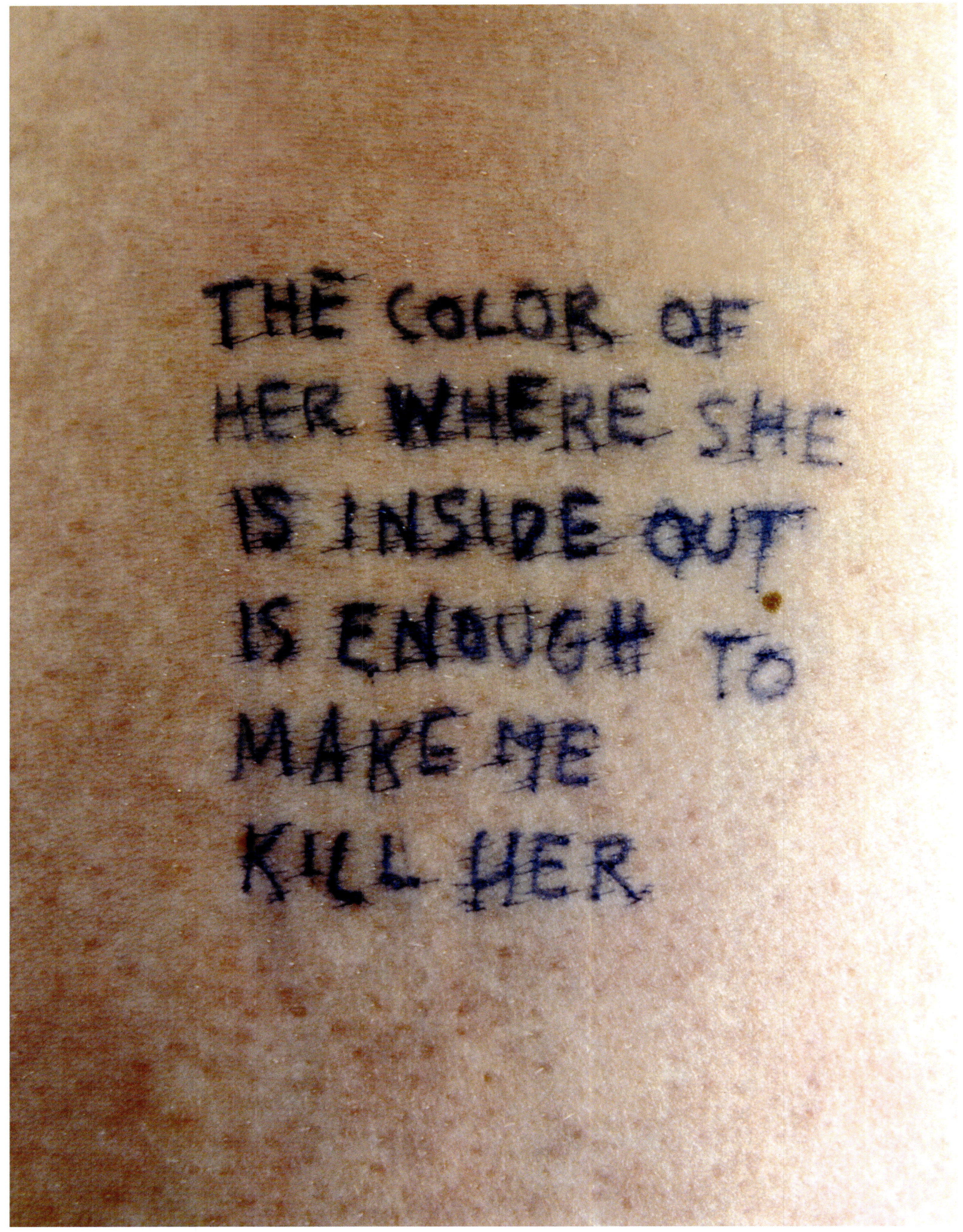
THE COLOR OF
HER WHERE SHE
IS INSIDE OUT
IS ENOUGH TO
MAKE ME
KILL HER

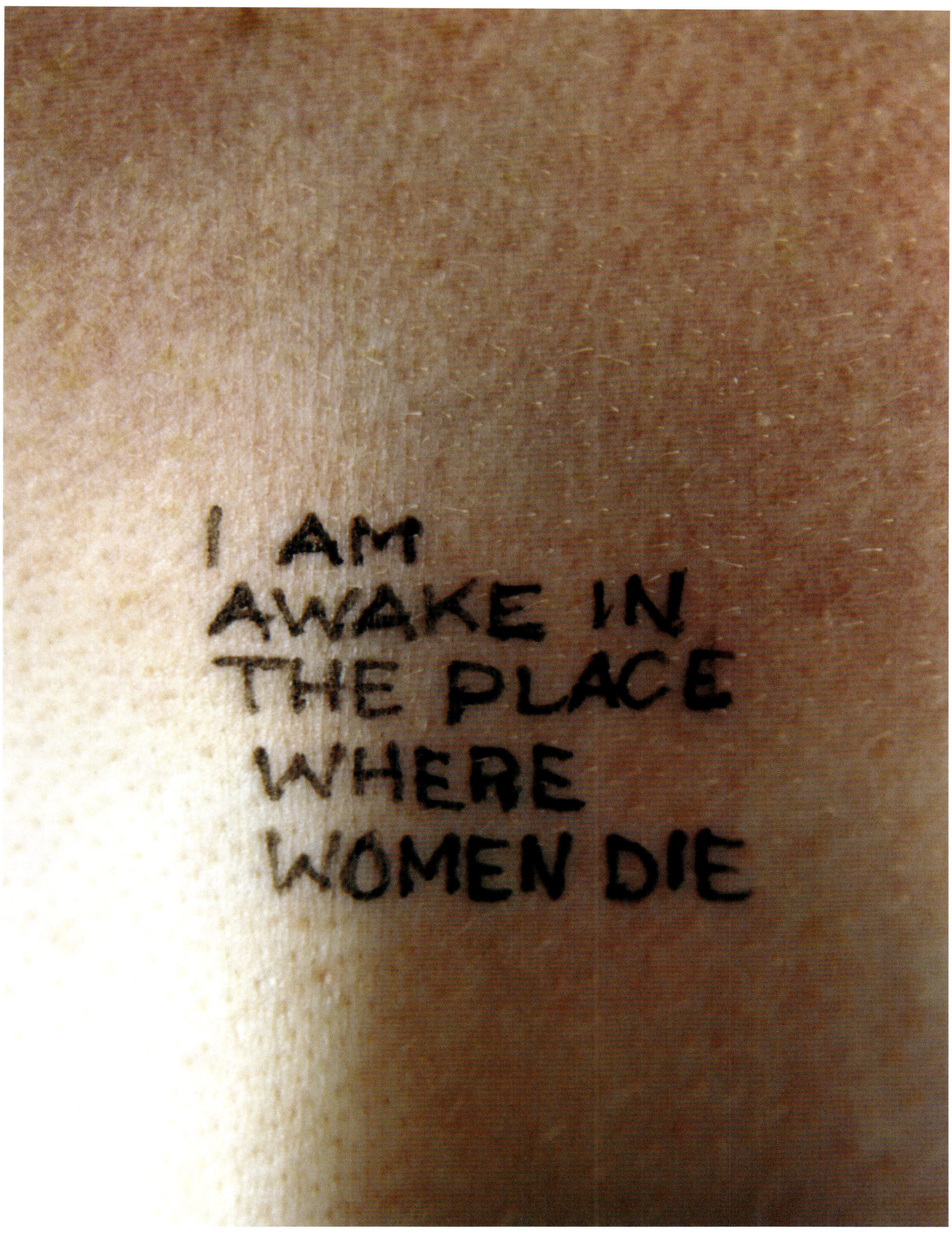
I AM
AWAKE IN
THE PLACE
WHERE
WOMEN DIE

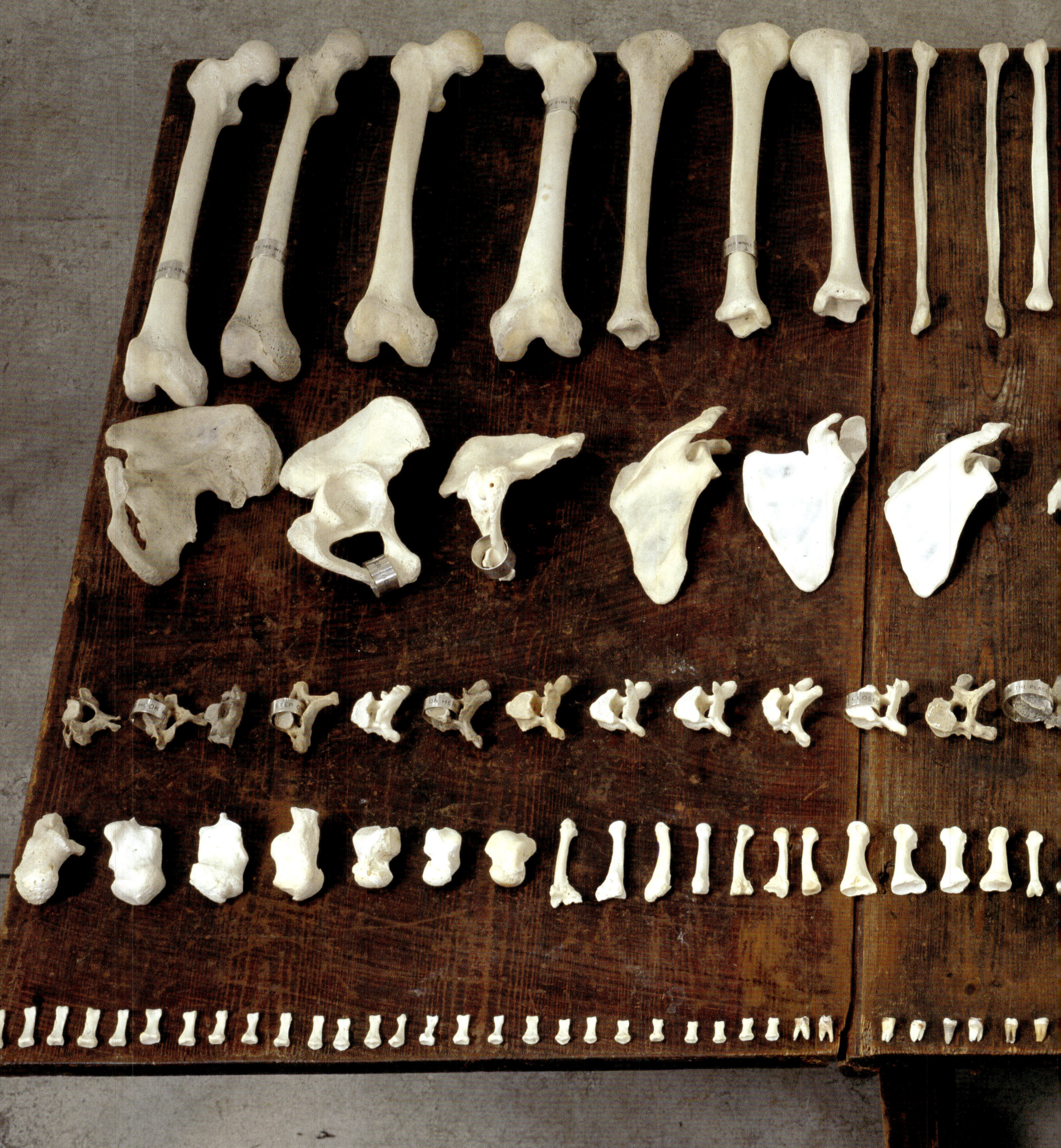

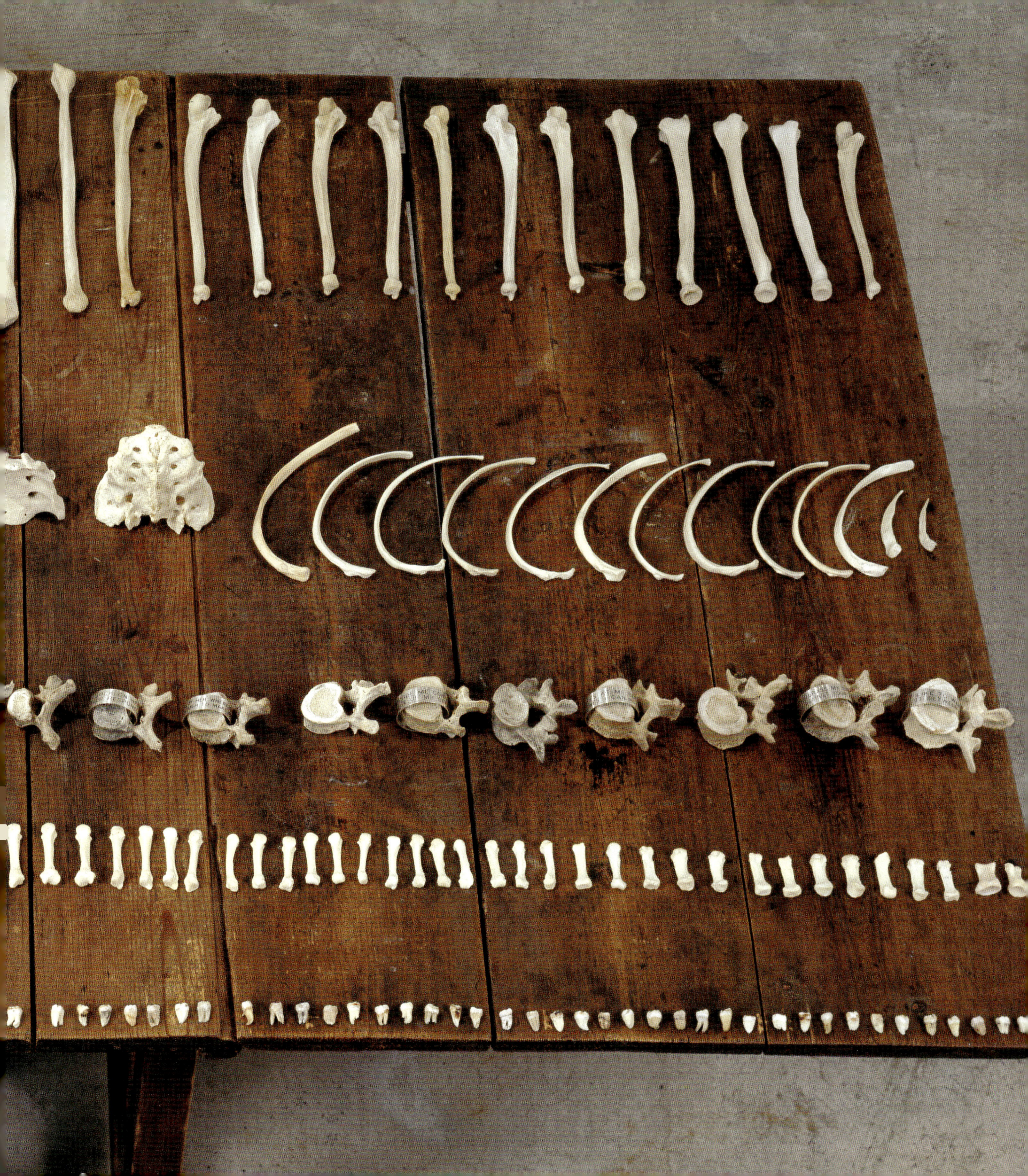

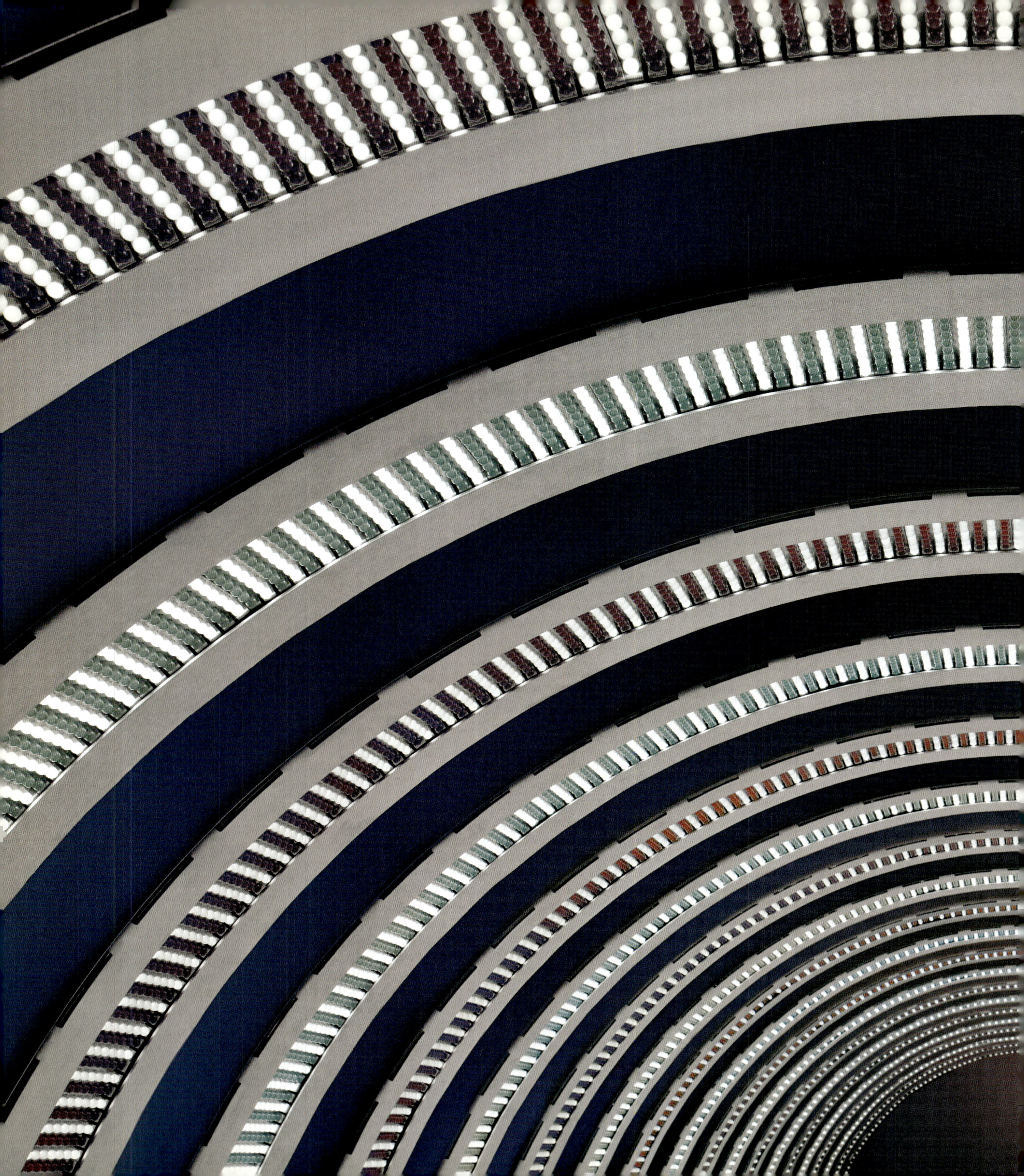

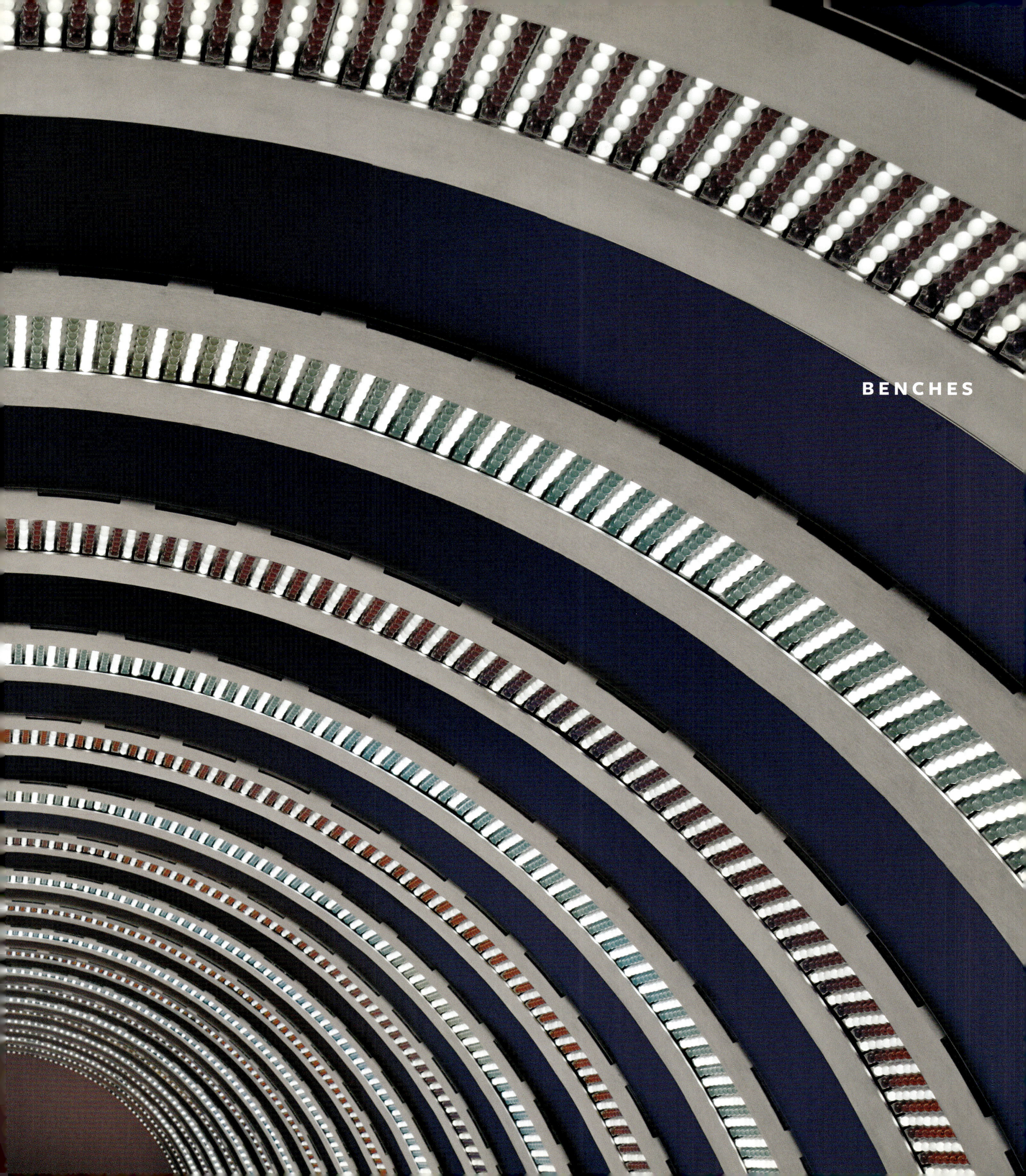

BENCHES

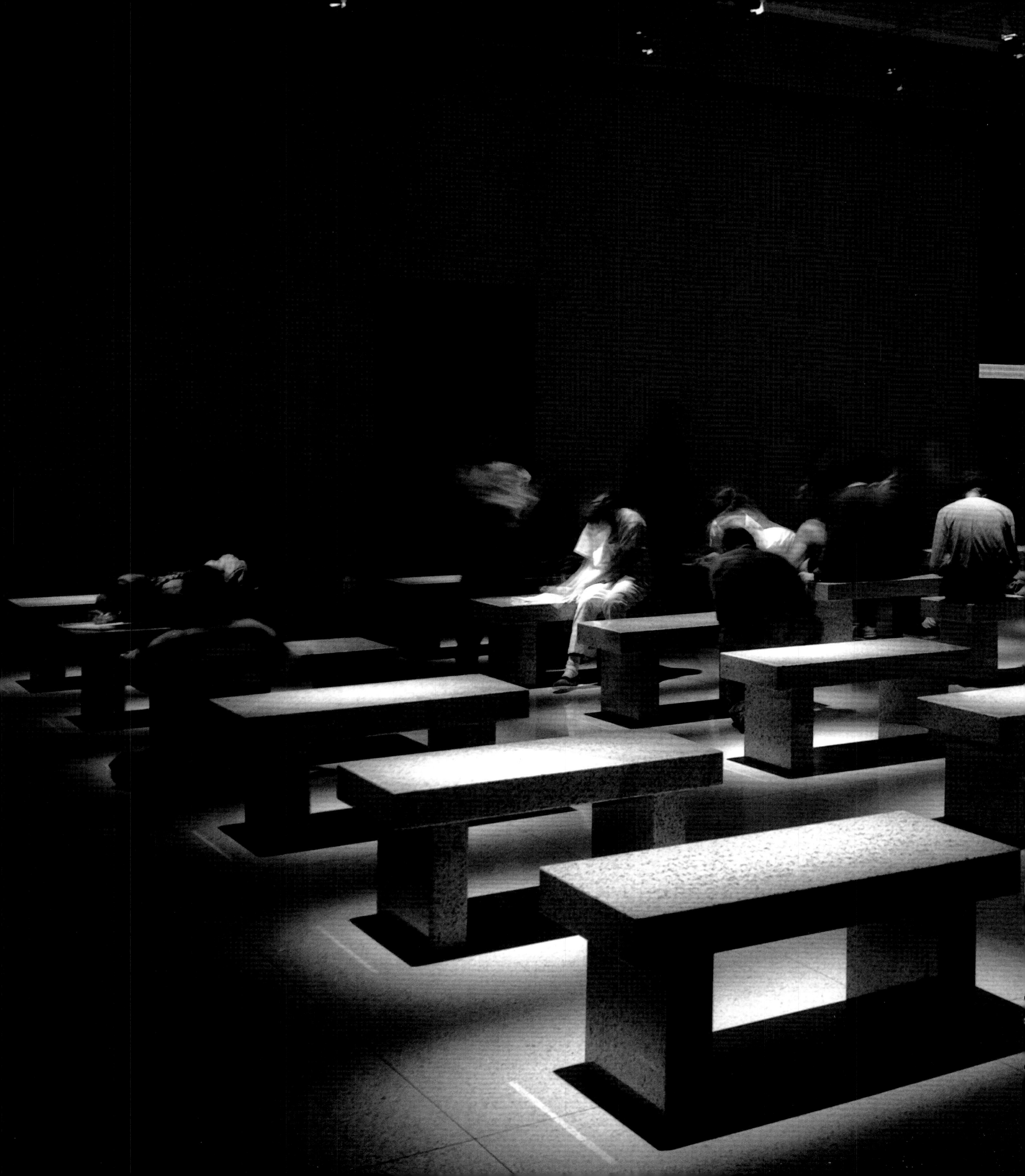

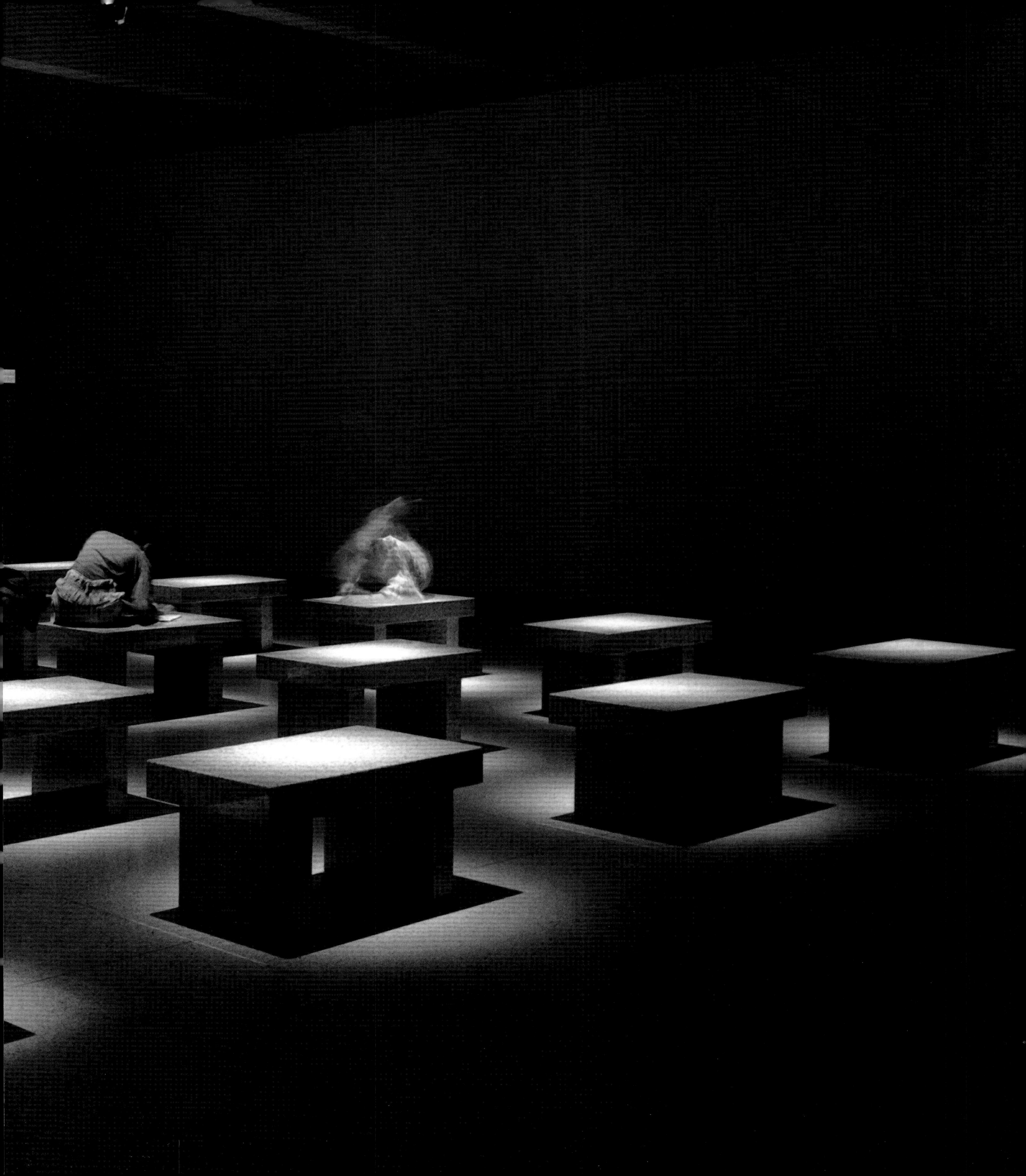

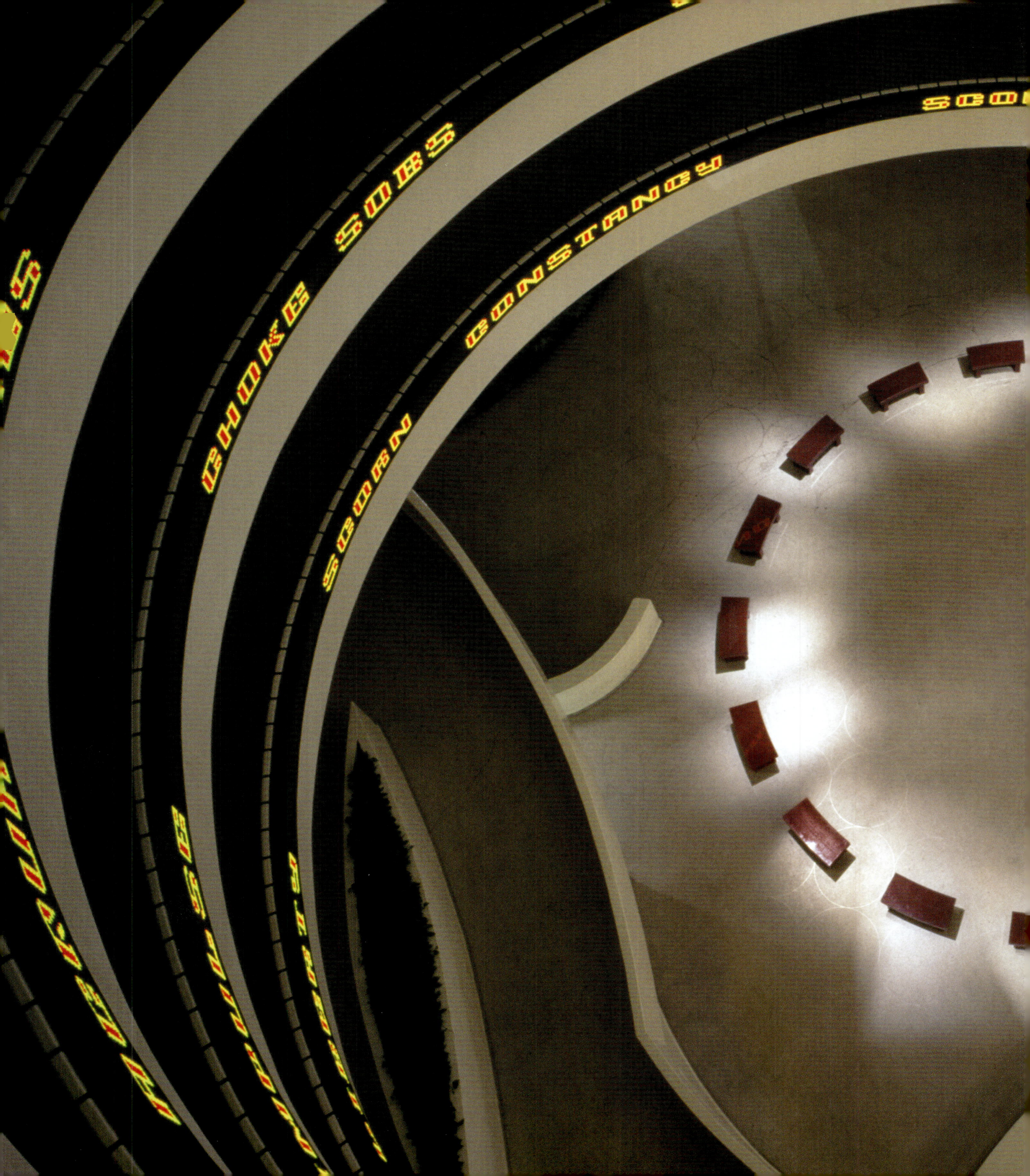
CHOKE SOBS
SCORN
CONSTANCY

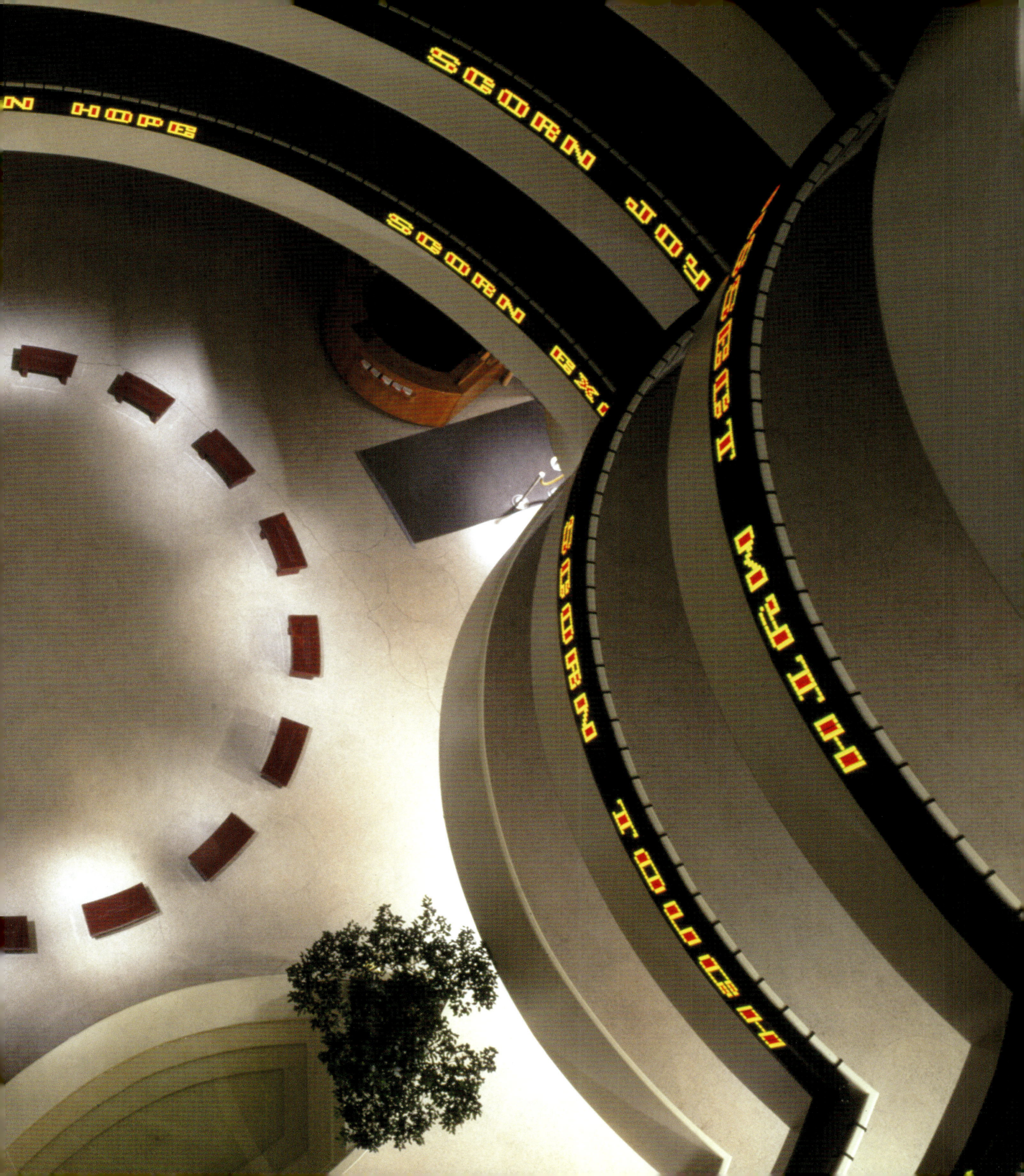
HOPE
SCORN
JOY
SCORN

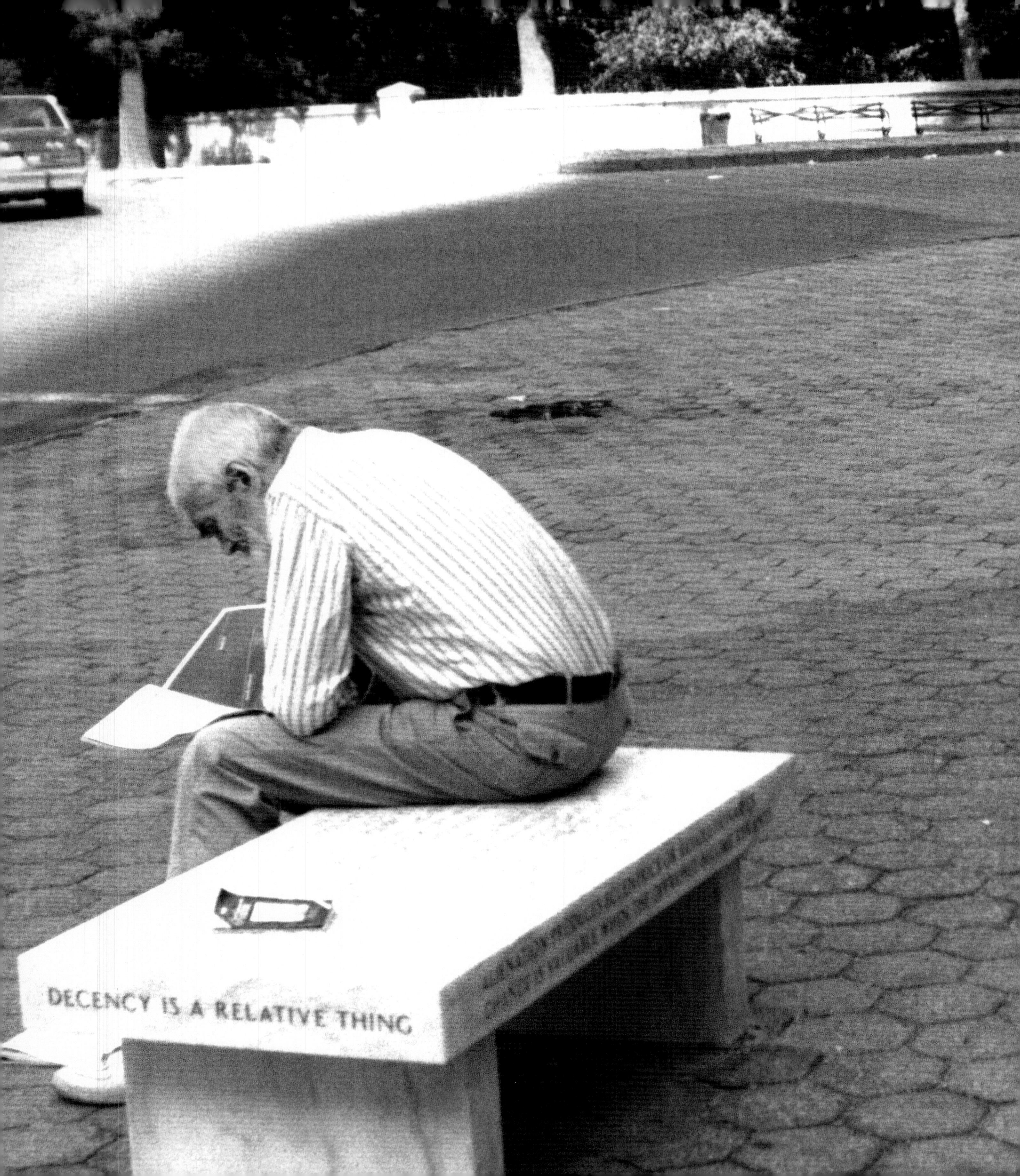
DECENCY IS A RELATIVE THING

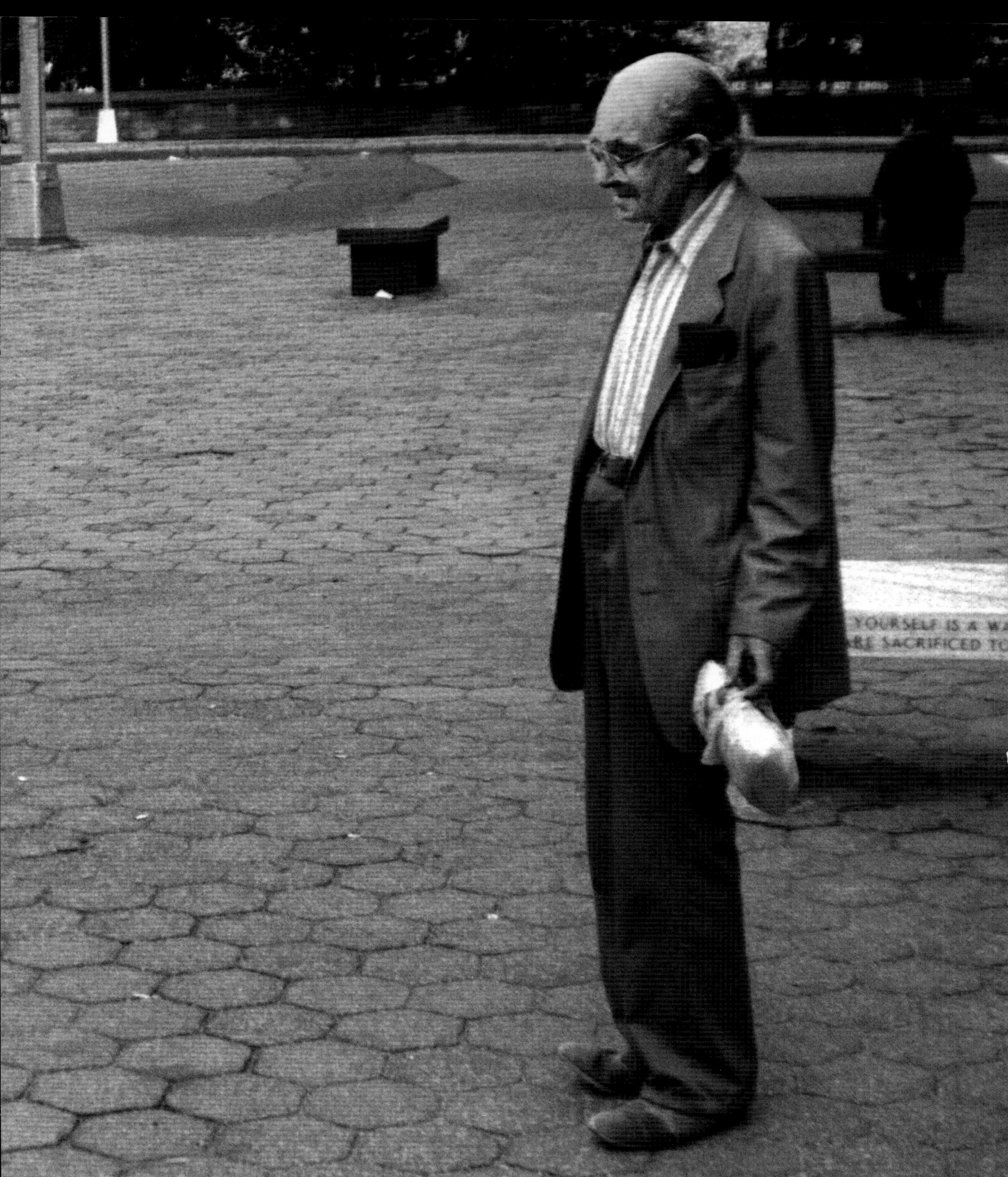
YOURSELF IS A
SACRIFICED

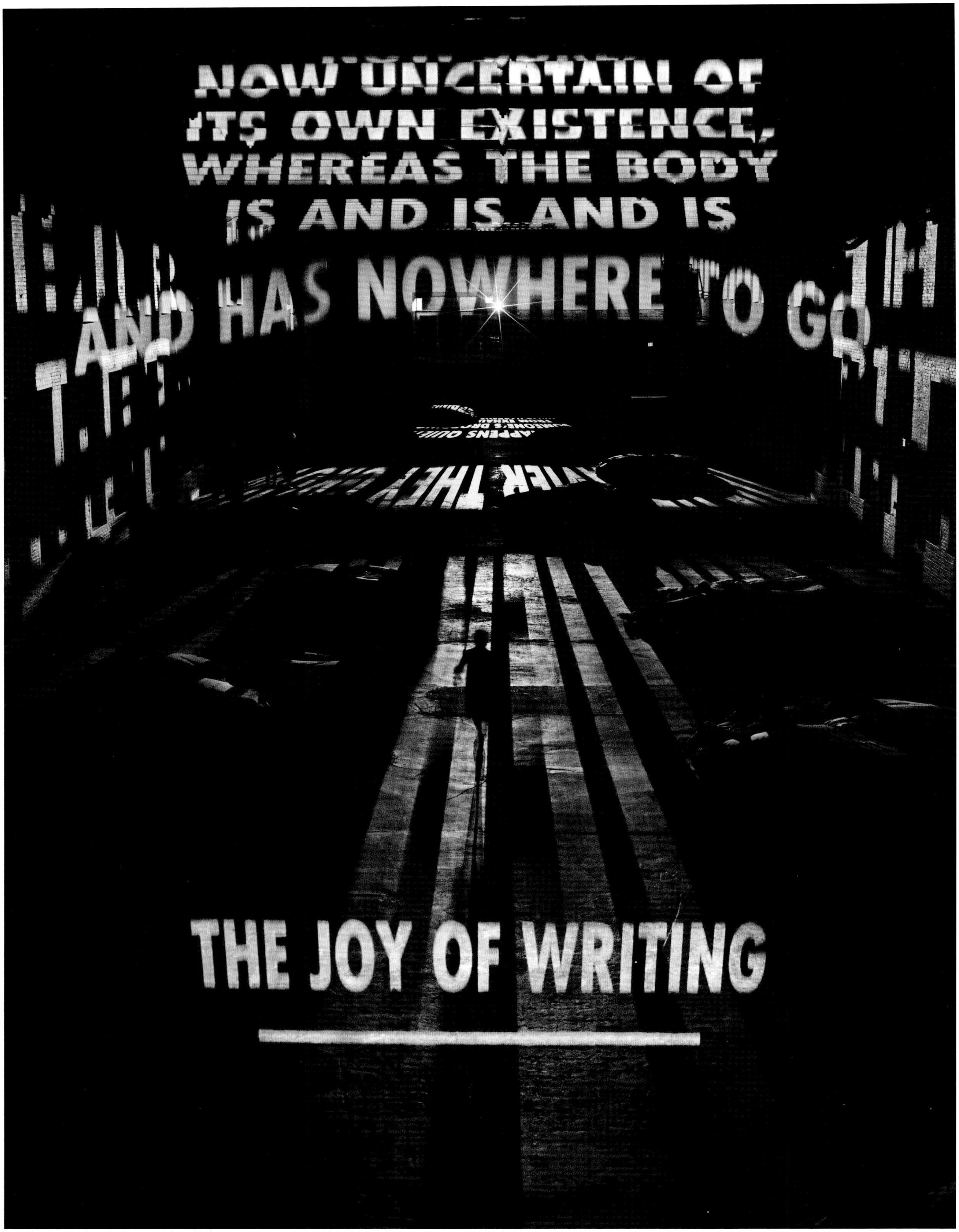

NOW UNCERTAIN OF
ITS OWN EXISTENCE,
WHEREAS THE BODY
IS AND IS AND IS
AND HAS NOWHERE TO GO

THE JOY OF WRITING

AN INTERVIEW WITH JENNY HOLZER

BENJAMIN H.D. BUCHLOH

BENJAMIN H.D. BUCHLOH: I remember a presentation that you gave of your work that began with images of a room whose surfaces were painted in heavily textured blue paint, almost as though it was encaustic.

JENNY HOLZER: When I was in graduate school at RISD, I painted my studio all white, including the windows, and then came in with an atmospheric Thalo blue acrylic wash to cover the floors, walls, ceiling, and the glass in the windows and door.

BB: If my memory is correct, does that work indicate that you started out as a painter at some point?

JH: I began with a little bit of everything including printmaking, conceptual work, assemblage, video, bad sculpture, inscrutable public pieces, and painting. I did try to become a painter proper at RISD.

BB: Would it be correct to suggest that it wasn't language at that time, but rather the shift into public architectural space that was at the forefront of your reflections on how to challenge painting and transcend its traditional parameters?

JH: Language appeared in my undergraduate conceptual work, and then left for a little while at RISD while I concentrated on painting. When I was unable to paint well enough, language returned as a way for me to continue working. I'm not sure that I wanted to challenge painting as much as I just wanted to make something decent for people. I wanted a lot simultaneously: to leave art outside for the public, to be a painter of mysterious yet ordered works, to be explicit but not didactic, to find the right subjects, to transform spaces, to disorient and transfix people, to offer up beauty, to be funny and never lie. I needed to offer something to be able to tolerate myself and to justify trying to become an artist. After time in New York City, I focused on what traditional painting couldn't do in public spaces and used language to carry the greater part of my content. Eventually, though, I tried to bring part of what appears in, say, a Rothko painting, into architecture and out to the public. I went some distance toward that with the warm amber LED installation in the Neue Nationalgalerie in Berlin, and with light projections in a number of cities. Text was there along with the light and the light's effect on people.

BB: From the perspective of a historian, it appears that your work emerges out of a dialogue with the governing forms of Conceptual art of the late 1960s and early 1970s. Often, these linear genealogies turn out to be deceptive or plain wrong. Nevertheless, would you want to address your relationship to Conceptual art at the time of your formation as an artist?

JH: I could be dead wrong, but I think my work was much influenced by painting, by artists who work in many media like Beuys and Nauman, by sculpture such as that by Judd and Flavin, and by other types of work including Conceptualism. I was a part-time if naïve Conceptualist in undergraduate school. When I was retreating from painting and learning about Conceptualism, I was most grateful to have that model before me. I am not certain that my redrawing hundreds of published captioned diagrams was a Conceptual practice, but I imagined that Conceptualism gave me the blessing for that odd study of text's relationship to image. I also thought it would look kindly upon my survey of the many subjects represented in these diagrams. I drew diagrams from physics, religion, biology, psychology, sociology, economics, and from kooks. (This survey was a precursor of sorts to the *Truisms*, given the multiple subjects and points of view.) I learned about Kosuth at RISD and had the notion that Conceptualism encouraged artwork that was dematerialized, and I liked that. I glimpsed more than read much of the attendant language but was reassured that words could be art. I had paid attention to words in Dada, in Cubist pieces, and in Renaissance paintings, but Conceptualism was especially instructive. By the time I was in NYC, I knew about Weiner's and Buren's practices, and this encouraged me to go outside to work for a general public, to make pieces that could be seen, then completed by people. I noticed that Yoko Ono was worth studying. I was attracted by LeWitt's work courtesy of its definition and systems, and because it was just beautiful. Same goes for De Maria's pieces.

BB: The theoretical language models underlying Conceptual art could be somewhat simplistically summed up as deriving from analytical philosophy (e.g., Joseph Kosuth) and language theories elaborated by the Structuralists and Noam Chomsky (e.g., Lawrence Weiner). Did looking at the work of artists such as Kosuth and Weiner make you reconsider the language models to be deployed in your own practice afterwards, and how did you perceive your definitions to be different from the language models of Conceptual art?

JH: I've read little about analytical philosophy and language theory, so I can't comment about that. I was attracted to the accessibility, inscrutability, intelligence, economy, and looniness of Weiner's work and wanted to emulate that somehow. I can't say exactly how Weiner's work influenced my writing—in part because I can't stand staying with my texts—but I thought about Larry's work when I was young and still do. About Kosuth's practice, it played as a general permission to go ahead, and I liked seeing his text in light. My writing had to be short to catch the attention of passersby, and I'm not an ace writer so there was no reason to ramble. Plus, most of the subjects I chose are hard to tolerate, so I had to be quick, concise in order to be able to write the texts, and also to be merciful to readers. For many series, including *Lustmord*, I would fall into the subject and see what would come without thinking too much. Once I had enough text, I would cut away at it so—hopefully—nothing distracting or stupid would remain. I also might drop into one or more personalities, and that would make the writing faster and easier.

opposite: ***PROJECTIONS*, 2008**

BB: In the late 1970s and early 1980s, you participated in the activities of a number of artists' collectives, some of which were co-founded by you, such as The Offices of Fend, Fitzgibbon, Holzer, Nadin, Prince and Winters. Collectives such as Group Material and Colab followed your example slightly later.

JH: I'd like to take credit for being early, but Colab existed before I joined. I was a founder of the short-lived Offices that was heavier on concept and absurdity than action. We had business cards and did one show in L.A. where Peter Fend surprised Frank Gehry, but I'm not sure what else we achieved.

BB: Many of the collaborative groups had a distinctly activist character and pushed definitions of artistic practice to the threshold of political practice, if not actually substituting the latter for the former (for example, offering legal services to immigrants and assisting with housing). What, if any, were your historical models for art as social activism at the time when you co-founded these collectives?

JH: I wasn't sure how and if art and activism worked and still am not, but I was aware of groups of artists, designers, and architects who envisioned much and worked hard, including the Dadaists, Futurists, Suprematists, the Bauhaus group, and the Fluxus people. I also knew a little about what happened with dance and performance at Judson Church and about mail art collectives.

BB: In hindsight, how do you view the extraordinarily utopian and optimistic character of the collectives with which you were involved?

JH: I know the most about Colab, so I'll talk about that. Colab was utopian, optimistic, occasionally squabbling, sincere, and practical. Working en masse or in small units let us realize complicated shows that none of us could have managed alone, when no one else was offering to support this sort of activity. Because we organized the exhibitions — often in spaces no one wanted — we didn't need to be cautious about content. Because most members liked to make and present work with outside-world vs. art-referential subjects, it was relatively straightforward to imagine and stage big exhibitions about difficult subjects in public zones. I liked working with other artists because so much of my practice was solitary.

It's hard to measure how socially and politically useful the activity was, but the *Manifesto Show* that Colen Fitzgibbon and I organized was an exercise of free speech and supplied a survey of classic political and art manifestos, as well as fresh visual and written shouts by over 100 people, plus a number of utopian propositions.

BB: Do you attribute the courage of these practices to a post-1968 radicalism still pervasive in some groups within the art world at that time? Or would you rather consider it to be the outcome of post-Conceptual artistic reflections (e.g., the work of Hans Haacke and Daniel Buren) which had recognized that different models of public space and social communication had opened up and that it was necessary to expand on these models in order for a cultural production in the present to remain credible?

JH: An accurate answer could be some of each. Sixties activism was familiar and well-regarded; many of us came of age in that decade. And Haacke and Buren were appreciated; I imagine they were influenced by the '60s as well. The groups formed naturally with artists of approximately the same generation with similar interests, subjects, and approaches. There were ancient subjects to treat — war, poverty, race, and the abuse of women — and relatively new topics, like the bomb and AIDS. Many artists were explicit about these subjects in their work, went directly to general audiences, and skirted theory.

BB: The traditional conception of the artist as single author was replaced in these collectives by a model of culture defined as the result of a group identity and its practices. More generally speaking, individual authorship was displaced by an emphasis on the collaborative nature of all social processes, including those of cultural production. But today, these collaborative models have all but disappeared from the cultural sphere, and we seem to have returned again to the idea of the artist as singular creative producer, if not genius. How do you explain that?

JH: Money is part of the answer, but not all. There was little support around for young artists in the late '70s and early '80s, at least for wild artists, and now there's money for solitary geniuses. The '60s influenced many of us when we began to work, and had something to do with working in groups.

An interesting feature of the "salon-hanging" style of the '70s and '80s was that it let individual artists show whatever they favored, represented the group effort, but then became something different that was satisfying visually and conceptually, and unusually deep in content. These hangs often were more successful than murals made by a number of artists. The visual simultaneity of group hangs seemed accurate and represented what really was out there in the world — the ideas, opinions, and images then present. Because artists chose the themes of the exhibitions, found and/or broke into the venues, made the works, and hung the shows, the presentations were cohesive against the odds, even though the work was all over the map: representational or abstract, cartoony, film, video, drawing, text, sculpture, kinetic, plumbing, sound, or not art, not ever. These presentations looked like my thinking when I was writing the *Truisms*, when I wanted to present everything at once.

BB: One of the most fascinating challenges for me when reading/seeing your work has always been the attempt to situate your language practices *within,* or rather in *differentiation from,* the more traditional conventions of language production (i.e., poetry, literature, journalism). While you use, in the more recent work, extensive quotations from poetry, literature, or public speech, one would never want to see your work declared as belonging to any of these conventions. Rather, one would want to insist on its affiliation with sculptural practices as a material intervention in public space. In that sense, your writing seems to occupy a similarly complex linguistic space to that of the work of Lawrence Weiner, whom I personally perceive to be your predecessor in a manner analogue to the way that Jasper Johns, for example, was a predecessor to Andy Warhol.

JH: I'm thrilled to be considered a follower of Lawrence Weiner. I am a longtime student and fan. His writing is almost impossible to classify or describe. Sometimes I get it, and I benefit when I don't.

BB: *Like* Weiner's language (who has always insisted on having his work understood as "sculpture"), yours is *not* easily identifiable as to its place in the universe of linguistic utterances. Nevertheless, *unlike* Weiner's work or that of Conceptual art at large, your linguistic interventions have, from the very beginning, claimed language as one of the prime sites where ideology is reproduced in the subject, or rather, where language as ideology *produces* the subject.

JH: I think that's correct, or at least I believe that language can produce and describe the subjects.

BB: Is it this conception of language that makes your texts since the late 1970s appear as both post-poetical and post-literary? Would you want to claim a similarly hybrid definition for your language practices, i.e., that they are placed (like sculpture used to be) in public spaces of seeing and reading?

JH: My writing might not be post-poetic or post-literary. It never was and won't ever be poetic or literary, other than accidentally or incidentally. I hope the practice is like sculpture and sometimes like painting.

BB: I see your language practices deliberately scrambling and diffusing any identifiable message or activist intervention on behalf of a particular political position so that the reader/spectator actually has to perform the work of critique, discernment, and identification herself in the process of reading. Is this a fair assessment?

JH: There can be a deliberate scrambling, or at least a heaping of many messages. Sometimes the messages are conflicting, and other times the language and the messages will be blunt and to the point. I routinely invite the reader to sort through the offerings and complete the thoughts, and to echo, amplify, or shrink from the feelings the work elicits. I tie the language to the visuals as an assist, and as a take-away gift.

BB: Even if your writings are challenging to place within the context of conventional language forms, it seems evident that your work, beginning with *Truisms,* deploys several strategies with regard to language. One of them seems to have been to construct texts as *citations* from the full range of linguistic registers that ideology and everyday life supply to an individual. Or could we say that these are texts as *citations* from the full range of contradictions and unresolvable conflicts that permeate an individual's conscious and unconscious thoughts as linguistic utterances?

JH: That seems right for a number of the series, such as *Truisms* and *Inflammatory Essays.* I didn't have the same approach in all the writing though. *Arno* could not be described as a series of citations, for example.

BB: I had always assumed that your motivation to construct these texts (or at least some of them) in the manner of the citation had been determined in a number of different ways. First, that you follow a model of language that is similar to what Louis Althusser defined as an ideological apparatus, i.e., the conviction that there is literally not a single form of knowledge or of linguistic articulation that could claim to be exempt from its participation in ideological interests.

JH: I imagine that's true of much, but I think that screaming can come straight from the body. The person screaming might have been hit courtesy of an ideology.

BB: I also thought that by suspending your texts in manifold and manifest contradictions, you wanted to avoid the readers'/spectators' easy responses and thwart premature identifications.

JH: The answer depends on the series and often on the site, medium, and installation, but as a general rule, I don't want people to go too quickly to simplistic conclusions.

BB: Would you rather generate systematic dis-identification than solicit affirmative consensus?

JH: Again, there is no one answer. With *Lustmord,* even though the voices of Victims, Perpetrators, and Observers are present, I am for affirmative consensus that rape and murder are criminal.

BB: Your writings seem to suspend the readers/spectators in a place of doubt and skepticism with regard to any linguistic utterance, even those that might have at first appeared as attractive conventions and affirmative of governing convictions.

JH: This is accurate about some of my writing but certainly not all. When I present a large number of declassified documents with conflicting accounts of a single event in wartime, I hope people pause to study.

BB: I find that your work consciously generates a treacherous liberalist slippage, an ambiguity that seems at odds with its agitational potential. Other artists of your generation engaged with the problems of linguistic and iconic representation as ideological powers in the service of subject formation (e.g., Martha Rosler or Allan Sekula) in explicit political criticism. By contrast, your work always gives its readers/spectators a considerable degree of responsibility to decide whether they would want to recognize their respective ideological suturing within the apparatus at large, or whether they would claim conscious choices as spaces of exemption and self-constitution.

JH: The readers already have this freedom and responsibility, so various texts of mine reflect as much as grant that. Often the most effective agitation—or at least the fastest—is not going to be art anyhow, and some political art is not likely to influence a general public because it's relatively impenetrable and not especially visual or sensual. I organized a project, *Sign on a Truck*—perhaps not art—but it did provide political criticism from various viewpoints as well as a chance to hope a little, and to think about how to vote and why in the 1984 presidential election.

BB: This generosity seems to originate in a political foundation of critical enlightenment thought, one that is driven by the liberal aspiration that readers/spectators would inevitably be free enough to determine their own ethical and political practices and behavioral patterns.

JH: Voting relies on this. Anyway, this seems an ideal, but I don't believe it's always possible to realize perfectly. Even so, it's worth imagining and representing and setting up situations in which something like that ideal can work. It seems worse to manipulate, trick, preach, make propaganda, or supply disinformation.

BB: When confronted with your constructions of ideological ambiguities, it seems the readers/spectators would choose those that correspond to their ethics in the present and dis-identify from those that would seem either outdated or fundamentally unacceptable at this point in history and social reality.

JH: Often I don't present ambiguities. I am more likely to present certainties simultaneously and hope people hear the competition and think about what comes next—a pounding or negotiation. But, yes, there could be a good result, depending on the ethics.

BB: This next question concerns the problem of the "distribution form" of your work. Obviously, as had been the case with Conceptual art, your decision to engage language as your primary medium of artistic communication in the mid-to-late 1970s entailed a transformation of the actual carriers of the messages that your work attempted to disseminate. Thus, you invented a whole new array of devices that served to distribute your textual production.

JH: Maybe it's that I found various things that were right for text? More often than not I chose everyday objects that would look normal until you read the writing.

BB: Initially, these were programmatically modest, e.g., inexpensively produced stickers and posters, pamphlets and books, and cheaply manufactured metal plaques, among others. These multiplications of textual signs in unlimited editions would aim at a much broader audience than even the Conceptual artists had addressed. Furthermore, all of these devices seemed to be defined by the desire to produce objects that could be displayed in any place and position that you or your readers would choose. These strategies thus affected both the aesthetic and economic *status* and the discursive and institutional *location* of the object, continuing the Conceptualists' critique of the commodity status of the work of art as much as subverting the restrictions within which the institutional frame had traditionally contained the object.

JH: I liked following the Conceptualist critique, plus I simply distributed the writing in practical, friendly, cheap ways. I needed these sentences to be in daily life on regular stuff available to many people who don't frequent museums.

BB: In a second phase, your work increasingly shifted to textual dissemination via electronic devices such as LED signs and complex, often monumentally sized projections. What do you think are the motivations and ramifications of this rather dramatic expansion of means and technologies from the 1970s to the 1980s and on to today?

JH: Initially, it was cheaper and easier to put writing on electronic signs, ones that were already installed in public places, than it was to produce and paste the posters. All that was required was advance art worry and a little programming time. (It was hard work not to be caught in the middle of the night with an armload of posters and a bucket of paste.) Often there was dead space on the big outdoor signs, so I didn't have to pay to exhibit because the operators welcomed content. With those outdoor signs, I was able to work without using any art materials, and the first little LED boards I bought were humble objects. When I began to install site-specific electronics in museums such as Wright's Guggenheim, Gehry's Guggenheim, Foster's Bundestag, and Mies van der Rohe's Neue Nationalgalerie and had to reply to the superb and even competitive architecture, fabrication complexity and material costs went up. Same expensive story when I wanted to make sculpture with LED arrays that were more intricate and visual. The move to electronic technology had to do with my needing to be where people look. I thought I should present many hard germane subjects as large, loud, and well as what's done for celebrity gossip, concerts, products, and the sometimes too cautious reporting of the news.

In the mid-1990s, it was good to find the projection equipment that could be rented, that didn't have to be purchased. And I very much like that the projected works are immaterial — light only. The projections are a way to deliver feeling and writing by a number of great poets, as well as a means to highlight the natural world and to create sculpture from architecture. Plus, many of the buildings chosen as projection screens have occupants and histories worth highlighting, and projections can invite benign gatherings of people at night.

BB: Would it be fair to argue that there is a concrete specificity in the first phase, analogous perhaps to the model of a grassroots organization?

JH: I am not certain about concrete specificity, but my first work in the streets was self-sufficient at least, and the Colab programs were kind of grassroots and do-it-yourself activities. Colab exhibitions were pretty large and sophisticated though, while the means were modest.

BB: Was the work, as it seems at least in retrospect, still driven by a perhaps naïve assumption about the possibilities of newly implemented activist art practices that would actually generate an immediate effect and response from its readers and spectators?

JH: I know that a fair amount of people stopped to read and to write on my posters, and people unscrewed and ran off with a few plaques. People stayed to look at my texts on the public electronics and were amused, angered, reinforced, bored, and wired. I don't know what they did next. The Colab shows seem more well-realized and influential than naïve. Colab activities elicited immediate responses, and I believe created lasting effects. Of course, art shows won't stop an invasion, and only holy people and ecstatics think something like art will — and I'm glad about them.

BB: Did the second phase, with its technologically complex and visually seductive innovations, pay tribute to an increasingly spectacularized public sphere, where a technological mediation in addition to an intense apparatus of visual seduction would be necessary to aspire to any communication at all — if communication still was possible.

JH: I don't know that I paid tribute to the spectacular, in the outdoor works anyway; I just kind of moved in with different content. My big electronics went into museum and gallery spaces first, and there I was thinking more about architecture and art than staged landings on aircraft carriers or halftime at the Super Bowl. Indoors, I wanted to build LED pieces with traditional qualities such as form, depth, and subtle color, and at times I needed to answer and meld with super and potentially overwhelming museum architecture. A way to reply effectively was to use a fair amount of gear, although I prefer that my installations appear relatively spare and minimalist when finished. At the 1990 Venice Biennale, I made a full and hyperactive LED room that included comment on media and information overload, but this was more the exception than the norm.

"Spectacular" has become a dirty word, perhaps rightly when astonishing events are designed to overwhelm the ability to think, to generate mass acceptance of iffy policies and goods. I don't believe that the light projections are tricky this way. I am reluctant to vouch for my work or even describe it at length because that feels awkward, self-involved, and maybe defensive, but here goes. I resorted to talking to my husband, the artist Mike Glier, and what's decent that follows is his:

Projections invite reading, which typically is a quiet, private activity. At a projection, reading is possible with many companions or solo, as preferred. There is no single point from which to watch; it's worth walking close to a façade where the light runs abstract or appears as a few enormous

Subject: RE: FW: Taskers

All:

Regarding the tasking—I am not a legal expert, but seems to me that everyone we are detaining at this point is an unpriviledged belligerent, since we have taken over the country and there is no longer any force opposing us that 1) wears recognizable uniform; and 2) bears arms openly. So I think everyone we detain is in that category.

As for "the gloves need to come off..." we need to take a deep breath and remember who we are. Those gloves are most definitely NOT based on Cold War or WWII enemies--they are based on clearly established standards of international law to which we are signatories and in part the originators. Those in turn derive from practices commonly accepted as morally correct, the so-called "usages of war." It comes down to standards of right and wrong--something we cannot just put aside when we find it inconvenient, any more than we can declare that we will "take no prisoners" and therefore shoot those who surrender to us simply because we find prisoners inconvenient.

"The casualties are mounting..." we have taken casualties in every war we have ever fought--that is part of the very nature of war. We also inflict casualties, generally many more than we take. **That in no way justifies letting go of our standards.** We have NEVER considered our enemies justified in doing such things to us. Casualties are part of war--if you cannot take casualties then you cannot engage in war. Period.

BOTTOM LINE. We are American soldiers, heirs of a long tradition of staying on the high ground. We need to stay there.

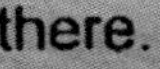

b62/7c2

Psalm 24: 3-8

above: ***Wish List/Gloves Off*** *pewter*, **2007 (detail)**

letters. The multiple perspectives available encourage individualized experience and interpretation. (I surprised myself by thinking about my mother's death while watching letters closely on a war memorial in Leipzig.) Sometimes you can hear kids reading out loud or watch people track text on the ocean or on dusty air. In a projection, there is not a hard split between what's presented and the audience, so people are not passive. They become the scene when they walk through poems or dive on heat-sensitive beanbags at an indoor projection; people color print where they've lain and can be startled to see they've contributed profiles or handprints. The writing chosen for projection invites responses from people and doesn't yell or sell. Projections will alter public space by changing the light, sound, and speed of the place to make it a reading room. (I adore the New York Public Library's Main Reading Room and wanted to create a mobile version.) Projected lines from superb poets lend a thinking sensuality that's not part of spectacle.

Because projections and big electronic installations take much content prep and hovering — my piece for the politician's entrance of the Bundestag jumps to mind with its research for, and transcription of, a hundred-plus years of parliamentarians' speeches — it has been a relief to paint again, to try to realize complex expression via simple means.

BB: Does the work participate in these historical processes of the spectacularization of the public sphere, or does it merely follow the determinations of its increasingly universal and inescapable laws to enable and enhance any form of communication?

JH: No. I've participated in a few spectacles in museums, but the outdoor projections function because they are not spectacular in that old bad way. I don't work in every form available, but I like the variety offered by white light, bones, black plants, diodes, cotton shirts, rocks, and oil paint.

BB: On that topic, you recently have returned to painting as a process, as a technique of display, and as a distribution form (a singular object on canvas in the most conventional manner). Does this departure from the increasingly complex apparatus of technology that you had developed for the dissemination and display of your work signal a change of attitude on your side, i.e., a certain degree of skepticism with regard to the media optimism of the 1970s?

JH: No, I continue to work with the electronics because people turn toward flashing light. Maybe because I am familiar with LEDs, I finally have made something like sculpture from this technology. And LED arrays work especially well for installations in and on architecture. I use electronics to display transcribed declassified documents because so much of this material can be stored in the signs' controllers, and I need the active programming that's possible on electronics to have the content hard to miss and leave.

BB: Is working with painting a decision that recognizes the necessity for a more expressive, if not expressionist, form and format to articulate messages of political protest and opposition at a moment of a seemingly endless war and increasing erosion of elementary civil liberties in the United States?

JH: Choosing painting had to do with an appreciation of the qualities of paint, and an odd thought that hand-rendered oil grounds were appropriate for silk-screened documents about the Middle East. I was looking at Warhol's Death and Disaster works while I was collecting the declassified and other sensitive pages. For the first paintings, I tried flat, somewhat tough and loud colors for the grounds. These were all right, but then I wanted more emotional substrates for first-person accounts — the pages in which a detainee or a soldier says "I was hit" or "I struck." I collected books on Goya's Black Paintings, looked at the colors and layering, and then sampled portions of the skies and landscapes. Later, I took pastel skies from Renaissance works to indicate hope. I also screened many documents in black on white paint to emphasize that the documents are real.

BB: From the outside, it has always appeared difficult to associate your work with any of the programmatic political positions that had been articulated by artists, writers, and philosophers since the 1960s (e.g., feminism, Situationism, Marxist cultural and political critiques). Yet at the same time, it was always evident, and continues to be strikingly clear, that you are — with Martha Rosler — one of the most politically conscious and explicit artists of your generation (if we agree that Louise Lawler, Cindy Sherman, Sherrie Levine, Martha Rosler, and Richard Prince form a historical peer group for your work).

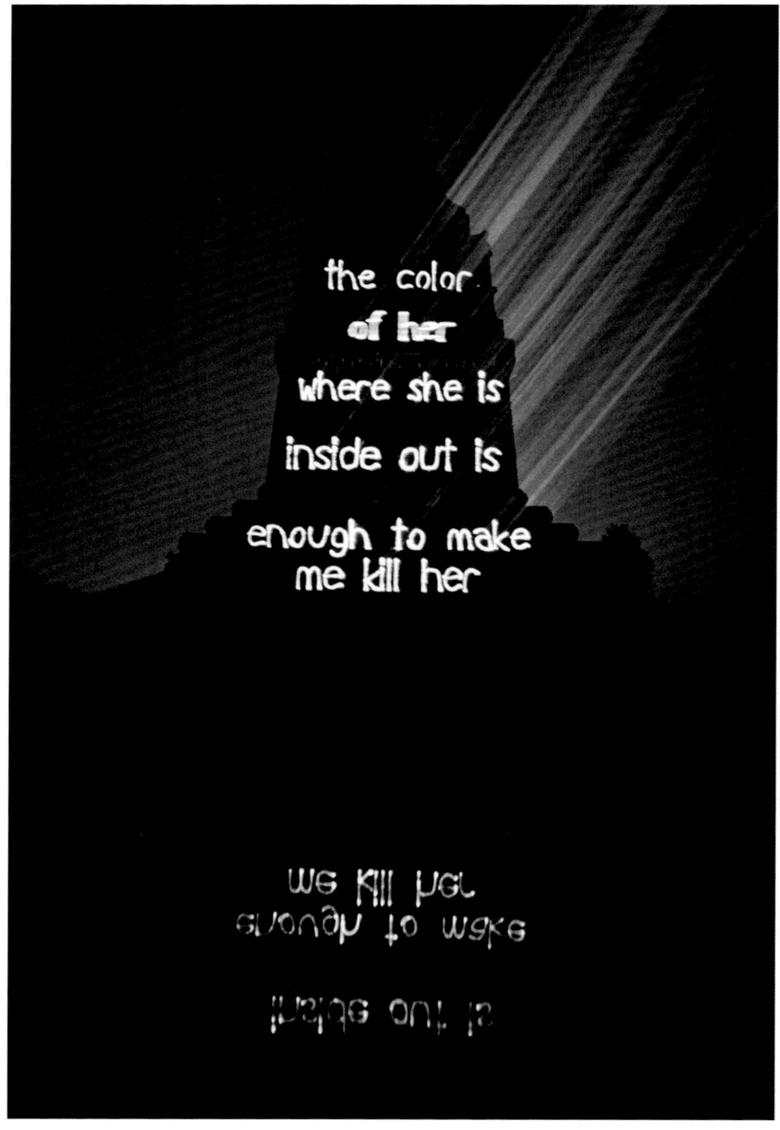

above: ***Kriegszustand*, 1996**; opposite: ***For Milan*, 2007**

JH: Thanks. I am uneasy about comparing consciousness, but my work can be explicit.

BB: How would you describe your positions in political terms, and what are the writers that you would claim as having provided you with a theoretical foundation for your work?

JH: I don't talk much about my politics because I don't like people to confuse my work and me, and I am old enough that it's not possible for me to reconstruct which readings did what. I can offer that I think the war in Iraq is a mistake and that the secrecy in advance of and after the invasion was and continues to be dangerous and reprehensible. The works with declassified material are from my sometimes frantic (witness the number of paintings) worrying about the war and the attendant changes in American society. There is an unusually close connection between this artwork and my private politics, as there was with the *Lustmord* pieces, for example.

BB: I always assumed that you had emerged from a classical American tradition of Anarchist thinking and writing that had its foundations in the 19th-century traditions of Thoreau and Emerson, and that more recent elaborations in European Anarchist thinkers like Jean Baudrillard had become important to you in the 1970s?

JH: I don't know much about Baudrillard, but I did read and appreciate Thoreau and Emerson, as well as Emma Goldman and Alexander Berkman. Long ago, I read Bakunin, Kropotkin, and others, as well as some Nihilist writing. For balance I studied Utopian ideals and read accounts of fairly successful and failed American and other utopian experiments.

BB: The same complexity, if not even a more difficult set of questions, emerges when one attempts to identify your position with regard to sexual politics. Clearly, your writings articulate a feminist position, but it is one that is far from the purist *doxa* of the feminist theoreticians and activists of the 1970s. That would be evident, for example, in your writings in which the phenomena of sexual and corporeal violence are addressed in terms of the bewildering ambiguities that are so essential to your work.

JH: Perhaps these are accurate, if bewildering? Or, more precisely, there's the concurrent presence of conflicting, or at least wildly varying, beliefs, motivations, and actions in the work — as there is in the world.

BB: Clearly these writings recognize power relations as a historical formation (of the sexuality of the subject and of social relations at large) whose realities cannot be simply overcome by a feminist emancipatory *doxa*.

JH: So far nothing has stopped the abuse of women — men won't give it up — and the failure is not that of feminism or art. No sort of artwork is immediately going to change men who abuse and kill their pregnant wives, rape and torture women in war, diminish and sandbag their lovers, assault their girl children or other girls they can catch, refuse to change their sheets, and pay peanuts.

BB: These ambiguities give your work at times a pessimistic dimension that would clearly be at odds with any of the radical feminist critiques, if not with any of the political activist projects with which one would otherwise want to associate you.

JH: I don't believe that my artwork is pessimistic. It is realistic, and perhaps the fact of it is encouraging to some women and men. And I wouldn't go to art to stop a man in his tracks.

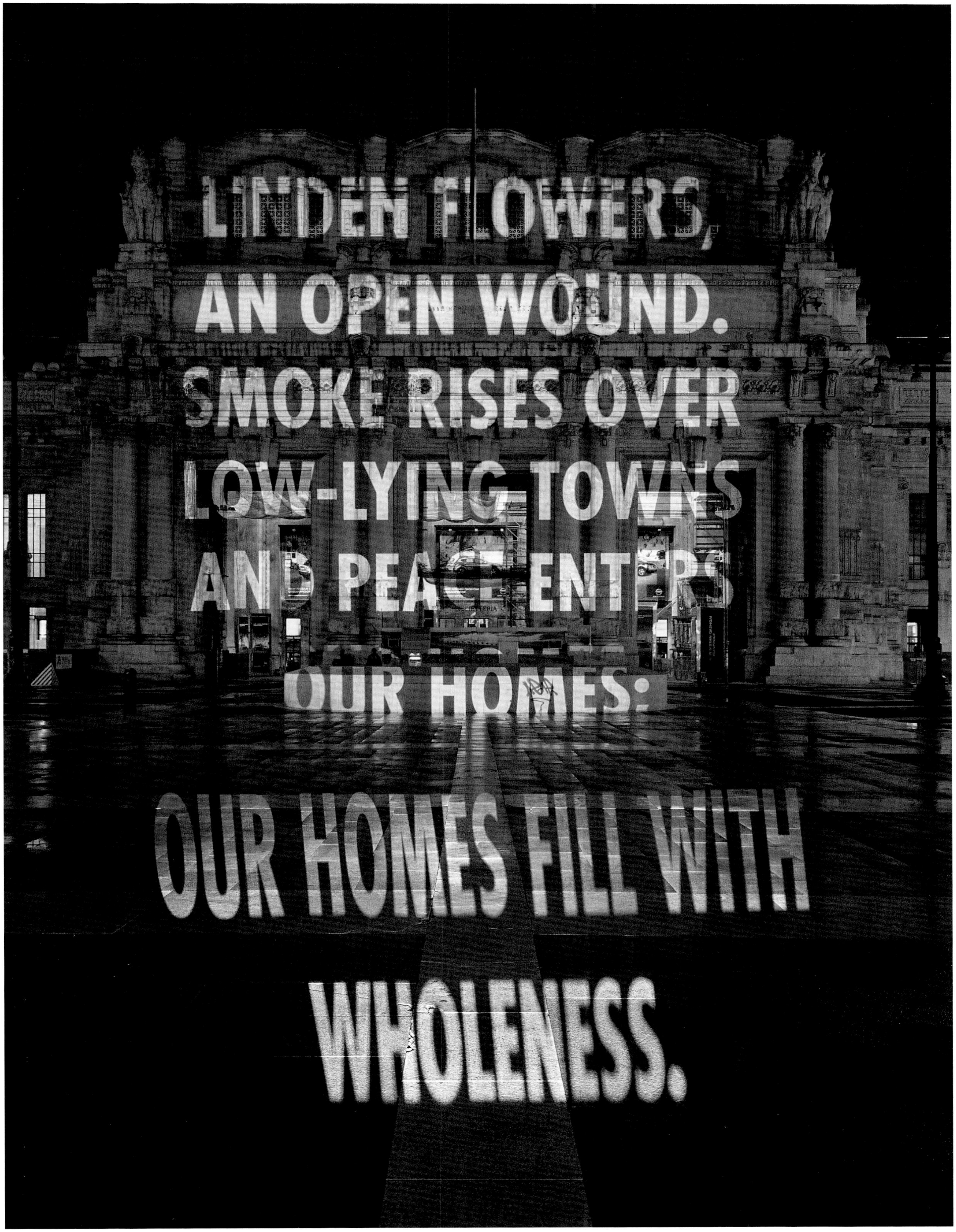

LINDEN FLOWERS,
AN OPEN WOUND.
SMOKE RISES OVER
LOW-LYING TOWNS
AND PEACE ENTERS
OUR HOMES:

OUR HOMES FILL WITH
WHOLENESS.

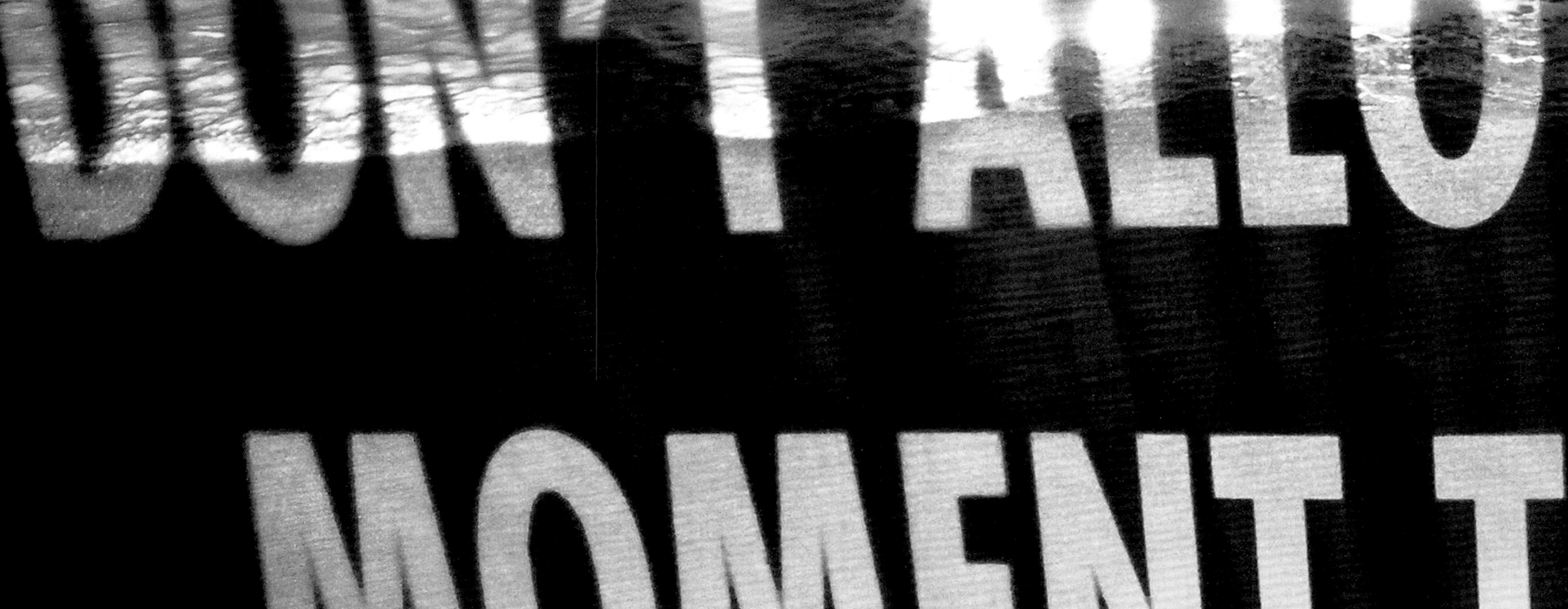
DON'T ALLO
MOMENT T

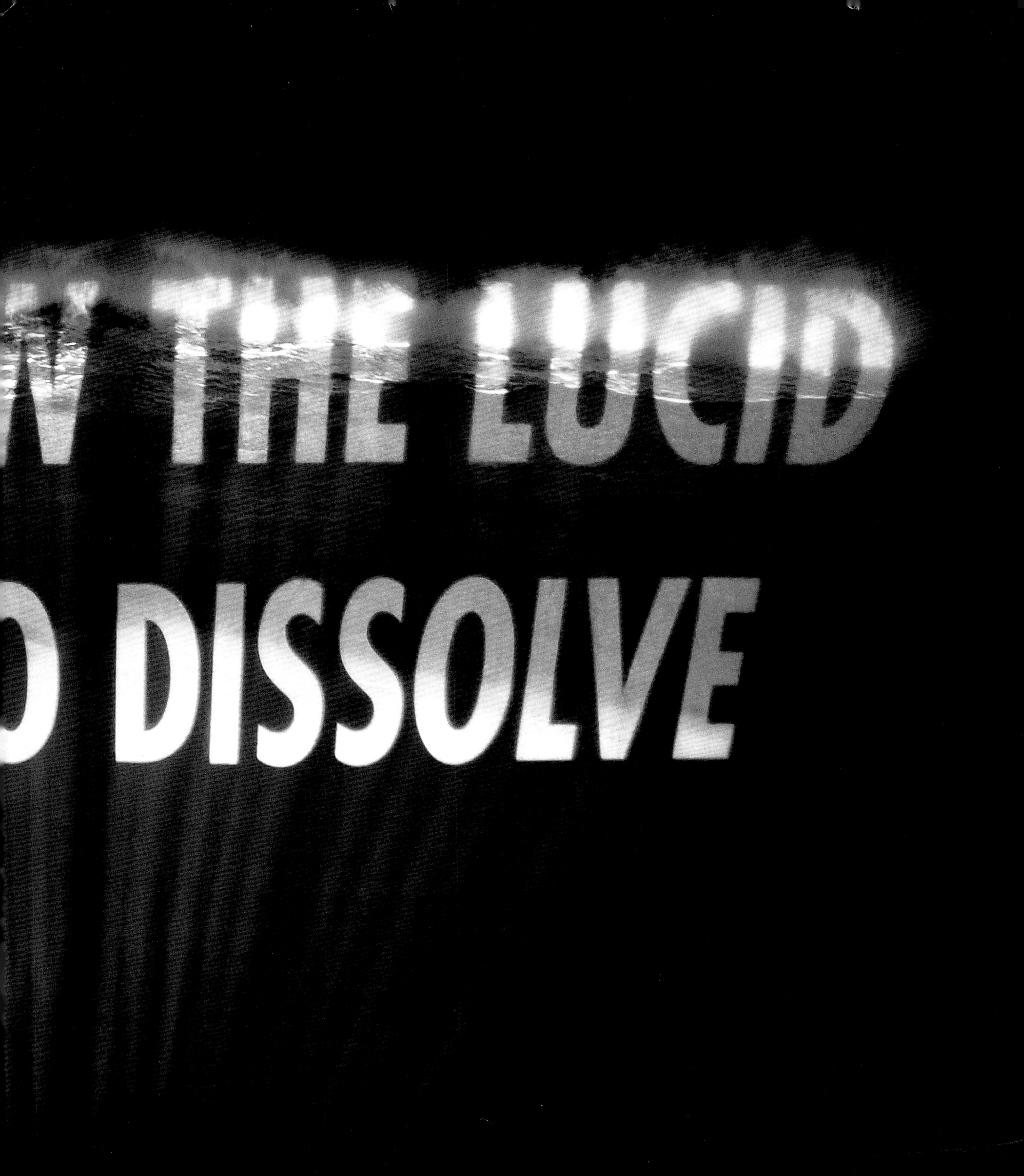

THE LUCID

DISSOLVE

JACKET

***MONUMENT*, 2008 (detail)**
22 double-sided, semi-circular electronic LED signs:
13 with red and white diodes; 9 with red and blue
diodes on front and blue and white diodes on back
194.3 x 57.8 x 28.9 in (493.5 x 146.8 x 73.4 cm)
Text: *Truisms*, 1977–79; *Inflammatory Essays*, 1979–82

FRONT

***For San Diego*, 2007**
Light projection
Text (pictured): *Arno*, 1996

ESSAYS

p. 10
***Purple Cross*, 2004**
10 double-sided electronic LED signs with red and blue diodes
126 x 122.6 x 100.7 in. (320 x 311.4 x 255.8 cm)
Text: "Blur," from *Middle Earth* by Henri Cole.
Copyright © 2003 by Henri Cole. Reprinted by permission
from Farrar, Straus and Giroux, LLC.

p. 11
from *Truisms*, 1977
Offset poster with graffiti, 36 x 24 in. (91.4 x 61 cm)
Text: *Truisms*, 1977–79

p. 12
***For 7 World Trade*, 2006**
Electronic LED sign with white diodes, stainless steel,
aluminum, etched glass, Dupont Sentry Glass Plus
13.5 x 65 ft. (4.1 x 19.8 m)
Text (pictured): John Lambert, from *Travels Through
Canada, and the United States of North America
in the Years 1806, 1807, 1808*

p. 12
***Rib Cage*, 2004**
8 double-sided, curved electronic LED signs with white
diodes on front and red and white diodes on back
93.3 x 58.3 x 37.1 in. (237 x 148.1 x 94.2 cm)
Text: "Beach Walk," from *Blackbird and Wolf* by Henri Cole.
Copyright © 2007 by Henri Cole. Reprinted by permission
from Farrar, Straus and Giroux, LLC.

p. 13
Hanging cage
Torture Museum, Amsterdam

p. 13
***Blue Room*, 1975**
Acrylic wash over latex paint, dimensions unknown

p. 14
from *Truisms*, 1982
Spectacolor electronic sign, 20 x 40 ft. (6.1 x 12.2 m)
Text: *Truisms*, 1977–79
Organized by Public Art Fund, Inc.

p. 15
***Installation for Neue Nationalgalerie*, 2001**
13 electronic LED signs with amber diodes
4 x 1,716.5 x 1,920 in. (10.2 x 4,360 x 4,867 cm)
Text (pictured): *Survival*, 1983–85

p. 16
***Xenon for Venice*, 1999**
Light projection
Text (pictured): *Blue*, 1998

p. 16
***The Venice Installation: First Antechamber*,
1990 (detail)**
Nero Marquina and Rosso Magnaboschi marble tile
in diamond pattern with Biancone marble border
370.5 x 253.8 in. (941.1 x 644.7 cm)
Text (pictured): *Truisms*, 1977–79

p. 17
***Black Garden*, 1994 (detail)**
Concentric rings of black plantings,
5 Bentheimer Red sandstone benches
Text: *War*, 1992

p. 18
***Erlauf Peace Monument*, 1995**
White plantings, Bethel White granite pavers,
searchlight set in Bethel White granite column
Text: *Erlauf*, 1995

p. 19
***For Pittsburgh*, 2005**
2 double-sided electronic LED signs with blue diodes
4,152 x 14 x 1.75 in. (10,546.1 x 35.6 x 4.4 cm), east sign;
4,104 x 14 x 1.75 in. (10,424.2 x 35.6 x 4.4 cm), west sign
Text (pictured, left): *Sent for You Yesterday*, © 1983 by
John Edgar Wideman, reprinted with the permission of
The Wylie Agency, Inc.; (pictured, right): *An American
Childhood*. Copyright © 1987 by Annie Dillard, published
by Harper & Row Publishers, Inc. Reprinted with the permission of Russell & Volkening as agents for the author.

p. 21
***For SAAM*, 2007**
Cylindrical electronic LED sign with white diodes
348 x 48 in. (883.9 x 121.9 cm)
Text (pictured): *Survival*, 1983–85

pp. 22–23
***COLIN POWELL GREEN WHITE*, 2006**
Oil on linen, 33 x 102 in. (83.8 x 259.1 cm)
Text: U.S. government document

p. 24
***Lustmord*, 1996 (detail)**
Human bones, engraved silver, wood table
Text: *Lustmord*, 1993–95

p. 26
from *Truisms*, 1983
T-shirt worn by Lady Pink
Text: *Truisms*, 1977–79

p. 27
Bruce Nauman
***Life, Death, Love, Hate, Pleasure, Pain*, 1983**
Neon, diameter: 70.875 in. (180 cm)
Museum of Contemporary Art, Chicago
Gerald S. Elliott Collection, 1995.74

p. 29
Leon Golub
***Mercenaries I*, 1979**
Acrylic on unstretched linen, 120 x 166 in. (304.8 x 421.6 cm)
Museum of Contemporary Art, Chicago
Gift of Lannan Foundation, 1997.39

p. 30
Louise Lawler
***War is Terror*, 2001/2003**
Cibachrome (museum box), 30 x 25.75 in. (76.2 x 65.41 cm)
Collection of Carla Emil and Rich Silverstein

p. 31
Barbara Kruger
***Untitled (Admit nothing/Blame everyone/Be bitter)*, 1987**
Photographic silkscreen/vinyl, 100 x 180 in. (255 cm x 457 cm)

p. 32
Dan Flavin
***monument 4 those who have been killed in ambush
(to P.K. who reminded me about death)*, 1966**
Red fluorescent light, 8 x 8 feet (243.84 x 243.84 cm)
Collection Dia Art Foundation, New York

L.E.D.

pp. 36–39
***Yellow Floor*, 2004**
4 x 786 x 589.6 in. (10.2 x 1,996.4 x 1,497.7 cm)
Text (pictured): Sherman Kent, "Estimates and Influence,"
in *Sherman Kent and the Board of National Estimates:
Collected Essays*, ed. Donald P. Steury (Washington, D.C.:
Center for the Study of Intelligence [C.I.A.], 1994).
First published in *Studies in Intelligence*, Summer 1968.

pp. 40–41
***Red Yellow Looming*, 2004**
143.9 x 109 x 52 in. (365.4 x 276.9 x 132.1 cm)
Text: U.S. government documents

p. 42
***Thorax*, 2008**
104.3 x 58.3 x 37.1 in. (264.8 x 148.1 x 94.2 cm)
Text: U.S. government documents

p. 43
***Torso*, 2008**
86.3 x 57.8 x 28.9 in. (219.2 x 146.8 x 73.4 cm)
Text: U.S. government documents

pp. 44–49
***MONUMENT*, 2008**
194.3 x 57.8 x 28.9 in. (493.5 x 146.8 x 73.4 cm)
Text: *Truisms*, 1977–79; *Inflammatory Essays*, 1979–82

INDOOR PROJECTIONS

pp. 52–53; pp. 60–61
***For MAK*, 2006**
Text (pictured): Elfriede Jelinek, "Die Liebhaberinnen."
Copyright © 1975 by Rowohlt Taschenbuch Verlag GmbH,
Reinbek bei Hamburg.

pp. 54–59
***PROJECTIONS*, 2008**
Text (pictured pp. 54–55): "Parting with a View," from
View with a Grain of Sand by Wisława Szymborska, copyright © 1993 by Wisława Szymborska, English translation by
Stanisław Barańczak and Clare Cavanagh, copyright © 1995
by Houghton Mifflin Harcourt Publishing Company, reprinted
with permission of the publisher and the author. Text (pictured
pp. 56–57): "The Terrorist, He's Watching," from *Poems New
and Collected* by Wisława Szymborska, English translation by
Stanisław Barańczak and Clare Cavanagh, copyright © 1998
by Houghton Mifflin Harcourt Publishing Company, reprinted
with permission of the publisher and the author.

PAINTINGS

pp. 64–65
***PALM, FINGERS & FINGERTIPS 000406*, 2007;**
***PALM, FINGERS & FINGERTIPS 000407*, 2007**
Oil on linen, 58 x 44 in. (147.3 x 111.8 cm), each
Text: U.S. government documents

pp. 66–67
***Left Hand (Palm Rolled)*, 2007;**
***Right Hand (Palm Rolled)*, 2007**
Oil on linen, 80 x 62 in. (203.2 x 157.5 cm), each
Text: U.S. government documents

pp. 68–69
***Protect Protect deep purple*, 2007 (detail)**
Oil on linen, 79 x 102.25 in. (200.7 x 259.7 cm)
Text: U.S. government document

pp. 70–71 (left to right, top to bottom)
Phase I – Force Laydown green
Phase II . . . Running Start Decisive Offensive operations violet
Phase II – Force Laydown dark purple
Shape the Battlespace
Phase III Complete Regime Destruction
Phase III Actions
Phase III Operations purple
Phase III – Decisive Operations
Force at End of Phase III (If Required) violet
Phase IV Actions green
Phase IV Post-Hostilities purple
1003V FULL FORCE – FORCE DISPOSITION PEWTER
(all 2007)
Oil on linen, 79 x 102.25 in. (200.7 x 259.7 cm), each
Text: U.S. government documents

pp. 72–73
***Midtown Massacre ochre*, 2007 (2 of 3 pictured)**
Oil on linen, 102.25 x 237 in. (259.7 x 602 cm)
Text: U.S. government documents

pp. 74–75
FINAL AUTOPSY REPORT
***DOD003235 DOD003241 GREEN WHITE*, 2006 (detail)**
Oil on linen, 66 x 25.5 in. (167.6 x 64.8 cm)
Text: U.S. government document

p. 76
***b. 1*, 2008**
Oil on linen, 58 x 44 in. (147.3 x 111.8 cm)
Text: U.S. government document

pp. 77–79
***Wish List/Gloves Off pewter*, 2007 (3 of 4 pictured)**
Oil on linen, 102.25 x 316 in. (259.7 x 802.6 cm)
Text: U.S. government documents

pp. 80–81
***As a Parent turquoise*, 2006**
Oil on linen, 33 x 51 in. (83.8 x 129.5 cm)
Text: U.S. government document

OUTDOOR PROJECTIONS

pp. 84–87
***Xenon for Rio de Janeiro*, 1999**
Text (pictured pp. 84–85): *Truisms*, 1977–79
Text (pictured pp. 86–87): *Arno*, 1996

pp. 88–89
***For the Academy*, 2007**
Text (pictured p. 88): "He Embraces His Murderer," from *Unfortunately, It Was Paradise* by Mahmoud Darwish, edited and translated by Munir Akash and Carolyn Forché with Sinan Antoon and Amira El-Zein. © 2003 Regents of the University of California. Published with permission of the University of California Press. Presented by the American Academy in Rome. Text (pictured p. 89): "In My Life, On My Life," from *Open Closed Open* by Yehuda Amichai, translated by Chana Bloch and Chana Kronfeld. Compilation copyright © 2000 by Yehuda Amichai. English translation © 2000 by Chana Bloch and Chana Kronfeld. Used by permission of Georges Borchardt, Inc.

p. 90
***Xenon for Berlin*, 2001**
Text (pictured): "Bürgerbrief," 1813

p. 91
***Xenon for Monterrey*, 2001**
Text (pictured): *Truisms*, 1977–79

p. 92
***Xenon for Paris*, 2001**
Text (pictured): *Erlauf*, 1995

p. 93
***For the City*, 2005**
Text (pictured): "Smoke," from *Without End: New and Selected Poems* by Adam Zagajewski, translated by Clare Cavanagh. Copyright © 2002 by Adam Zagajewski. Translation copyright © 2002 by Farrar, Straus and Giroux, LLC. Reprinted by permission of Farrar, Straus and Giroux, LLC. Presented by Creative Time, Inc.

pp. 94–95
***For San Diego*, 2007**
Text (pictured): "The End and the Beginning," from *View with a Grain of Sand* by Wisława Szymborska, translated by Stanisław Barańczak and Clare Cavanagh. © 1993 by Wisława Szymborska. English translation copyright © 1995 by Houghton Mifflin Harcourt Publishing Company, reprinted with permission of the publisher and the author.

pp. 96–97
***For the Capitol*, 2007**
Text (pictured): John F. Kennedy, "Address Before the General Assembly of the United Nations," September 25, 1961

LUSTMORD

pp. 100–105
***Lustmord*, 1993**
Ink on skin
Text: *Lustmord*, 1993–95

pp. 106–107
***Lustmord*, 2007**
Human bones, engraved silver, wood table
34 x 70 x 44.5 in. (86.4 x 177.8 x 113 cm)
Text: *Lustmord*, 1993–95

BENCHES

pp. 110–111
***The Venice Installation*, Walker Art Center, 1992**
17 x 36 x 18 in. (43.2 x 91.4 x 45.7 cm), each bench
Text: *Living*, 1980–82

pp. 112–113
***Installation for the Solomon R. Guggenheim Museum*, 1989**
14 x 6,369.5 x 4 in. (35.6 x 16,178.5 x 10.2 cm), LED sign;
17 x 42 x 18 in. (43.2 x 106.7 x 45.7 cm), each bench
Text (pictured, LED): *Inflammatory Essays*, 1979–82;
(pictured, benches): *Survival*, 1983–85

pp. 114–115
***Installation for Doris C. Freedman Plaza*, 1989 (detail)**
17 x 54 x 25 in. (43.2 x 137.2 x 63.5 cm), each marble bench;
17.25 x 48 x 21 in. (43.8 x 121.9 x 53.3 cm), each granite bench
Text (pictured): *Truisms*, 1977–79

INTERVIEW

p. 116
***PROJECTIONS*, 2008**
Light projection
Text (pictured): "Tortures" and "The Joy of Writing," from *View with a Grain of Sand* by Wisława Szymborska, translated by Stanisław Barańczak and Clare Cavanagh. © 1993 by Wisława Szymborska. English translation copyright © 1995 by Houghton Mifflin Harcourt Publishing Company, reprinted with permission of the publisher and the author.

p. 121
***Wish List/Gloves Off pewter*, 2007 (detail)**
Oil on linen, 102.25 x 316 in. (259.7 x 802.6 cm)
Text: U.S. government document

p. 122
***Kriegszustand*, 1996**
Laser projection
Text (pictured): *Lustmord*, 1993–95

p. 123
***For Milan*, 2007**
Light projection
Text (pictured): "Smoke," from *Without End: New and Selected Poems* by Adam Zagajewski, translated by Clare Cavanagh. Copyright © 2002 by Adam Zagajewski. Translation copyright © 2002 by Farrar, Straus and Giroux, LLC. Reprinted by permission of Farrar, Straus and Giroux, LLC.

BACK

***For San Diego*, 2007**
Light projection
Text (pictured): "Don't Allow the Lucid Moment to Dissolve," translated by Clare Cavanagh, from *Without End: New and Selected Poems* by Adam Zagajewski. Copyright © 2002 by Adam Zagajewski. Translation copyright © 2002 by Farrar, Straus and Giroux, LLC. Reprinted by permission of Farrar, Straus and Giroux, LLC.

Exhibition

JENNY HOLZER: PROTECT PROTECT

co-organized by the Museum of Contemporary Art, Chicago,
and the Fondation Beyeler, Riehen/Basel

Museum of Contemporary Art, Chicago
October 25, 2008 – February 1, 2009

Whitney Museum of American Art, New York
March 12, 2009 – May 31, 2009

Fondation Beyeler, Riehen/Basel
November 1, 2009 – January 24, 2010

Conception and realization:
Elizabeth A.T. Smith, Museum of Contemporary Art, Chicago,
with Philippe Büttner, Fondation Beyeler, Riehen/Basel

Major support for *Jenny Holzer: PROTECT PROTECT* is provided by Donald and Brigitte Bren, Anne and Burt Kaplan, The Andy Warhol Foundation for the Visual Arts, and the National Endowment for the Arts.

Additional support is generously provided by Andrea and Jim Gordon, Penny Pritzker and Bryan Traubert, Gretchen and Jay Jordan, the Kovler Family Foundation, Cari and Michael Sacks, Howard and Donna Stone, Kathy and Steven Taslitz, Helen and Sam Zell, Lannan Foundation, the Graham Foundation for Advanced Studies in the Fine Arts, Barbara Ruben, Irving Stenn, Jr., Lynn and Allen Turner, and The Orbit Fund.

For Chicago (2007) has entered the MCA Collection through the generosity of the Edlis/Neeson Art Acquisition Fund.

Support for the exhibition catalogue is generously provided by Sara Szold, Cheim & Read, Monika Sprüth Philomene Magers, and Yvon Lambert.

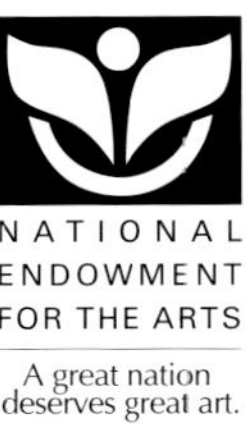

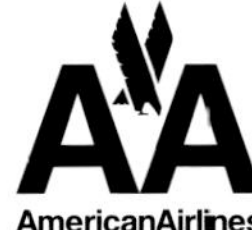

Official Airline of the Museum of Contemporary Art, Chicago

In Basel, the Fondation Beyeler would like to thank the following for their continued support: Bank Sarasin & Cie AG; Basler Kantonalbank; Basler Zeitung Medien; Bayer; Fondation BNP Paribas; Gemeinde Riehen; ISS; Kuhn & Bülow; Kultur Basel-Stadt; kulturelles.bl; Manor; and UBS.

Fondation Beyeler extends special thanks to the Hansjoerg Wyss Foundation for the crucial support they provide for their exhibition activities.

Elizabeth A.T. Smith would like to thank David Breslin, Celine Kopp, and Kate Kraczon for their crucial assistance with the preparation of her essay.

Jenny Holzer wishes to thank the following: Jason Best, Emily Blanchard, Robert Blanton, Thomas Blanton, David Breslin, Marc Breslin, Benjamin Buchloh, Berta Burr, Walter Burr, Philippe Büttner, John Cheim, Delia Ciuha, Henri Cole, Ben Diep, Paul Donohue, Jennifer Draffen, Alanna Gedgaudas, Gilles Gingras, Hanspeter Giuliani, Mike Glier, Jon Grizzle, Madeleine Grynsztejn, Remo Hobi, Lili Holzer-Glier, Sam Keller, David Kiehl, Helmut Lang, Yvon Lambert, Louise Lawler, Simon Liu, Merrick Ketcham, Philomene Magers, Mindy McDaniel, Mark Nelson, Carolyn Padwa, Charles Passarelli, Jason Pereira, Brenda Phelps, Howard Read, Adam Sheffer, Joan Simon, Elizabeth Smith, Benjamin Snead, Monika Sprüth, Kerin Sulock, Robert Vinas, Jr., Adam Weinberg, Ben Wickerham, Jon Wise, and David Zaza, just for starters.

This book is dedicated to Paul Miller who is missed every day.

Published in conjunction with the exhibition.

Editor: David Breslin

Copyediting: Jason Best

Designed collaboratively by McCall Associates, New York, NY (Mark Nelson, David Zaza) and Jenny Holzer Studio, Hoosick Falls, NY (Jon Grizzle, Brenda Phelps).

Typeface: Freight Sans
Paper: Galaxi Supermat, 150g/m²
Binding: Conzella Verlagsbuchbinderei, Urban Meister GmbH, Aschheim-Dornach
Reproductions and printing: Dr. Cantz'sche Druckerei, Ostfildern

Benjamin H. D. Buchloh's interview with Jenny Holzer took place via email during the summer of 2008.

Photo Credits: Emmanuelle Bernard, Mary Boone Gallery, Stephen Brayne, Christopher Burke, Art Evans, Beto Felício, Megan E. Foldenauer, Roberto Ortiz Giacomán, Vassilij Gureev, David Heald © The Solomon R. Guggenheim Foundation, Jenny Holzer, Lili Holzer-Glier, Lisa Kahane, Hans-Dieter Kluge, Salvatore Licitra, Werner Lieberknecht, Attilio Maranzano, Paul Miller, Yurij Pokrovsky, David Regen, Alan Richardson, Philipp Scholz Rittermann, Städtische Galerie Nordhorn, Christian Wachter, Walker Art Center, Gene Young

A publication of the Beyeler Museum AG (Fondation Beyeler)
Baselstrasse 101
4125 Riehen/Basel
Switzerland
Tel. +41 61 645 97 00
Fax +41 61 645 97 19
www.beyeler.com
fondation@beyeler.com

and the Museum of Contemporary Art, Chicago
220 East Chicago Avenue
Chicago, Illinois 60611
Tel. 312 280 2660
Fax 312 397 4095
www.mcachicago.org

Published by
Hatje Cantz Verlag
Zeppelinstrasse 32
73760 Ostfildern
Germany
Tel. +49 711 4405-200
Fax +49 711 4405-220
www.hatjecantz.com

Hatje Cantz books are available internationally at selected bookstores. For more information about our distribution partners, please visit our homepage at www.hatjecantz.com.

Museum editions:

Fondation Beyeler
ISBN 978-3-905632-72-9 (English)

Fondation Beyeler
ISBN 978-3-905632-73-6 (German)

Museum of Contemporary Art, Chicago
ISBN 0-933856-87-3

Trade editions:

ISBN 978-3-7757-2301-5 (English)
ISBN 978-3-7757-2300-8 (German)

Printed in Germany